THE ABERCROMBIE & FITCH LIBRARY

THE ABERCROMBIE & FITCH LIBRARY

NARRATIVE OF

AN EXPEDITION INTO

SOUTHERN AFRICA

Sir William Cornwallis Harris

ARNO PRESS

New York · 1967

A Note to the Reader

Sir William Cornwallis Harris (1807-1848) spent most of his lifetime with the Bombay engineers and he was knighted June 7, 1844, for diplomatic services in establishing relations between Britain and the ancient Abyssinian highland kingdom of Shwa, but he is best remembered for the books he wrote about his travels and hunting adventures in southern Africa.

After his first thirteen years in India, he was invalided to the Cape for two years. At that time, 1836, South Africa was a center of world attention as the result of the exodus of Dutch colonists and their strife with the Zulus. On his voyage to the Cape, Harris made the acquaintance of another devoted sportsman, Richard Williamson, and together they planned the expedition into the interior that provided this *Narrative of an Expedition into Southern Africa* (Bombay, 1838). Later editions of this book are titled *The Wild Sports of Southern Africa.* Two years after the publication of the *Narrative*, another work by Harris appeared, a magnificent folio containing thirty fine colored plates based upon the drawings Harris made during the expedition; this second book, *Portraits of the Game and Wild Animals of Southern Africa*, has long been a highly prized and highly priced collector's item.

Harris's contributions were a landmark in the literature of African sport and travel, as explained by John G. Millais, himself a noted painter and big-game hunter, "Harris was a capable artist and an excellent writer. . . . He at once inspired many hunters to follow in his footsteps and several of these wrote either books of great value or portions of standard works." Among the writers directly influenced by Harris were R. Gordon Cumming and Sir Francis Galton.

At first one wonders how this narrative could have inspired other sportsmen to make the arduous trek into the African interior. The terrible tedium of travel in Africa 130 years ago combined with the hostility and treachery of natives made the Harris expedition a grinding and prolonged ordeal. But tremendous challenges spelled fabulous rewards. After the terrors of the road came the revelations of a natural paradise, scenes of fantastic beauty, and wonderful days of sporting adventure. Also, as the expedition proceeded, Harris used his skills to put together the impressive collection that he describes on page 340.

Harris sums up, "In spite of all hardships and privations, toilsome and tedious as our journey frequently was . . . we were more than amply repaid by the unparalleled magnificence of the sport that we enjoyed; and I can safely say that some of the happiest days of my existence have been passed in the wilds of Africa." Harris returned to India after his memorable African experience—"a passage in my life which time can never efface . . . a green spot in memory's waste." In later years, following the special mission to Abyssinia that won him knighthood, he became superintending engineer of the northern provinces of India. There, near Poona, he died of fever at the age of thirty-nine.

C. A. P.

Dean & Munday, Lithog^{rs},   40 Threadneedle St London.

MOSELEKATSE,
KING of the AMAZOOLOO.

NARRATIVE

OF AN

EXPEDITION

INTO

SOUTHERN AFRICA,

DURING THE YEARS 1836, AND 1837,

FROM

THE CAPE OF GOOD HOPE,

THROUGH

THE TERRITORIES OF THE CHIEF

MOSELEKATSE,

TO

THE TROPIC OF CAPRICORN,

WITH A SKETCH OF THE RECENT EMIGRATION OF THE

BORDER COLONISTS,

AND A ZOOLOGICAL APPENDIX.

BY

CAPTAIN W. C. HARRIS,

H. E. I. COMPANY'S ENGINEERS.

Member of the Bombay Branch, R. A. S.; and of the Geographical Society of Bombay.

Illustrated by a Map and Drawings.

BOMBAY:

Printed

AT THE AMERICAN MISSION PRESS.

1838.

TO

DR. JAMES BURNES,

F. R. S.

KNIGHT OF THE GUELPHIC ORDER,

THIS NARRATIVE,

IN THE PROGRESS AND PUBLICATION OF WHICH HE HAS

EVINCED THE MOST LIVELY INTEREST,

IS INSCRIBED,

WITH EVERY SENTIMENT OF FRATERNAL REGARD

BY HIS AFFECTIONATE FRIEND,

THE AUTHOR.

" Afar in the Desert I love to ride,
  With the silent Bush-boy alone by my side :
  Away—away from the dwellings of men,
  By the Antelope's haunt, and the Buffalo's glen ;
  By valleys remote where the Ourebi plays ;
  Where the Gnoo, the Sassayby, and Hartebeest graze ;
  And the Eland and Gemsbok unhunted recline,
  By the skirts of grey forests o'er hung with wild vine ;
  Where the Elephant browses at peace in his wood,
  And the River Horse gambols unscared in the flood ;
  And the mighty Rhinoceros wallows at will
  In the pool where the Wild Ass is drinking his fill ;
  Where the Zebra wantonly tosses his mane,
  As he scours with his troop o'er the desolate plain ;
  And the stately Koodoo exultingly bounds,
  Undisturbed by the bay of the hunter's hounds ;
  Where the timorous Quagga's wild whistling neigh,
  Is heard by the fountain at fall of day ;
  And the fleet footed Ostrich over the waste
  Speeds like a horseman who travels in haste ;
  Hying away to the home of her rest,
  Where she and her mate have scooped their nest,
  Far hid from the pitiless plunderers view,
  In the pathless wilds of the parched Karroo."

                                        PRINGLE.

CONTENTS.

CONTENTS.

CAHPTER X.

CHAPTER XXX.

DIRECTIONS TO THE BINDER.

INTRODUCTION.

FROM my boyhood upwards, I have been taxed by the facetious with *shooting madness,* and truly a most delightful mania I have ever found it. My first essay in practical gunnery was made at the early age of six, by the discharge of an enormous blunderbuss, known to the inmates of my paternal mansion by the familiar soubriquet of "*Betsy.*" A flock of sparrows perched upon the corner of a neighbour's pigstye, were the only sufferers; but information was maliciously laid against me, and I underwent severe corporal chastisement. About a year afterwards I took ample revenge upon my ill-natured neighbour, by *pinking* his ducks and geese with a cross-bow of my own construction; but my catapult was unfortunately discovered, seized, and confiscated. I next clubbed my Christmas capital with that of two sporting confederates, and raised a sufficient joint stock to purchase a condemned musquet, with which during the holiday vacation,

we shot, and *tyed*. But the partnership proving un-
satisfactory, it was soon dissolved by mutual consent,
and I found myself sole and undisputed *Master of
the Ordnance*. From this eventful and dignified
epoch in my life, I date my rapid improvement in
the noble science of projectiles.

After this sketch of my puerile biography, it is
scarcely necessary to inform the reader that I was considered by my partial friends to be fitting food for
shot and powder. Accordingly I was entered at
the Military College, where my worthy superiors
having pronounced me competent for a commission
in the Engineers, I found myself at the early age of
sixteen, an officer of that distinguished Corps in
Western India; one of the not least valued of my
distinctions being the possession of a rifle, before
the deadly grooves of which a kite had but little
chance at one hundred and fifty yards. Armed with
this weapon, I had ample opportunities of indulging
in my favorite pursuits, and may safely affirm, that
during many years, I enjoyed ball-practice in perfection.

But whilst silently stealing on the recent tracks
of the " antlered monarch of the waste," or perse-
veringly stalking a stately buck—whilst urging my
elephant to his utmost speed in pursuit of a retreating tiger, or contemplating with delight the grizly
figure of a prostrate lion—how frequently did my

thoughts wander to the wilds of Africa, the tales of
sport connected with which had ofttimes reached my
ears, and how impatiently did I long to make the
acquaintance of her motley group of four footed
denizens. Often in my dreams, did I see at the extremity of a long vista of years, that intervened betwixt me and my furlough, the slender and swan-
like neck of the stately Giraffe, bowing distantly to
our better acquaintance; Behemoth, with his square
and mirth-exciting snout protruded from the yellow
waters of a vast river, acting the part of master of
the ceremonies; whilst a host of Rhinoceroses, supported by gigantic Elephants, eccentrically horned
Antelopes, and other fascinating strangers, awaited
their turn of presentation with evident impatience.

With such strong impressions, it will easily be believed that I scarcely regretted the sentence of a
Bombay Medical Board, transporting me for two
years to the Cape of Good Hope; and as this was
accompanied with a welcome recommendation to
travel, I made preparations before quitting India, to
penetrate into the interior of Africa. It would be
injustice to myself, however, to leave an impression
that sport was my only object—for both from edu-
cation and taste, I possessed an ardent desire to
contribute my mite to the Geography and Natural
History of the countries I was about to explore.

At the period of my arrival at the Cape of Good

Hope, public attention was much excited by an event which has probably no parallel in our Colonial history. I allude to the emigration of a large body of Dutch Farmers, who voluntarily forsook the British protection and territory, to effect an establishment in the wilderness, where it was believed—as indeed the result fully proved—they would encounter the severest hardship; and it was no small additional spur to my spirit of enterprise, that I might trace the steps of these wanderers, and, without mingling in politics, investigate on the spot, the origin of so remarkable an expatriation. The map that accompanies this volume, for the outlines of which I am indebted to Arrowsmith's Atlas, published in 1834, is principally illustrative of the history of this singular event. Many interesting Geographical chasms however, have also been filled up, and numerous additions made, either from personal observation, or from materials obligingly furnished by missionaries and intelligent traders, upon whose correctness I could rely. Nothing has been inserted upon vague report; and although it will be remarked that my inconvenient mode of travelling would not admit of my making a strictly scientific survey, I trust that I have been enabled to embody information of interest and importance, in a manner sufficiently accurate to answer the object in view.

My passion for *venerie* had long afforded me opportunities of discovering that the delineations given in popular books of Natural History, of many of the larger quadrupeds, were far from being correct; and I had during my service in India, devoted a portion of my leisure to making more accurate portraits of them with appropriate scenery. A wide field for the gratification of this taste lay before me in Africa, of which I did not fail to avail myself, nor do I despair of being enabled shortly to lay before the Public, the result of my labours in this department.*

These pages were originally written for the perusal of some of my brother officers in India, with whom I have oft stalked the forest, and scoured the plain, and it is to them chiefly that I still present them, trusting that in the scenes described, they will recognize their friend and brother huntsman, and participate with him in the emotions which the overpowering excitement of African wild sports naturally produced in his breast. I knew them to be persons equally attached to the pleasures of the chase with myself, but generally unacquainted with African story, which will account for the occasional introduction of information derived from works already published. My journal having however casually fallen into the hands of others, not sportsmen, whose opinions I respect, and to whom it afforded

*See Prospectus attached to the end of this volume.

gratification, I have ventured to submit it to the public, being assured that my habits of life, and occupation in the details of military duty, will afford a ready excuse for the imperfections it contains, more particularly when I add that it has passed through the press without my personal corrections and at a distance of some hundred miles from the cantonment in which I am quartered.

From my absence also, I have been unable to superintend the printing of the lithographed drawings, for the appearance of which, to those who know the state of the lithographic art at Bombay, I need offer no apology; while to my readers at a distance from India, I can only say that no labor was wanting on my part to render them creditable, and that, before the originals left Belgaum, they had received the approbation of qualified judges, whatever may be now thought of the impressions. They have in fact been destroyed by natives to whom they were unavoidably entrusted, and I lament that the prevalence of the rainy season precludes the possibility of my supplying others.

W. C. HARRIS.

Belgaum, 15th July, 1838.

POSTSCRIPT.

AUGUST 1st 1838.—Recent files of the Graham's Town Journal, which have been received in India since the following pages were printed, contain a tragic sequel to the History of the Border Colonists. It appears that in February last, an advanced party of the Emigrants, led by Retief, having negociated a formal treaty with Dingaan, had been suffered to pass unmolested through the territories of that chieftain, to Port Natal, in the neighbourhood of which they had proposed to establish themselves. Being lulled into perfect security by the friendly reception they had experienced, many families imprudently detached themselves from the main body, and were actively engaged in the division of the land; when, on the fifth day after their separation, they were treacherously attacked by the crafty savage, and man, woman and child, indiscriminately butchered. It is confidently reported that Retief, together with two hundred and seventy souls, had thus miserably perished; and the intelligence of the dreadful catastrophe having been conveyed to Maritz, he was exerting himself to obtain reinforcements from among the Emigrants who were still on the Reit and Modder rivers, with the design of taking summary vengeance on the despot, and succouring the remnant of Retief's unfortunate party; but so great had been the panic created, that his endeavors had hitherto proved unsuccessful; and the escape of the survivors from their hampered position among hostile tribes, and natural barriers, being next to impossible, as a glance at the map will show, it is too probable that accounts will shortly be received of still further massacres.

In the mean time our Colonial authorities were using their utmost exertions to check further emigration, as will appear from the following extract of a proclamation by the Governor, dated Cape Town, the 26th April last. "His Excellency earnestly exhorts the Civil Commissioners and all Public Functionaries throughout the Colony, as well as all ministers of religion, and other persons of sound views, who cannot but foresee the inevitable result of the prevailing mania of emigration, to endeavour by every means in their power, to dissuade intending emigrants from the prosecution of plans which cannot fail, sooner or later, to involve themselves, and their families who are prepared to accompany them, in certain and irretrievable ruin."

W. C. H.

EXPEDITION

INTO

SOUTHERN AFRICA.

CHAPTER I.

VOYAGE FROM INDIA TO THE CAPE OF GOOD HOPE,
AND THENCE TO ALGOA BAY.

On the 16th March 1836, I sailed from Bombay in a large Indiaman, advertised to be a fast sailer, fitted up expressly for passengers. Amongst many others who, like myself, had been attracted by this inviting announcement to enter upon a voyage to the Cape of Good Hope, was William Richardson, Esquire, of the Bombay Civil Service, a gentleman whose acquaintance I had never before had the pleasure of cultivating, but who had long been known to me by repute as a devoted sportsman. To him I communicated my intention of penetrating as far into the interior of Africa as my limited leave would permit, and he immediately agreed to

1

accompany me, embarking from that moment heart, hand, and purse, in the plan I had projected. The usual duration of the voyage is six weeks, but in our case it was protracted to eleven, nor did we reach Simon's Bay until the 31st May.

The first glimpse of the shores of Africa awakened in my bosom the strongest emotions. I already saw realized those fairy dreams which had haunted my imagination, and felt within my grasp the substance of those shadows which had long strewed my path. On arriving at Cape Town, I was so fortunate as to meet with Dr. Andrew Smith, the well known talented leader of the scientific expedition which had just returned from the interior, who afforded me information of the highest value, and gave me accounts of what I should see in the way of sport, which determined me to lose no time in taking the field. A few days sufficed to complete our arrangements and purchases. The former were confined to obtaining passports, visiting the children of Missionaries whom we expected to meet, and engaging a servant, whose name will frequently appear, in lieu of a Mahomedan whom I had brought from India, and who, having already seen enough of the Cape of Good Hope, preferred returning to eat his curry with true believers, to undergoing contamination amongst accursed Kafirs or infidels. Our purchases comprised every article that we fancied could be of service to us in a country where few of the necessaries, and none of the luxuries of life can be obtained, in which no circulating medium exists, and where even mercantile transactions are conducted exclusively by barter. Beads, buttons, brass wire, common trinkets, cheap gewgaws, and ornaments of the baser metals, formed no inconsiderable items of our expenditure, not forgetting an abundant supply of snuff and tobacco. I had brought with me from India pots, kettles, and camp furniture, together with my tent, and an ample stock of gunpowder; and a Parsee servant, named Nesserwanjee Motabhoy, who had accompanied my friend Richardson, declared his determination of following our fortunes.

By Dr. Smith's kind advice, we ordered from a tailor in Cape-town, as a present, amongst others, to the redoubted Chief Moselekatse, called by some *Umsiligas*, whom we proposed to visit, a great coat, in itself so perfectly unique that I may be excused for describing it. Of dimensions suited to the figure of a portly gentleman, pointed out by the Doctor, as resembling the Chief, it was composed of drab *Duffel*, a coarse shaggy cloth commonly worn by the colonists, surmounted by six capes, and provided with huge bone buttons, and a ponderous brazen clasp in the shape of a crest, the whole being lined and fancifully trimmed with scarlet shalloon in a manner calculated to captivate the taste, and propitiate the esteem, of the most despotic and capricious of savages.

With this curious investment, we embarked on the 2d July in a small schooner bound for Algoa Bay, one of our fellow passengers from India accompanying us to the pier, unable to persuade himself, until the boat had fairly pushed off, that we really intended to venture upon a second voyage in such a craft so immediately after the troubles we had undergone. In addition to a mate, a cook, and a Mozambique negro, dignified with the appellation of steward, our crew consisted of three men and a boy; our fellow passengers being two adventurers, who occupied the berth opposite to our own in the only cabin, and a tailor, with his wife and nine daughters, some marriageable, others at the breast. This unfortunate family, every member of which was sea-sick during the whole voyage, located themselves in the steerage, an apartment about eight feet square, ventilated only by the hatchway. The passage up the Coast at that season seldom occupies more than three days, but the fates decreeing that our progress should still be opposed, adverse winds had taken the place of the north-wester, which had been blowing without intermission during the preceding six weeks, and which, had it but continued a day longer, would have wafted us to our destination.

The little vessel was usually gunwale under.

Stormy seas breaking over her, obliged the tailor to seal up his family hermetically; heavy lurches during the night ejected us from our narrow precincts, and more than once brought my companion, who slept in a shelf above me, and myself, into awkward and violent collision; whilst the rolling during the day repeatedly swept the table, and deposited the viands in our laps. Being the whole time within sight of land, no observations were taken, and on the afternoon of the eighth day we entered St. Francis' Bay, in mistake for that of Algoa, not discovering our error until we were about to let go the anchor. The opinions on the subject were various and conflicting. The tailor, who had made the voyage before, courageously ascended the mast-head, in spite of the remonstrances of his love-sick spouse, to make an attempt at recognition: and regaining the deck gravely asserted that we were in Plettemberg's Bay, nearly two degrees to the westward. Doubts being entertained of the soundness of his opinion, we were consulted. The chart was produced, and being satisfied that we were close to Cape Recif, a dangerous reef of rocks, we advised the ship to be hove to; but sail having been again made during the night, we contrived to weather the point, and having narrowly escaped foundering on the Bird Islands, floundered by good fortune into the harbour of Port Elizabeth.

CHAPTER II.

JOURNEY FROM PORT ELIZABETH TO GRAHAM'S
TOWN.

ALGOA Bay is exceedingly open and exposed, and
the anchorage very insecure. During high winds
ships not unfrequently go on shore, a tremendous
surf often rendering it dangerous, and at times even
impossible, for boats to land. We were fortunate in
being able to prevail on the Port Captain to take us
ashore in his barge, a favor which our uncouth habiliments rendered him somewhat cautious in vouch-
safing. The town of Port Elizabeth, though rapidly
increasing, does not consist of above one hundred
and fifty houses. It is built along the sea shore on
the least eligible site that could have been selected.
The soil in the neighbourhood is a sandy loam, producing fine crops of wheat and barley without irriga-
tion, its contiguity to the sea affording sufficient mois-
ture.

We tarried a week at Mrs. Scorey's fashionable
hotel, and were actively engaged in an attempt to
purchase horses, which we understood were to be ob-

tained in the adjoining districts in considerable numbers, and of an excellent quality. It was with inconceivable difficulty, however, that we at length succeeded in procuring two miserable quadrupeds, that appeared to have scarcely sufficient stamina to carry us to Graham's Town. The recent Kafir war having trebled the price of every thing, and of live stock in particular, the demands upon us were exorbitant. With the assistance of Colonel Tripp, the Commanding Officer at Algoa, from whom we experienced great kindness and hospitality, we also became the proprietors of a comfortable travelling waggon, seventeen feet in length, and a span or team of twelve tough little *Faderland* oxen. The former owner, an honest Yorkshireman, named Matthews, whom I specially recommend to all persons requiring a similar conveyance, was with difficulty induced to part with it, and after twelve months experience of its comforts we had no hesitation in pronouncing it to be a cheap and valuable purchase.

With this vehicle, driven by a drunken Hottentot, we took the road to Graham's Town under convoy of Joe Butler, a merry Irishman, of whom we had hired a second waggon for the conveyance of our wares. The activity and skill displayed by Joe in the guidance of his straggling team of oxen, and the unerring dexterity with which he wielded his long and formidable whip, did not fail to excite in us the same astonishment that has been expressed by every traveller in South Africa. Richard, my new valet, voluntarily assumed the office of cook, conceiving himself also, in virtue of the experience he had acquired during a trip to Litakoo, a few years before, with a party of Indian gentlemen, specially charged with our safety. On this occasion, however, he had strangely forgotten to lay in supplies for the road, and we fared badly in consequence.

In the course of the journey few incidents occurred worth mentioning. With the assistance of Butler's team, making in all twenty-four oxen, we ascended the Zwartcop mountain by a steep and difficult acclivity during the first night, and encamped near an extensive grove of aloe trees in full blossom. Thence, a rugged and circuitous track of about one hundred miles in length constituted the road, the scenery comprising a mixture of barren, unprofitable vallies, and stony, uninteresting hills, varied occasionally by deserted farms, where depopulation had stayed the hand of the husbandman—and the blackened walls of roofless cottages which had been sacked by the Kafirs during their late irruption.

Throughout this miserable country, which had been described to us as abounding with game of every description, our diligent researches were only once repaid by a glimpse, on the distant horizon, of three ostriches, and about a score of spring bucks.

This event occurred at a place called Quaggas flat, where we halted a day, and were treated with hospitality by three English settlers, brothers named Pullen. Besides gin-shops, there are two inns on the road; the first at Sunday River, the second at Bushman's Hill; but at neither of these could we procure bread or forage, and the country not producing a single blade of grass, our cattle daily presented more finished specimens of anatomy. Old Pollard, the loquacious landlord of the last mentioned inn, endeavored by his wit to supply the want of cheer, gravely assuring us that had we employed him we might have obtained horses, waggons, and oxen, at a tenth of the price. This worthy Boniface's daughter here joined our party, proceeding to Graham's Town on a matrimonial expedition, or in other words, to be present agreeably to colonial custom, when her marriage banns were proclaimed in church.

Whilst descending a steep hill by night, one of the oxen contrived to strangle himself—a circumstance only remarkable from the great sensation produced by the Parsee's steady refusal to partake of the flesh. We often overheard our followers afterwards talking of the cow-worshipper, who was not allowed to eat beef.* It rained repeatedly and heavily during our

* The well known objection on the part of the Parsees, or fire-worshippers of India, to eating beef, is believed to have arisen from a compact formed with the Hindoos on their first arrival. A respect for Mahomedan prejudices is

journey, the roads in an instant becoming so slippery that it was impossible to proceed a single step until the water had run off. At a place called Assegai Bush, the ground in the morning was white with hoar frost; and all the brooks were frozen over, a sight we had not witnessed for years. It was piercingly cold, and even at 7 A. M. the thermometer stood at 34°. When within a few miles of Graham's Town, which we reached on the seventh day, the baggage waggon was accidentally upset in a deep hole by the road side, and the upper works completely broken, although little injury occurred to the contents, beyond the destruction of our chairs and crockery.

Graham's Town is situated at the source of the Cowie River, at a distance of six hundred and fifty miles from Cape Town, and thirty from the nearest point of the Coast. It is well built, and contains nearly seven hundred houses, with about three thousand inhabitants, principally English. Here we made further purchases, and with difficulty obtained two additional horses, residing four days at Parke's excellent hotel. We also made a valuable friend in the person of Captain Stanford, of the 27th Foot, who introduced us to two intelligent men, David Hume and Robert Scoon, both of whom had

understood to influence them equally against partaking of the unclean beast.

performed several journies into the interior, for the purpose of trading in ivory, and who afforded us much valuable information. Hume provided us with a new driver, a pensioned private of the Cape Rifle Corps, minus a right eye and a fore-finger, proud of his ancestry as a Hottentot, and glorying in the name of Andries Africander. This highly favored individual had already made no less than five trips with Hume and others into Moselekatse's country, and besides being well acquainted with that Chief, possessed a fair smattering of the English and Sichuana languages. He was, moreover, according to his own account, a crack-shot, an intrepid elephant hunter, and a finished waggon driver ; thus professing to combine, beneath a mutilated and unprepossessing exterior, every qualification that could be required in a servant by men in our situation. Had but the virtues of this man kept pace with the accomplishments to which he laid claim, he would indeed have been a valuable acquisition: but unfortunately the result proved that he had not a single redeeming quality that we could discover. A coward, a mutineer, and a liar, it will be seen that Andries caused more mischief and trouble to us by his pernicious example and rebellious conduct when beyond the reach of the law, than can be well conceived by those who have never had the misfortune to be exposed to the machinations of so dangerous a ruffian.

Wherever we were likely to obtain recruits to join our expedition, we hoisted our standard, in the hope and expectation that numbers would flock around it. But whilst some had married wives, and others had purchased farms, we saw too plainly written in the countenances of all, that they felt convinced of the impossibility of two poor Indian gentlemen, who had been only three weeks in the colony, achieving alone and unassisted amongst savage nations in South Africa, a long and perilous journey, which had never been undertaken except by a few persons whose experience of the country might be traced back almost to their cradles, and even by them had been accomplished with great difficulty and hazard.

CHAPTER III.

JOURNEY FROM GRAHAM'S TOWN TO GRAAFF
REINET.

For the moderate remuneration of one hundred Rix
dollars, equal to about seven pounds sterling, Mr.
Pollard junior, the innkeeper's son, volunteered to
accompany us with his waggon as far as Somerset, a small town about half way to Graaff Reinet,
where his maternal uncle resided ; but by dint of
attending the market every morning, we contrived,
on the 26th of the month, to obtain a return vehicle for one fourth of the sum. When we had
proceeded about a mile, one of the lately purchased
horses deserted, and I did not succeed in re-captur-
ing him until he had re-entered Graham's Town.
After travelling ten miles, our waggon having been
carelessly driven by Andries, became entangled in a
wiry unyielding bush, and could not be extricated without the assistance of hatchets. John Strydom, the fat
good natured proprietor of the waggon that we had
hired, took advantage of this delay to ride back upon
a horse that he borrowed from us, in order to recover
a cash receipt of some importance, which he fancied

he had dropped, and returned about the middle of the night, having completely knocked up the steed. What added to our vexation was that he found the missing document in his waistcoat pocket. The leader of our team having stolen a horse during our sojourn at Graham's Town, had been incarcerated, and our difficulties had not been a little multiplied by the impossibility of finding a substitute. Fortunately, however, in the course of the second day's journey, a Hottentot, whom we found sunning himself by the way side, consented to enter our service in the vacant capacity.

The country was still of the same barren, uninteresting character as that already described, but generally more level, less abundantly watered, and more thickly covered with brushwood and succulent dwarf trees, called by the Colonists speck-boom. We travelled at the rate of thirty miles a day, twice passing the night without water for the oxen—saw several small herds of spring bucks, of which beautiful little antelope I killed three—and arrived late on the evening of the 29th at the home-sick Strydom's cottage on Mynheer De Klerck's farm, where his doating young *vrouw* received him with overflowing eyes and open arms. On the journey we had picked up a disconsolate wheelwright, whom we overtook plodding his weary way along the road, with a green veil over his face, and a saddle, bridle, and bundle, on his head; his horse having most unceremoniously abandoned

him under cover of the night, an event by no means
uncommon in the annals of South African travelling,
and one to which our dismounted equestrian was so
well accustomed that he had lost no time in precarious
search, but had set out forthwith in the pedestrian
order I have described, well convinced that if his
truant horse were not already at home, he would
shortly return thither.

John Strydom having messed with us on the road,
his good *vrouw* insisted in return on entertaining us
at supper. Mynheer De Klerck, and several of the
members of his family, visited our host after the repast was over, and were very slow in taking the hint
conveyed by his violent yawnings, that he was anxious
to retire to rest. We slept in the waggon as usual,
and were amused during the greater part of the night
by the drunken merriment and boisterous singing of
a lame Irish cobler, who was " keeping it up" in a
roofless mud outhouse, with two Hottentot " boys,"
neither of whom was under fifty years of age. The
cobler apologized next morning for not inviting us
to the wassail, on the score that we were *gentlemen*,
adding that not being at the time altogether " com-
pos mentis," he hoped we would excuse his apparent
want of politeness.

We halted one day, in order to enjoy the diversion of
wild Guinea fowl shooting on De Klerck's farm, where
we found these birds in abundance; and on the 31st,

continued our journey about five miles, to Somerset, at which we hoped to obtain another waggon; the uxorious John Strydom having been proof against the most tempting bribes offered to induce him to transport our baggage beyond it. The paltry little town of Somerset consists only of about two dozen English houses, and stands in a swamp at the western base of a mountainous range called the Zuur-berg, being completely environed on three sides by the Little Fish river, in attemping to cross which treacherous stream, my horse was suddenly engulphed in a quick sand, and nearly drowned before I could extricate him.

My recollections of Somerset, a place through which I have twice passed, are, I confess, far from pleasing. After I had thrown off my wet garments, we prosecuted our search for a vehicle, and literally visited in succession every house in the village, taking Jackson the Tinman first in order, to whom we had brought a strong letter of introduction from the crippled cobler, but who, nevertheless, received us with marked contumely, turning us from his door with dirt upon our beards, as our Persian friends in India would say. The proprietors of no less than nine out of the twenty-four mansions, were surnamed Smith, an appellation by no means less common in the Cape Colony than in other parts of the British dominions. But although all the Messrs. Smith had waggons, not one of them could

be induced to accede to our request. One of the several John Smiths, a straight haired methodistical
little man, was sitting down to dinner with Mrs.
Smith and the children, when we called to pay our
respects, and, bowing to the ground ventured to seat
ourselves on a vacant sofa; but though the young
Smiths stared abundantly at us, neither the master
nor mistress even condescended to look at us, the lady
after a time informing us, whilst she shovelled down
the pease and gravy with her knife, that she could not
think of allowing her poor dear oxen to go another
journey so immediately after their return from the
country.

In the course of our perambulations through the
town, we stumbled upon a waggon discharging a
cargo of oranges, which was to return the very next
day to within a few miles of Graaff Reinet; yet
strange to say, the bull headed proprietor after taking
an hour to consider of our offer, preferred returning
empty to receiving our freight and fifty Rix dollars.
In the end, being utterly discomfited, we had no alternative but to avail ourselves of an offer obligingly
made by a Mr. Thomas Butler, to deposit our effects
in his warehouse; and having strictly enjoined him to
forward them to us by the first opportunity, we crossed the Little Fish river a second time, and, shaking
the dust from off our feet, departed from Somerset.

3

The following morning, according to arrangements previously made, Mr John Campbell, a kind and obliging friend whom we had met at Graham's town, and to whom we had been introduced by Colonel Tripp, overtook us, and shared one gipsey breakfast on his way to Graaff Reinet. The road over Bruintjes Hoogte, comprises a succession of formidable acclivities and perilous descents, and we were frequently obliged to lock both hind wheels at the same time, the path skirting the very brink of yawning chasms several hundred feet in perpendicular depth, over some of which the clumsiness of Andries, more than once, nearly precipated us.

It was pitch dark before we had cleared this mountain barrier, and the oxen being greatly in want of water, I groped my way in advance, directed by a light, to the dirty cottage of a neighbouring boer, and with some difficulty obtained unwilling permission from the owner, who gloried in the virtuous appellation of Erasmus, to unyoke on his farm. Here a trial of temper awaited us, that immeasurably eclipsed all that we had been destined hitherto to experience. A strong disagreeable wind was blowing, which added to the impossibility of obtaining on the spot more than barely sufficient fire wood to boil the water in the kettle, caused every one to retire early to bed, and the oxen having literally tasted nothing since leaving De Klerck's, were

left at liberty to graze upon the farm during the
night, instead of being secured as usual to the wheels
of the waggon.   On our awakening the next morning
they were no where to be found, and the stony character of the country, in every part clothed with a
high thicket of speckboom, added to the violent wind
that had blown during the night, and effaced the trail,
rendered utterly fruitless our diligent search for them
during the whole day.

A combination of circumstances led us to suspect
that Erasmus was concerned in the abstraction of
our cattle, with the design of extorting a reward for
their restitution.   He had been seen lurking about
the waggon with some of his associates the preceding
evening, and now, far from rendering us any assistance towards their recovery, turned a deaf ear to our
application, and studiously absented himself from the
house.   The sequel proved that our suspicions of his
dishonesty were not unfounded.   The promise of a
reward induced him on the 3d August to return
four of the oxen, but as these were insufficient to draw
the waggon, we proposed that he should furnish us on
hire with a team of his own.   To this he at first
consented, but altered his mind upon some frivolous
pretext, even before the operation of yoking was completed.   Our own provisions, on which we entirely
depended, were by this time exhausted, and I considered myself fortunate in killing two spring bucks.

On the third day, the accidental and opportune arrival of a field cornet named Cornelius, a centurion
having soldiers under him, gave a favourable turn to
our affairs, at the very moment that I had resolved
to ride on to Graaff Reinet for magisterial assistance.
We stated our case to this worthy individual, who
forthwith accompanied us to the nest of theives a-
mongst whom we had fallen, and having threatened
them with legal retribution, sent to our aid two of his
own servants, who succeeded the following day in
recovering the twelfth ox, the other seven having
been in the mean time cunningly restored by Erasmus, whose finished villany we could not help admiring, however much we had suffered by it. Leaving him to the tender mercies of the field cornet,
who prohibited us from paying any reward, we
pursued our journey on the morning of the 5th.
Before dismissing Erasmus from these pages, I may
add that on our way back through the colony, about
twelve months afterwards, we were forced by heavy
rain, I need scarcely say contrary to our wishes,
again to halt at his farm. The hand of fate had fallen
heavily upon him and his race; the house was deserted and its inmates extinct—a small group of graves
before the door being all that remained instead of a
numerous and well favoured family.

As we advanced, the country became more open and
practicable, and was covered with large herds of

elegant spring bucks, bounding playfully across the road. Whilst vainly pursuing some of these antelopes, a favorite dog belonging to my companion ruptured a blood vessel, and died shortly after. On the 6th we rode on at noon in advance of the waggon, but darkness overtaking us, we had great difficulty in finding our way. Crossing the Sunday river three several times we at length arrived at Graaff Reinet, having ridden six and thirty miles, and thus completed a total of two hundred miles from Graham's Town.

CHAPTER IV.

GRAAFF REINET—AND FINAL PREPARATIONS FOR
OUR JOURNEY INTO THE INTERIOR.

THE picturesque little Dutch village of Graaff Reinet, with its adjoining gardens and fields, is nearly surrounded by the Sunday river, which takes it
source in the Sneuwbergen, a lofty range of mountains immediately to the North—and flowing through
the districts of Camdeboo and Uitenhage, falls into
the sea at Algoa bay. The village is sheltered
on each side by high conical mountains decorated
with perpetual verdure, which is derived from the
abundance of speckboom that covers their rocky de-
clivities. The serpentine banks of the river are lined
with willows and acacias—many of these latter are
overgrown with mistletoe, and both with evergreen
creepers, which climbing to the very topmost branches fall gracefully in festoons adorned with a profusion
of fragrant white flowers, not unfrequently concealing
the tree upon which they have entwined themselves.

The district of Graaff Reinet was formed in 1786
under the administration of Governor Van-der-Graaff,
whose name it received with the adjunct of that of

his lady. Nothing can exceed the neatness of the quaint little Dutch houses; and whilst the salubrity of of the climate has no rival in Southern Africa, the produce of the gardens and vineyards may vie with those of Europe. Fruits and vegetables of all kinds grow here in abundance and perfection. I have before said that we entered the village after dark; on looking out of the window in the morning, we saw the street carpeted with snow, while garden hedges of quince, and a row of lemon trees on either side, bending beneath a load of ripe fruit, formed decorations as beautiful in themselves as they were novel to an Indian eye.

We considered Graaff Reinet to be the starting point or base of our operations. Our object now was to sweep rapidly over a great extent of country, in order to reach the most distant point that our time and the duration of our supplies, would permit us to visit. This method of proceeding not only greatly increased the probability of romantic peril, adventure, and discovery, but also enhanced our prospect of sport. We therefore resolved to reach Kuruman or New Litakoo, a missionary station of importance, four hundred miles to the northward, with all practicable expedition, and to proceed thence to the country of Moselekatse, king of the Abaka Zooloos or Matabili, a powerful and despotic monarch, whose dominions were known to abound with game, and possessed the additional advantage of having been little traversed by our countrymen. Arriving there, time and circumstances would enable us to form a further programme of our proceedings, but I determined at all events to extend my researches to the tropic of Capricorn, and even if possible also to visit the Great Lake which is reported to exist considerably beyond it in the interior—fiinally forcing my way back to the colony by the hitherto unexplored routé of the Likwa or Vaal river, which though the most direct, had hitherto in consequence of Moselekatse's interdiction, remained unexplored by Europeans, and which I intended to survey. I need scarcely say that at this time the result of Dr. Smith's recent enquiries had not been made public, and even while I now write, his work has not reached India.

At the time of our arrival at Graaff Reinet, the rage for emigration beyond the boundary was rapidly spreading, and waggons being consequently at a high premium, we had no little difficulty in obtaining a second one for our journey. This will appear strange to those who know that in the Cape colony five out of every six tradesmen, are wheelwrights or waggon builders; but Gert Maritz, the principal waggon maker at Graaff Reinet, a wealthy and discontented man, who, it will be seen, afterwards took a prominent part in the proceedings of his expatriated countrymen—being about to emigrate, had not only purchased as many as he could obtain, but was also busily engaged in manufacturing for himself.

To our surprize, we found that the various wares we had obtained at Cape Town, and which we had unfortunately been obliged to relinquish at Somerset, could easily have been procured at Graaff Reinet. Unwilling however, to incur fresh expense, or to be delayed beyond the 1st September, the day we had fixed for our departure, we despatched a cart to Somerset with instructions to Mr. Butler to forward the articles under his charge: and were not a little mortified to find that during our short absence they had been devoured, as he asserted, by the rats and other vermin, and were consequently not forthcoming. So that in the end we were not only saddled with the extra charge for the cart, but also obliged to make further disbursements for a fresh supply.

The agent we employed here was Mr. John Burnet Biddulph, a trader who had some years before visited Sobiqua, king of the Wangkets, and whose name in conjunction with that of Mr. Bain, will be found referred to in Arrowsmith's map of South Africa. Knowing exactly what we required, he succeeded in obtaining for us from one *Naudé*, a capital waggon with thirty draught oxen: and we had in the mean time completed our stud of horses to twelve of sorts and sizes, conceiving that these would suffice, though in this supposition we were greatly mistaken.

4

Our waggon, fitted up with water casks, tar buck-
ets, side chests, beds, pockets, and other appurte-
nances for the long journey before us, during which it
was to be our only abode, might now not inaptly be
compared to a ship proceeding to sea. Besides ourselves and our personal conveniences, it contained
with the addition of a barrel of gunpowder, and the
commodities for barter already enumerated—six sacks
of flour, two bags of rice, and two of sugar, with
chests of tea and bales of coffee. The baggage
waggon carried tent, camp stools, table, and cooking
utensils: hams, tongues, and cheeses in profusion: salt
and dried fish, biscuits, wax candles, soap, and oilmans
stores, or in other words, sauces and pickles. The
luxury of beer, so palatable to an Anglo Indian, we
were compelled to dispense with in consequence of
its bulk: but we provided ourselves instead with a few
dozens of brandy, and a small barrel of inferior spirits
for the use of the followers. Crevices and empty
spaces were filled up with spades, pickaxes, hatchets,
sickles, and joiner's tools, together with nails, screws,
spare bolts, and linchpins; and as if all these were not
weight sufficient, no less than eighteen thousand leaden
bullets duly prepared—to say nothing of a large additional supply of that precious metal in pigs, to be
converted into instruments of destruction as occasion
required—were added to our stock.

At Graaff Reinet we engaged six additional

Hottentots under a formal contract of service for six months, executed in presence of the Clerk of the Peace. As these were our only associates for many months, and will occasionally appear in prominent relief, I may be here excused consigning them to print, under the appellations of Piet-van-Roy, a man of mixed breed, Cobus Jacobus, John April, Claas September, Frederick Dangler, and Ethaldur Wildman. Nearly all of these being *tronk volk,* or in other words discharged criminals, no agreement less binding than the one we had made, would have answered our purpose. But scarcely a day had elapsed, before we had reason to regret our part in the contract: for perpetual drunkenness and debauchery found their way into our peaceful family, and while our cattle were left to stray in the fields, their keepers were generally reposing in a happy state of oblivion by the road side. The result was that two of our oxen died, and most of the others lost their condition. The characters of these baboon faced gentlemen however, as they became gradually developed to their masters, will be sufficiently unfolded in the course of these pages.

Before quitting Graaff Reinet, we obtained from Mr. Ryneveldt, His Majesty's Civil Commissioner, a further passport, claiming protection for us in the wards of the different field cornets on our route: together with introductory letters to Captains Waterboer and Cornelius Kok, two Griqua chieftains in alliance with the colonial Government. Without such an official authority, we could not have ventured to carry across the frontier so large a supply of ammunition, the policy of Government rendering the transit of gunpowder into the territories of the native princes, altogether contraband.

Our party now amounted in all to eleven. As a body of men intended to resist a hostile tribe, this number was very insufficient; but with due prudence and courage, we felt confident of repelling any predatory attack: and with the advantage of fire arms, of withstanding even a multitude of such opponents as those by whom we were likely to be assailed.

CHAPTER V.

————

Every preparation for our final departure was completed on the 1st September; but that day so auspicious to sportsmen in Europe, "looked lowering upon us," —dawning with a tremendous deluge of rain, which continued until afternoon, and afforded the Hottentots more than sufficient leisure to indulge in their vicious propensities. In accordance with advice that we had received, but the futility of which we were not long in discovering, they had each been furnished with a musquet, as a defence against the wild beasts and savages; and it will be seen hereafter, that whilst their pusillanimity prevented their turning these weapons to our advantage, they employed them but too successfully in scaring the game from our encampments. On the present occasion our astonishment may be conceived, when on preparing to start in the evening, one half of the musquets were found to be already in pawn, and the proceeds squandered in the gin shop. As a consequence, most of the Hottentots themselves,

were discovered to be in such a brutal state of in-
ebriety, that we were obliged—after various ineffec-
tual attempts to rouse them, on our own part and that
of their more sober brethren, who beat them without
mercy—to transfer them like pigs into the waggons
which they had been hired to drive.

In this comfortable condition we commenced our
march—but had scarcely passed the outskirts of the
village when the rain descended in torrents, and left
us no alternative but to return : in doing which, one of
the less intoxicated Hottentots, civilly carried off the
corner of a house, by propelling the heavily laden vehicle against it. Dreading further mishaps, and satisfied that no dependence could be placed upon our
followers, if once allowed to recover their sobriety
and liberty, we finally quitted Graaff Reinet at six
p. m. and by ten o'clock had formed our camp ten
miles off.

The morning's dawn did not find the Hottentots
much gratified at their transportation into the desert,
coupled as it was with the prospect of a long and tedious separation from gin and bitters; and to add to
their distress, we insisted also that they should part
from their *vrouws* or wives, before crossing the snowy
mountains. As we ascended the acclivitous road
leading over Sir Lowry Cole's pass into that range,
the farewells were abundantly affecting. John April's
interesting spouse in particular, a negress possessing

all the Hottentot peculiarities fully developed, clung round the neck of her " dear man" and half smothered him with kisses.

Before we had proceeded many miles, we were met by a Hottentot riding post to Graaff Reinet for medical assistance: his master, a young Dutch boor, having been fearfully clawed in a clumsy attempt to destroy a leopard. Soon after, a courier overtook our cavalcade, having been hired at an expense of *four* Rix dollars, to gallop after us to recover a debt of *five*, which, in the hurry of departure we had neglected to settle—an ominous proof that the good people of Graaff Reinet had little expectation of seeing us again. Our friend Mr. Campbell, together with Mr. Lloyd His Majesty's Special Justice, and several other gentlemen, joined our party in the evening, and remained with us until the following day.

As we advanced through the elevated region of Sneuwberg Proper, the vegetation became visibly more abundant, and the air sensibly colder. That greatest of all rarities in South Africa, a real turf or sod, was to be seen, interspersed with mat rushes. Around, nothing presented itself in the landscape but rocky mountains, of which the summits were enveloped in mist and snow: the unsettled state of the weather heightening in no small degree, the sublimity and frowning grandeur of the scene. Peak towering above peak, the lofty and broken mountains appeared

to crowd in one upon the other—the Spitscop, a remarkable and pre-eminently lofty crag, soaring above
the whole: whilst the rude and bold features of nature
were for miles unmingled with any trace of human
works, beyond the beaten track that we were following
along steep acclivities. But for this, and an occasional wreath of smoke, ascending from the bosom of
some sunken valley, no one could have supposed that
the abode of man was to be found in a region, apparently so deserted and inhospitable.

A chilly mist overtaking us, we resolved to halt for
the night at a kraal* of Fingoes or tame Kafirs,
where barely a sufficient quantity of fuel, from a
shrub called the Rhinoceros bush, could be obtained for culinary purposes. Although still within the
Cape Colony, our tobacco here proved of use in the
purchase of goats' milk; and I may here remark that
this precious weed, which may be denominated the
current coin of the realm, is carried about in Africa twisted in long thin ropes, which are coiled up
in rolls. A roll is considered a splendid oblation to
a prince—and an inch, a handsome present to a

* Notwithstanding that it has been the habit to employ the
terms *Kraal, Caross,* and *Assegai,* as respectively indicating a
native village or cattlefold, a skin cloak, and a dart or spear
—not one of them have any signification in the native languages, but are supposed to be a corruption of Dutch and
Hottentot.

commoner; meted out by the span in traffic, it will purchase whatever this most benighted of countries can produce.

The following day, after passing the residence of Piet Van-der Merwe, yclept Dickwang or double chin, —a soubriquet with which a large wen on the throat has saddled him, as a distinction from his neighbours of the same name—we cleared the Sneuwbergen, and arrived at a deserted farm, named Dassies fontein. Here we were struck with the sight of an old kafir smoking dacca, or the narcotic wild hemp, in which the natives greatly delight. Seated at the door of a miserable hovel, a squalid picture of poverty, the decrepit wretch was inhaling the pernicious drug through water from a bullocks horn. Volumes of smoke were forced into his stomach by draughts of water, and the result was a violent fit of coughing, attended by raving delirium. We actually saw him throw off his slender apparel, and rush forth into the plain like a wild beast or a maniac from Bedlam.

At noon on the 5th the thermometer stood at 32°, the snow falling in quantities during the whole of the day. We however travelled twenty-five miles, and reached Vogel valley, where the following morning, the whole of the brooks were frozen over with ice a quarter of an inch thick, and the manes of the horses, and the herbage around, were decorated with icicles. The glass at 7 A. M. had sunk to 18°, yet the cold to

5

the feeling was neither intense nor disagreeable.
Here for the first time, we saw large troops of those
eccentric animals the Gnoos, † three of which we killed, having hemmed a herd into a valley, and obliged
them to run the gauntlet.

Of all quadrupeds, the Gnoo is probably the most
awkward and grotesque. Nature doubtless formed
him in one of her freaks, and it is scarcely possible
to contemplate his ungainly figure without laughter.
Wheeling and prancing in every direction, his shaggy
and bearded head arched between his slender and
muscular legs, and his long white tail streaming
in the wind, this ever wary animal has at once a ferocious and ludicrous appearance. Suddenly stopping,
showing an imposing front, and tossing his head in
mock defiance, his wild red sinister eyes flash fire, and
his snort resembling the roar of a lion, is repeated
with energy and effect. Then lashing his sides with
his floating tail, he plunges, bounds, kicks up his heels
with a fantastic flourish, and in a moment is off at
speed, making the dust fly behind him as he sweeps
across the plain.

On the 7th we reached Boks fontein, where, during
the night, two of the horses absconded. Having been
bred in the neighbouring district. called New Hantam,

† *Catoblepas Gnoo.* Delineation in Captain Harris's African views. Vide appendix.

to the grass of which cattle are much attached, it was surmised that they had strayed thither : and whilst Piet and Andries were despatched in pursuit of them we continued our journey to the Seven Fountains. Here the face of the country was literally white with spring bucks,* myriads of which covered the plains, affording us a welcome supply of food. When hunted, these elegant creatures take extraordinary bounds, rising with curved backs high into the air, as if about to take flight : and they invariably clear a road or beaten track in this manner, as if their natural disposition to regard man as an enemy, induced them to mistrust even the ground upon which he had trod.

The *trek bokken*, as the occasional immigration to the abodes of civilization, of countless swarms of these antelopes, is called by the colonists, may be reckoned amongst the most extraordinary examples of the fecundity of animal life. To offer any estimate of their numbers would be impossible : pouring down like locusts from the endless plains of the interior, whence they have been driven by protracted drought, lions have been seen stalking in the middle of their compressed phalanx, and flocks of sheep have not unfrequently been carried away with the torrent. Cultivated fields which in the evening appeared proud of their promising verdure, are in the course of a

---

* *Gazella Euchore.* Delineated in the African views.

single night, reaped level with the ground, and the despoiled grazier is constrained to seek pasture for his flocks elsewhere, until the bountiful thunder clouds restore vegetation to the burnt up country. Then the unwelcome visiters instinctively retreat to their secluded abodes, to renew their attacks when necessity shall again compel them.

Two of our oxen having become exhausted, we presented them to Frederick Mark Graaff, an itinerant pedagogue and masonic brother, whom we here met, and from whom in return we received a handsome and powerful dog. At Vendussie Kuilen, a waterless station, at which we encamped the next day, Piet returned, not only unsuccessful, but having completely broken down, and so deeply galled the back of one of the best horses, that he was utterly useless during the rest of the trip. Andries still remained to carry on the search for those that had strayed.

Three tedious marches through an arid level country, quite denuded of herbage, and nearly destitute of water, brought us across an extensive tract impregnated with salt, to the residence of the frontier Field Commandant, whose domains are situated on the extreme border of the Colony, and are bounded by the Nu Gareep, (one of the two principal branches of the Great Orange river,) where we encamped to enjoy the luxury of bathing, and having our linen washed. This day, three more of our oxen dropped down on the road, and being unable from fatigue and want of sustenance to advance another step, we had no alternative but to leave them a prey to the wild beasts. A forlorn traveller whom we overtook, might have shared the same fate had we not succoured him, for his horses agreeably to Colonial usage, had absconded, leaving him to pursue his journey on foot.

We were at first rather coolly welcomed by the Field Commandant, to whom we presented the Government letter. He received it with great respect, and putting on his spectacles, laboured hard to decipher its contents: but after halting at every word of more than two syllables—taking his leisure to comprehend the meaning of each sentence—overrunning the stops, and making a pause to reconsider them— he consigned it to his wife, who, although scarcely a better scholar than himself, reported so favorably of its purport, that the worthy Warden of the Marches at once invited us to join his evening meal. In the course of conversation, we found that Mynheer, although ignorant of all languages except Dutch, claimed a Scottish extraction. His board was graced by many sturdy scions of his stock, the younger of whom adhered to the primitive custom of standing behind and attending on their parents and guests. Before supper commenced, a slave made a circuit of the room with a tub filled with water, offering it to us, and to the members of the family, who each, according to seniority washed their feet therein—a custom not very congenial to our tastes, and with which we declined to comply—considering that the same water served for all, and that the operation was followed by a general appropriation of the table cloth instead of a towel. After a long grace—repeated, or rather sung, with the most puritanical countenance and tone by one of the young men, who occupied an elevated position behind his father's chair—the Field Commandant gave the order for the onslaught, and commenced his revel with an earnest. A scene of conglomeration and tobacco smoke ensued, from which we were unceremoniously dismissed at 9 o'clock, by an intimation from our landlord that he was about to proceed to bed.

After great solicitation on the following day, the Commandant consented to dispose of one hundred of his wether sheep to us, but in the end did not supply us with more than sixty. These we purchased from him at three Rix dollars per head, and being on the opposite side of the river, their transit across the stream gave us the greatest trouble and annoyance. No less than thirteen persons were engaged in the attempt to bring them over, but it was not until one of Mynheers son's had brought a large black goat, which headed the flock, and strange to say took the water like a Newfoundland dog, that we got them transported. On enquiry we found that the old goat was a Palinurus frequently employed for the same purpose. I may here remark that although the merino sheep has been introduced, the Cape Colonists continue to be attached to the African breed, the large tails of which, composed of solid fat which literally trails on the ground, producing a luxury that is essential to the comfort and enjoyment of every South African settler.

CHAPTER VI.

FROM THE BOUNDARY OF THE COLONY, ACROSS THE
GREAT ORANGE RIVER TO KURUMAN.

W E had now fairly quitted civilization, and were
entering upon a sterile inhospitable region sparingly
inhabited by Bushmen—the remnant of Hottentot
hordes, and the wild aborigines of the country—who,
gradually receding before the encroachments of the
European Colonists, have long since sought refuge in
the pathless desert. Unblessed amongst the nations
of the earth, the hand of these wandering out-casts
is against every man, and every man's hand is against
them. Existing precariously from day to day—heedless of futurity, and forgetful of the past,—without
either laws, arts, or religion—only a faint glimmer-
ing ray of instinct guides their benighted path. Depending for subsistence upon the produce of the
chase or the spontaneous gifts of nature, they share
the wilderness with beasts of prey, and are but one
grade higher in the scale of existence.

From this point until we reached Kuruman, a distance of three hundred miles, the number of our

oxen became daily diminished by the effects of a drought which had prevailed, and which had so completely removed every vestige of vegetation, that they were frequently compelled to pass two days without tasting food or water. Extensive—to the eye boundless, plains of arid land with neither eminence nor hollow, were on all sides expanded to the view : of these the prevailing color was brownish yellow, variegated with a few black and sickly shrubs. Scarcely an object met the straining eye but an ostrich sometimes striding in the distance, or a solitary vulture soaring in the sky. Over the wide desolation of the stony waste not a tree could be discerned, and the only impression on the mind was—that of utter and hopeless sterility. Occasionally however as we advanced, the sameness of the scene was varied by a wide stretching undulation. Our caravan was then the only object in the landscape upon which the eye could repose. Waggon after waggon slowly rising to view, the van was to be seen advancing over the swell, whilst the cattle and sheep were yet hidden from the sight. The world before us was still nought but earth and sky—not a green herb enticed the vision, not a bird winged through the air: the loud cracking of a whip rolling in suppressed echo along the sun-baked ground alone disturbed the silence of the sultry atmosphere, which gave to the azure vault

6

of heaven [the semblance of an unnatural elevation from the globe.

Whilst the days were oppressively hot, and the sky unveiled by a cloud, the nights were piercingly cold— our feelings during the latter indicating as well as the thermometer, that the temperature was near the freezing point : and to add to our discomfort, fuel was rarely procurable. In the morning, the ground was sometimes covered with hoar frost : but the absence either of vapour or cloud to diminish the heat of the sun, soon dispelled the appearance, and rendered visible the nakedness of the land. Mirage in these regions, flickering in the distance, presents to the thirsty traveller an illusion as tempting as tantalizing. Blue and delusive lakes of which the surface seems agitated by a ripple, recede as he advances—and ultimately disappearing, "leave not a wreck behind."

But the monotony of this wearisome journey was not always unbroken by events. We halted the first day on the borders of what appeared to be a body of water many miles in circumference—an oasis in the desert, towards which after a sultry march of twenty miles, lured by the appearance of several waggons on its brink—both man and beast rushed with impetuosity. We soon perceived to our disappointment that we had been deceived by a saline deposit of immense extent at which a party of Boors

were engaged in obtaining salt for the use of the
Colonists : but it was long ere the broken hearted
oxen discovered that what they had understood to
be water, was a mere mineral efflorescence in the
desert.

The fourth day brought us to the magnificent
Orange river—the only stream within many hundred
miles that is entitled to the appellation. Emerging
from desolation and sterility the first glimpse that we
obtained of it realized those ideas of elegant and
classic scenery which exist in the minds of poets.
The alluring fancies of a fairy fiction, or the fascinating imagery of a romance, were here brought into
actual existence. The waters of this majestic river,
three hundred yards in breadth, flowing in one unbroken expanse, resembled a smooth translucent lake;
and as its gentle waves glided past on their way to
join the restless ocean, bearing on their limpid bosom
as in a polished mirror, the image of their wood clothed borders, they seemed to kiss the shore before bidding it farewell. Drooping willows clad in their
vest of vernal freshness, leaned over the bank—and
dipping their slender branches into the tide which
glistened with the last rays of the setting sun—seemed
fain to follow : whilst at intervals, the wrecks of
stately trees that had been torn from their roots by
the violence of the torrent during some vast inunda
tion, of which the traces on the shore gave evidence—

reared their dilapidated heads in token of the then resistless fury of that flood, which now appeared so smooth and tranquil. To those who may conceive this description overcharged I will only remark, that the sight of water after days in the desert, is probably one of the most delightful sensations that a human being can experience.

Our transit across the Orange river was highly amusing. In consequence of the depth of water, we were obliged to make an elevated platform within the waggons, on which to place our baggage. The double line of oxen stoutly stemming the current, the frantic gestures of the drivers, and the singular appearance of the followers , now wading, now swimming, laden with the lighter baggage, and urging on the loose horses and sheep, altogether presented a picture which I shall not readily forget.

Before reaching Campbellsdorp, a missionary station, we observed a large party of Corrannas engaged in an attempt to run down an ostrich on foot— a prodigy of speed which these people sometimes achieve. Their prevailing dress is a cloak and cap of leather, bedaubed, in common with their own skins, with an unguent of grease and red ochre; but the exhortations of the missionaries have, in some instances, caused this primitive garb to be supplanted by leathern jackets and trowsers of European fashion. At Campbellsdorp we were kindly received by Mr.

Bartlet the missionary, but were disappointed at learning that the Chief Waterboer was not at Griquastaad. Captain Cornelius Kok was also absent, but his *locum tenens* being desirous of purchasing finery for his wife, obliged us with three fat oxen in return for a glaring stamped tablecloth, to which we added a pound of tea. Mr. Bartlet considered himself well repaid for a sturdy ox by a small canister of gunpowder.

When near Daniels kuil—a kraal of Griquas, or Mulatto Hottentots, we met their Chief, Captain Dowd, whose mouth watered at the appearance of our waggons, and who requested particularly that we would not transact any business with his people until the morrow. This man is remarkable as being one of the only two Griquas who escaped the general massacre of their army by Moselekatse's warriors in 1831, the particulars of which we obtained from himself. From him also we received five fresh oxen, in lieu of our six lame ones and a cast off surtout coat of Richardson's, which he immediately donned with great exultation.

At Kramers Fontein next day, a horrible spectacle presented itself to us in the form of an emaciated old Bushwoman, who had come down from her kraal five miles distant, to fill two ostrich egg shells with water. "Grim misery had worn her to the bones," and it is no exaggeration to say that her attenuated form appear-

ed a skeleton covered with a wet cloth. Those rounded proportions which are given to the human form
divine, had no existence in her. Her skin resembled
wrinkled leather, and I can compare her legs and
arms to nothing but straightened sticks, knobbed
at the joints. Her body was actually crawling with
vermin, with which she was constantly feeding a
little half inanimate miniature of herself in arms.

> ———"Withered and wild in her attire,
> She looked not like a habitant of earth,
> And yet was on it."

We were glad to bribe her to depart by a present of
tobacco, and the wretched creature's countenance
evinced thankfulness at our liberality.

The pigmy race of which this woman was a char-
acteristic specimen, usually reside in holes and cran-
nies of rocks, and sometimes in wretched huts in-
capable of protecting them from the inclemency of
the seasons. These, their constant fear of discovery
induces them to erect in secluded spots at a great distance from water : a precaution to which they are further prompted by a desire to leave the pools open for
wild animals, which they occasionally shoot from an
ambush with poisoned arrows, and devour on the spot.
They possess neither flock nor herds—are unacquainted with agriculture—and the most wealthy can
boast of no property beyond his weapons and his
starving dog. With no cares beyond the present moment, they live almost entirely upon bulbous roots,

locusts, reptiles, and the larvæ of ants, by the habitations of which latter the country is in many places
thickly strewed. Not a trace of their hovels could
be seen from the road, and a traveller might even
pass through their country without seeing a human
being, or suspecting that it was inhabited. Such is
their general distrust of visiters, that the males would
never willingly approach us, evincing great trepida-
tion when forced to do so—no object being more unwelcome to their sight than a troop of horsemen on
the plain.

The stature of both sexes is invariably below five
feet. The males are usually meagre, bow-legged, and
ill made : yet they display a singular ease of motion
and flexibility of joint. The rapidity with which they
drive off a herd of cattle is perfectly astonishing.
Their complexion is sallow brown, darkened by dirt
and grease : their only dress a piece of leather round
the waist, and their sole defence a diminutive bow,
with poisoned arrows, rather resembling childrens'
toys than mortal weapons.

The women, who were much less shy, and who never failed to follow the tracks of our waggons when
they happened to come upon them, with the hope of
obtaining tobacco in exchange for ostrich eggs, are
of small and delicate proportions, with hands and feet
of truly Lilliputian dimensions. Their foot prints
reminded us of Gullivers adventures, and are not

larger than those of a child. When young they have
a pleasing expression of countenance, which they
take care to render as captivating as possible by be-
daubing their flat noses and prominent cheek bones
with a mixture of red ochre and fat.   The toilets of
many were made with scrupulous attention, the effect of the paint being enhanced by necklaces composed of the fresh entrails of wild beasts—a few cow-
ry shells, old bones and buttons, being also interwov-
en with their matted hair; but the life they lead, their
frequent long abstinence, and constant exposure to
the wind and glare of light in a dry open country,
soon inducing the habit of keeping their naturally
small eyes more than half closed, their comeliness is
very ephemeral, and never extends beyond youth.
The females possess much greater volubility and ani-
mation of gesture than the men—but the sounds
they utter are a succession of claps of the tongue
produced by forcing that unruly member against different parts of the teeth and palate : and whilst the
enunciation is thus rendered troublesome and full of
impediment, it resembles rather the chattering of
monkeys than the language of human beings.

    At Koning on the 25th, we had the unexpected
pleasure of meeting Captain Sutton of the 75th Foot,
—a mighty Nimrod, and a man after my own heart—
who was returning to the Colony from a successful
expedition against the Elephants.   Together with a

seasonable addition to our stud, and soul stirring accounts of what he had seen, we obtained from this
gentleman the first unwelcome intelligence that Moselekatse was embroiled with the emigrant Farmers.

The following day we entered Kuruman or New
Litakoo, a lovely spot in the waste by which it is
completely environed.   Here we received a very cor-
dial welcome from a missionary of the London Society—the Rev. Mr. Moffat—whose children amongst
others we had visited in Cape Town.   To this excellent Clergyman, who together with his amiable
lady, has devoted his life to the cause of Christianity,
we were indebted during our stay at Kuruman, for
hospitality and kindness which we shall never be enabled to repay.

7

CHAPTER VII.

FROM KURUMAN TO LITTLE CHOOI.

Twenty days had now elapsed without any tidings of Andries, when at last that worthy follower of our fortunes was seen approaching in equestrian order. Whilst however, he had undoubtedly brought back the horses, he had contrived to render them unserviceable for some weeks by galling their backs: and had besides sacrificed the mare upon which he had set forth on his quest. Had the accounts that he gave of the privations he suffered on the road, and of his personal combats will surly Boors, who had opposed themselves to the fulfilment of his mission, been correct, his claims to our everlasting gratitude might have been acknowledged; but, unfortunately for him, we subsequently discovered that they had no foundation in truth; and on the contrary, that having speedily recovered the fugitives, he had embraced the opportunity of surreptitiously paying a visit to his mother, and some of his cronies who resided at a distance.

Mr. Moffat confirmed the reports that we had heard from Captain Sutton respecting the attacks made upon the emigrant Farmers by Moselekatse, of whose history it will be expected that I should here offer a brief outline. He is the despotic ruler of a powerful tribe called Abaka Zooloo, or Matabili. His father was a chieftain whose territories lay at some distance to the North eastward of Natal, but being attacked and totally defeated by a neighbouring tribe, he took refuge with Chaka, the Zooloo tyrant, (predecessor of Dingaan,) with whom he remained till his death in a servile state, resembling that of the Fingoes amongst the Kafirs. Moselekatse, however, succeeded in gaining the favor and confidence of Chaka, and in process of time was intrusted with the command of an important military post, and the charge of a large number of cattle. Seizing his opportunity he revolted, and fled with his people and the booty towards the North west, eating up in his progress the several tribes which then occupied that country, and soon becoming so exceedingly formidable that his very name inspired terror through a vast region. Having completely subjugated or destroyed every tribe from whose opposition he had any thing to dread, he ultimately selected the country near the sources of the Molopo and Moriqua rivers for his permanent residence, where he now reigns, the terror of the surrounding nations.

Bidding adieu to the worthy missionary, we resumed our journey on the 29th of September, towards

Mosega, the capital of Moselekatse, distant about two hundred miles in a North easterly direction. As we were now entering upon a country hitherto little explored, and as far as I know, only partially described by Mr. Campbell on his journey towards Kurrechaine, I shall be excused being a little more minute in my descriptions.

The road from Kuruman to our intended halting ground was so circuitous that we despatched the waggons in advance, and rejoined them by a more direct route accompanied by Andries, who, after all his achievements, was not a little mortified at perceiving that the sorriest horse of all had been reserved for him. Naturally of an unassuming disposition, he humbly conceived himself entitled to the best : and thus disappointed, unhesitatingly declared his inability to shew the way, which nevertheless to his disgust we contrived to find for ourselves. The presentation of an old waistcoat in the evening however, had the effect of soothing his feelings.

The next morning, a messenger arrived with letters for us from Mr. Moffat to the missionaries at Motito and Mosega. A Bechuana gentleman of quality to whom we had been introduced at Kuruman, came at the same time with his two daughters, having conceived a desire to join our mess as far as Motito. We had received a bad character of this personage, but as far as our experience of him went,

he was very orderly, and afforded a fund of enter-
tainment by his ridiculous attempts to colloquise in
Dutch. His skin was blacker than a boot, and in
texture resembled a Rhinoceros hide : yet he studiously interposed a parasol composed of ostrich plumes,
betwixt the sun and his nobility, leaving his little
daughters to bestride a pack bullock, and their com-
plexions to take care of themselves.

Our march was a very hot one, over measureless
plains, bounded only by the distant horizon : the
fading blue summits of the Kamhanni mountains near
the Kuruman, only slightly breaking the evenness of
the line from which we were receding. The soil
consisted chiefly of red sand, abounding at intervals
with long coarse grass, which being dry, gave to the
plains the delusive appearance of ripe corn-fields.
Fourteen miles brought us to the Matluarin—a periodical river, with a few detached pools of hardly
drinkable water—where bulrushes, and a scanty turf,
afforded barely sufficient pasture for the oxen.

We had hitherto failed in our endeavors to obtain
an interpreter to accompany us—the only available
person in that capacity being a Bechuana residing at
Motito, against whom we had been particularly warned by Captain Sutton as a mischief-maker; but in
default of a better, we had resolved by the advice of
Mr. Moffat to entertain this man. It unfortunately
so happened however, that he passed through our

camp during the night on his way to Litakoo (whither he had been despatched by Mahura, chief of that place) a circumstance which the Hottentots carefully *concealed*, from motives of their own, until he was far distant.

The weather was piercingly cold when we resumed our journey in the morning. Our people had for once taken the precaution of filling the casks, and we were thus enabled to obtain breakfast although we came to no water. About noon we also halted for half an hour at a muddy pool, which the cattle drained to the dregs, whilst a sheep was being slaughtered to satisfy the cravings of our guest's stomach, to the empty state of which he had repeatedly by drawn our attention.

During the early part of the day our road continued across a boundless ocean like expanse, the surface being broken only by ant hills, or occasional dwarf bushes, amongst which troops of ostriches were grazing. Proceeding, we passed through many extensive areas of waving grass, and the country gradually became decorated with larger shrubs, bearing a profusion of yellow flowers. Occasionally too, straggling clumps of mimosas, from ten to fifteen feet in height, afforded a pleasing relief. The day was intolerably hot, dusty, and disagreeable: we saw Motito indistinctly in the distant glare some hours before we reached it. This we did about sunset, having travelled altogether twenty-two miles. We were immediately welcomed by Mr. Lemue, the French Missionary, who, with his agreeable wife, evinced by great attention and kindness to us, the gratification they experienced from the arrival of two civilized strangers in the desert, in which from motives of the highest nature, they have immured themselves. The elder of this interesting young couple did not appear to be more than twenty-two years of age.

I have not hitherto referred to the dress and appearance of the Bechuana tribes, of which the remnants have been collected by the Missionaries. Of the habiliments of the men little need be said, as they have generally adopted a rude imitation of the European costume. The females however, almost invariably retain the garb of their ancestors. The appearance of these ladies is masculine, and far from attractive. Fat and grease of all kinds form their delight: their bodies and skin cloaks being also plentifully anointed with *sibilo*, a grey iron ore sparkling like mica, procured from mines in the neighbourhood, which are visited from from all parts of the country. Their naturally woolly hair is twisted into small cords, and matted with this substance into apparently metallic pendules, which being of equal length, assume the appearance of a skull cap or inverted bowl of steel. Tobacco having undergone considerable depreciation by the introduction of the plant—beads are the medium through which exchanges are usually effected amongst the Bechuana. The more wealthy of their women are adorned with a profusion of these, hung in cumbrous coils round the waist and neck, along with ivory tooth-picks and gourd snuff-boxes : but even the indigent are not altogether without them. An apron of leather, cut into thin strips and clotted with an accumulation of grease and filth, reaches to the ancles—and with a rude skin cloak, completes the costume.

We were subjected to continual interruptions from the visits and curiosity of crowds of these ladies, who appeared to have no domestic concerns to attend to : and, although the assertion may subject me to the accusation of want of gallantry, I am compelled to state that the effluvia arising from their persons, which are not always free from vermin, was far from agreeable. Their language, termed *Sichuana*, is exceedingly melodious. Few syllables end with a consonant, and the remarkable abundance of vowels and liquids give it a smoothness of sound to which both sexes do ample justice by the gentle tones of their voice.

Early the following day our waggons were surrounded by natives with skins and *carosses* * for sale. Foremost in the motley group was Mahura,

* *Vide* note at Chapter V.

the Batlapi Chief—brother of Motibe, King of that
tribe—a portly personage of exceedingly forbidding
manners, and unprepossing exterior. He was habited in a thread bare braided jacket and leathern trowsers, with a broad brimmed white hat which obscured
a large portion of his sinister physiognomy. His A.
D. C.—another prominent figure, had inducted his
shrivelled frame into a green surtout and military
chaco, being withal the least martial character I
ever beheld. We made them propitiatory offerings,
and handed round the snuff box : but far from meeting our advances, they seemed disposed to quarrel,
more especially when they discovered that we knew
exactly how many yards of brass wire were esteemed an equivalent for a caross. At length, finding it
impossible to come to terms, we closed our little shop,
and were preparing to depart—when on a sign made
by Mahura, a tall gaunt savage pounced upon a
drinking cup, and declared his intention of retaining
it in compensation for alleged injury to the fence of
his field. Deaf to our remonstrances, he was moving off with his prize, when Richardson seized it from
him, and threw it to the right owner. In the mean
time another obtrusive savage deliberately seated
himself on the pole of the waggon, from which he
refused to move, although civilly requested to make
way for the oxen. In this posture of affairs I found
it necessary to resort to personal violence, which so

exasperated him that he sprung at me, brandishing his weapons, and exclaiming that I had kicked him on his own premises. The clamour now became fast and furious, and the threatening attitudes of our assailants obliged us to protrude the muzzles of two or three fowling pieces from the waggons, so as to bear upon their masses—when they instantly dispersed, leaving us to pursue our journey.

Mahura and Moselekatse are bitter foes. Shortly after Dr. Smith's expedition arrived at Kuruman, the former, who had carried off several head of cattle from the Matabili, expressed his determination of opposing the Doctor's advance—a threat which he did not however carry into execution. From that period, until within a few days of our arrival at Motito, this boaster, dreading the vengeance of Moselekatse, had ignominiously concealed himself—now, for the first time, venturing from his hiding place. Before we had proceeded many miles, a savage, breathless with haste, met us as if by accident, and implored the waggon drivers to turn back—representing Moselekatse as highly incensed—and stating that that Prince had attacked a party of Farmers with great slaughter, and that the same fate awaited us if we advanced farther into his territory. He then decamped, leaving every face blank with dismay. We instantly suspected that the whole was a plot of Mahura's, and it had the effect he desired of creating such a panic among the people, that they positively refused to advance another step. Andries was the first to declare this determination, repeating the savage's story with fifty exaggerations of his own, and confidently predicting an attack during the night. The spirits of the bolder were damped by the gloomy forebodings of the more cowardly, nor would they have proceeded if John April had not fortunately, though unwarrantably, presumed to broach the grog cask during the night: getting so drunk himself, that we were obliged to leave him to come on behind, whilst the rest became sufficiently courageous to resume the journey in the dark—not however, until they had broken the pole of the waggon, which we soon replaced.

As the morning's dawn slowly withdrew the curtain from the landscape, we perceived the aspect of the country completely changed. Instead of the dreary waste over which we had lately passed, we might now imagine ourselves in an extensive park. A lawn, level as a billiard table, was everywhere spread with a soft carpet of luxuriant green grass, spangled with flowers, and shaded by spreading *mokaalas*—a large species of acacia which forms the favorite food of the Giraffe. The gaudy yellow blossoms with which these remarkable trees were covered, yielded an aromatic and overpowering perfume—while small troops of Striped Quaggas or wild asses, and of Brindled Gnoos, which were for the first time to be seen through the forest, enlivened the scene. After travelling four hours we reached Little Chooi, an extensive salt lake, surrounded by troops of ostriches and spring bucks, attracted thither by the luxuriant, yet crisp and sour grass, which our cattle refused to eat—and by a small pond of intolerably alkaline water, which we found it impossible to purify.

Several armed natives of the Barolong and Batlaroo tribes, branches of the Bechuana, visited us for the purpose of begging *muchuco* or tobacco, causing great consternation by their approach. Poor Richard in particular, who till yesterday had considered himself a perfect Bayard, " sans peur et sans reproche," had been rapidly sinking since the affair of the flying savage, and now felt convinced that the threatened attack was at hand. Enveloped in a great coat, with a red night cap on his raven pate, he sat on the box of the baggage waggon looking the very picture of despair—and as he thought of his wife and helpless family with the improbability of his ever seeing them again, his feelings quite overpowered him and he wept aloud. Never was the heart of a hen partridge concealed beneath so bushy and so black a beard. We dubbed him *Cœur de Lion,* and he bore the surname ever afterwards.

CHAPTER VIII.

FROM LITTLE CHOOI, TO THE MERITSANE RIVER.

THE true Zebra* is exclusively confined to mountainous regions from which it rarely if ever descends : but the extensive plains of Southern Africa abound with two distinct species of the same genus, the Quagga, † and the Striped Quagga or Burchells Zebra.‡ These differ little from each other in point of shape or size, both having the tail and ears of the horse, whilst the Zebra has those of the ass. Of a pale red colour, the Quagga is faintly striped only on the head and neck—but Burchells Zebra is adorned over every part of the body with broad black bands, which beautifully contrast with a pale yellow ground. The Gnoo and the Quagga delighting in the same situations, not unfrequently herd together—but I have seldom seen Burchells Zebra unaccompanied by troops of the Brindled Gnoo, §—an animal differing materially from its brother of the same genus, from which, though scarcely less ungainly, it is readily distinguishable

---

* *Equus Zebra*
† *Equus Quagga*
‡ *Equus Burchellii* } Delineated in the African views.
§ *Catoblepas Gorgon*

at a great distance by its black mane and tail, more elevated withers, and clumsier action.

We were preparing to leave Chooi, when a party of Griquas arrived with three waggons. They had been hunting Giraffes on the Molopo, and having expended their ammunition, were returning to Daniel's Kuil with the spoils. Their horses and oxen were perfect skeletons, and their waggons literally tumbling to pieces. Tireless wheels were lashed together with strips of raw hide, and festoons of sun dried meat, termed *Biltong*, occupied the place of the awning: whilst a number of filthy women and children were stowed away with an odoriferous *melange* of garbage and fat. These people had approached to the western limit of Moselekatse's territory without molestation—a circumstance which seemed to inspire our timid followers with confidence. Large parties are annually formed for the purpose of hunting the Cameleopard and Eland—the flesh of these animals being held in great estimation, and the skins applied to the manufacture of shoes and a variety of uses. We would gladly have purchased some of the miserable horses, but the owners declined receiving any thing in exchange but gunpowder, which we could not have given without incurring the risk of twelve months imprisonment on our return to the Colony.

After crossing the Saltpan, we passed a long line of pitfalls used for entrapping game. Upwards of sixty of these were dug close together in a treble line: a high thorn fence extending in the form of a crescent a mile on either side, in such a manner that Gnoos, Quaggas, and other animals might easily be driven into them. They are carefully concealed with grass, and their circumscribed dimensions render escape almost impossible. Heaps of whitened bones bore ample testimony to the destruction they had occasioned.

We now entered upon the Chooi desert, an extensive flat, denuded of trees, but occasionally broken by low ridges. After travelling twenty miles, across this " region of emptiness," we reached Loharon, at which there was a prospect of obtaining water, but unfortunately the only tank in the country was exhausted. The small supply that we had brought in the waggons was barely drinkable even in coffee: but *our* sufferings were nothing compared with those of the unhappy oxen, which although tired to death with the sultry march, ran franticly in quest of some pool where they might slake their thirst—making the air resound with their mournful lowings. During the night the Hyænas, attracted by the smell of our mutton, actually devoured a spring buck within the limits of our camp.

As we advanced, the game became hourly more abundant although still exceedingly wild. Groups of Hartebeests*, Quaggas, and Brindled Gnoos, were

---

* *Acronotus Caama.*   Delineated in the African views.

every where to be seen. A short chase was sufficient
to seal the fate of three Quaggas—all males averaging
thirteen hands high. During the run I had not seen
a human being, and fancied myself alone : but I had
scarcely dismounted to secure my game, when a woolly head protruded itself from every bush, and in an
instant I was surrounded by thirty Barolongs, who
having by signs expressed their approbation of my
performance, proceeded to devour the carcase with
the greatest avidity—greedily drinking the blood, rubbing the fat upon their bodies, and not leaving so much
even as the entrails for the birds of prey.

Our unfortunate cattle had now tasted no water for
six and thirty hours, and we resolved to travel day and
night in search of this necessary of life. The sun at
length departed, darkness overtook us, and no moon
succeeded to guide our course: when by a singular
instinct, the two horses that we had obtained from
Captain Sutton, and which were consequently acquainted with the road—suddenly separated themselves
from us, and galloped off. Following them up, the
screaming of water fowl sounded like music in our
ears, and we had the gratification of perceiving a pond
of mephitic water a little to the right of the road.
Both man and beast appeared simultaneously apprised
of the cheering discovery—water was the universal
cry—the Hottentots rushed to the edge of the pond,
and throwing themselves on their faces, swallowed

large quantities—indifferent to the crowd of horses, oxen, and sheep, which followed close upon their heels. The oxen in the waggons were with difficulty restrained until the yokes had been removed, when impatient of their burning thirst, they also rushed headlong into the now muddy pool.

An accident deprived us of the handsome dog that we had obtained from Brother Mark Graaff, the itinerant tutor : no bush presenting itself, which could shelter him for a moment during the long march, from the scorching rays of a vertical sun, he had sought an asylum beneath the waggon, the wheel of which passed over his body.

In order to recruit the exhausted strength of the oxen, we halted a day at Great Chooi, another extensive salt lake, which we reached early the following morning. No pen can describe the scene that here took place. The Hottentots, having first mutinied against Richardson, deputed Andries—who, advanced to me with a step of defiance—to acquaint me with their determination not to obey his orders : the contracts having, to save trouble, been made in my name only. The discussion having been suppressed by me, led to a disagreement amongst themselves; they fought with inconceivable fury for half an hour, and were with difficulty prevented from murdering each other. With blood streaming from many a ghastly wound, they at length retired

9

to ablute themselves, and returned better friends
than ever. The engagement had been witnessed
by a party of savages, who carried umbrellas of ostrich
feathers, twisted round a long stick so as to resemble the nodding plumes of a hearse. In honour of
their own courageous bearing, the Hottentots purchased a number of these for a small piece of tobacco, and binding them round their hats, strutted forth
Knights of the sable plume.

The scattered inhabitants of this part of the country
are the remnants of various Bechuana tribes, which have
been conquered by Moselekatse—and consist principally of the Barolong, Wangkets, Batlapi, and Baharootzi. These poor wretches live in small communities, and being destitute of cattle, depend entirely for
subsistence on locusts, or such game as chance may
direct to their pitfalls. Crowds of them attracted by
prey, now hovered around me in my hunting expeditions, which were here particularly successful; and
having obtained a supply of meat, with the luxuries
of snuff and tobacco, for which they were constantly
begging, under the denominations of *lishüena* and
muchuko, they composed themselves to sleep, appearing to be in the enjoyment of as much happiness as man
in a state of mere animal existence probably ever
attains. Our little band was also instinctively attended by a host of hungry vultures, who, little disturbed
by the presence of man, divided the office of carrion

scavengers with hyænas and jackals. Wheeling in circles high above our heads, like small specks in the firmament, these voracious birds were ever ready to pounce upon game that might be shot, or upon the carcases of oxen that perished on the road—devouring the largest bodies with a promptitude truly surprising.

We had now crossed the unvaried level expanse of the Chooi desert, and were entering upon a country, which, though equally remarkable for its sameness of appearance, presented a different character. Immense sandy flats with a substratum of lime, were uniformly covered with Mokaala trees, low thorn bushes, and long grass, interspersed with numerous dry tanks: but no hill or conspicuous object that could direct the footsteps of a wanderer. Before reaching the Siklagole river, twenty-two miles, we passed many extensive villages totally deserted: rude earthen vessels, fragments of ostrich egg-shells, and portions of the skins of wild animals, however, proving that they had been recently inhabited. During the whole of this and the following day we saw no human being, a circumstance which I note here, because it added in no small degree to the troubles I am about to detail.

On the morning of the 9th October, when the waggons had started on their way to the Meritsane river, our next stage, I turned off the road in pursuit of a troop of Brindled Gnoos, and presently came upon another, which was joined by a third still larger—then by a vast herd of Zebras, and again by more Gnoos, with Sassaybys * and Hartebeests, pouring down from every quarter, until the landscape literally presented the appearance of a moving mass of game. Their incredible numbers so impeded their progress, that I had no difficulty in closing with them, dismounting as opportunity offered, firing both barrels of my rifle into the retreating phalanx, and leaving the ground strewed with the slain. Still unsatisfied, I could not resist the temptation of mixing with the fugitives, loading and firing, until my jaded horse suddenly exhibited symptoms of distress, and shortly afterwards was unable to move. At this moment I discovered that I had dropped my pocket compass, and being unwilling to lose so valuable an ally, I turned loose my steed to graze, and retraced my steps several miles without success: the prints of my horse's hoofs being at length lost in those of the countless herds which had crossed the plain. Completely absorbed in the chase, I had retained but an imperfect idea of my locality, but returning to my horse, I led him in what I believed to be a North-easterly direction, knowing from a sketch of the country which had been given me by our excellent friend Mr. Moffat, and which, together with drawing materials I carried about me, that that

* *Acronotus Lunata.* Delineated in the African views.

course would eventually bring me to the Meritsane. After dragging my weary horse nearly the whole of the day under a burning sun, my flagging spirits were at length revived by the appearance of several villages.   Under other circumstances, I should have avoided intercourse with their inhospitable inmates, but dying with thirst, I eagerly entered each in succession, and to my inexpressible disappointment, found them deserted.   The same evidence existing of their having been recently inhabited, I shot a Hartebeest, in the hope that the smell of meat would as usual attract some straggler to the spot.   But no.   The keen-sighted vultures, that were my only attendants, descended in multitudes, but no woolly headed negro appeared to dispute the prey.   In many of the trees I observed large thatched houses resembling hay stacks; and under the impression that these had been erected in so singular a position by the natives as a measure of security against the Lions, whose recent tracks I distinguished in every direction, I ascended more than one in the hope of at least finding some vessel containing water.   Alas, they proved to be the habitations of large communities of Social Grosbeaks, * those winged republicans of whose architecture and magnificent edifices, I had till now, entertained a very inadequate conception.   Faint

---

* *Loxia Socia.* Delineated in the African views

and bewildered, my prospects began to brighten as the shadows of evening lengthened. Large troops of Ostriches running in one direction, plainly indicated that I was approaching water: and immediately afterwards, I struck into a path impressed with the foot-marks of women and children—soon arriving at a nearly dry river, which, running East and West, I at once concluded to be that of which I was in search.

Those only who have suffered as I did during this day from prolonged thirst, can form a competent idea of the delight, and I may add, energy, afforded me by the first draught of the putrid waters of the Meritsane. They equally invigorated my exhausted steed, whom I mounted immediately, and cantered up the bank of the river, in order if possible to reach the waggons before dark. The banks are precipitous—the channel deep, broken, and rocky: clusters of reeds and long grass indicating those spots which retain the water during the hot months. It was with no small difficulty, after crossing the river, that I forced my way through the broad belt of tangled bushes which margined the edge. The moonless night was fast closing around, and my weary horse again began to droop. The Lions, commencing their nightly prowl, were roaring in all directions, and no friendly fire or beacon presenting itself to my view, the only alternative was to bivouac where I was, and to renew

my search in the morning. Kindling a fire, I formed
a thick bush into a pretty secure hut, by cutting
away the middle, and closing the entrance with
thorns; and having knee haltered * my horse to prevent his straying, I proceeded to dine upon a Guinea
fowl that I had killed, comforting myself with another
draught of *aqua pura*. The monarchs of the forest roared incessantly, and so alarmed my horse, that
I was obliged repeatedly to fire my rifle to give him
confidence. It was piercingly cold, and all my fuel
being expended, I suffered as much from chill as I
had during the day from the scorching heat. About
3 o'clock, completely overcome by fatigue, I could
keep my eyes open no longer, and commending my-.
self to the protecting care of Providence, fell into
a profound sleep.

* Knee haltering is the colonial method of securing a
horse when turned out to graze; a leathern thong attached
to the neck, is passed round the knee, and tied.

CHAPTER IX.

HUNTING AT MERITSANE.

On opening my eyes, my first thought was of my horse. I started from my heathy bed in the hope of finding him where I had last seen him, but his place was empty. I roamed every where in search of him, and ascended trees which offered a good look out, but he was no where to be seen. It was more than probable he had been eaten by Lions, and I had almost given up the search in despair, when I at length found his foot-mark, and traced him to a deep hollow near the river, where he was quietly grazing. The night's rest, if so it could be called, had restored him to strength, and I pursued my journey along the bank of the river, which I now re-crossed opposite to the site of some former scene of strife, marked by numerous human skeletons, bleached by exposure. A little further on I disturbed a large Lion, which walked slowly off, occasionally stopping and looking over his shoulder, as he deliberately ascended the opposite bank. In the course of half an hour, I reached the end of the dense jungle, and immediately discovered the waggon road: but as I could detect no recent traces upon it, I turned to the Southward, and

after riding seven or eight miles in the direction of
Siklagole, had the unspeakable satisfaction of perceiving the waggons drawn up under a large tree in the
middle of the plain. The discharge of my rifle at
a little distance, had relieved the anxiety of my companion and followers, who during the night had entertained the most gloomy forebodings on my account, being convinced that I had either been torn
piecemeal by Lions, or speared by the assagais of
the cannibals! A cup of coffee was immediately
offered me, which, as I had scarcely tasted nour-
ishment for thirty hours, proved highly grateful; and
I learned that Richardson had been obliged to halt
in the plain the preceding night, in consequence of
the great length of the march, and the darkness
overtaking him. This accounted for my not meeting him on the river bank, which we again reached
in about two hours, encamping under a grove of
spreading Mokaala trees.

Both the Siklagole and the Meritsane take their
source in the low range of hills called Kunuana,
considerably to the Eastward of the point where
we crossed them; and, joining about the same distance to the Westward, empty themselves into the
Molopo. Near their confluence the camp of Mr.
Bain, a trader to whose name I have already alluded,
was attacked in 1834 by Moselekatse. A party of
marauding Griquas, whom he had imprudently
10

taken with him to assist in hunting, entered the territories of that Prince, and succeeded in capturing several head of cattle, with which they had made good their retreat. A large party of warriors, however, overtook them when within sight of the camp; nearly all the followers fled in disorder on the first alarm, leaving their master to shift for himself, who finding the camp surrounded and resistance vain, jumped on his horse, and accompanied by four of his people, narrowly escaped with life, by riding through and killing some of the assailants. After travelling several days, and suffering dreadfully from want of food and water, the party reached Motito nearer dead than alive.

The reports of four savages of the Batlapi tribe, who joined us yesterday, determined us to halt a day for the purpose of hunting. Richardson and myself left the waggons at day break, attended by these men, and crossing the river, took a North-westerly direction through a park of magnificent camelthorn trees, many of which were groaning under the huge nests of the social grosbeak; whilst others were decorated with green clusters of misletoe, the bright scarlet berries of which were highly ornamental. We soon perceived large herds of Quaggas and Brindled Gnoos, which continued to join each other until the whole plain seemed alive. The clatter of their hoofs was perfectly astounding, and I could

Dean & Munday, Lithog 40 Threadneedle St London.

compare it to nothing, but to the din of a tremendous charge of cavalry, or the rushing of a mighty tempest.   I could not   estimate the accumulated numbers, at less than fifteen thousand; a great extent of country being actually chequered black and white with their congregated masses. As the panic caused by the report of our rifles, extended, clouds of dust hovered over them; and the long necks of troops of ostriches were also to be seen, towering above the heads of their less gigantic neighbours, and sailing past with astonishing rapidity. Groups of purple Sassaybys, and brilliant red and yellow Hartebeests, likewise lent their aid to complete the picture, which must have been seen to be properly understood, and which beggars all attempt at description.   The savages kept in our wake, dexterously despatching the wounded Gnoos by a touch on the spine with the point of an assagai, and instantly covering up the carcases with bushes, to secure them from the voracity of the vultures, which hung about us like specks in the firmament, and descended with the velocity of lightning, as each discharge of our artillery gave token of prey.   As we proceeded, two strange figures were perceived standing under the shade of a tree; these we instantly knew to be Elands,* the savages at the same moment exclaiming

* *Boselaphus Oreas.* Delineated in the African views.

with evident delight, *Impoofo*, *Impoofo*, and pressing our horses to the utmost speed, we found ourselves for the first time, at the heels of the largest
and most beautiful species of the antelope tribe.
Notwithstanding the unweildy shape of these animals, they had at first greatly the speed of our jaded
horses, but being pushed, they soon separated ; their
sleek coats turned first blue and then white with froth;
the foam fell from their mouths and nostrils, and the
perspiration from their sides.   Their pace gradually
slackened, and with their full brilliant eyes turned
imploringly towards us, at the end of a mile, each
was laid low by a single ball.   They were young
bulls, measuring upwards of seventeen hands at the
shoulder.

I was engaged in making a sketch of the one I
had shot, when the savages came up, and in spite of
all my remonstrances, proceeded with cold blooded
ferocity to stab the unfortunate animal, stirring up
the blood and shouting with barbarous exultation,
as it issued from each newly inflicted wound, regardless of the eloquent and piteous appeal, expressed
in the beautiful clear black eye of the mild and inoffensive Eland.

In size and shape, the body of the male Eland resembles that of a well conditioned Guzerat ox, not
unfrequently attaining the height of nineteen hands,
and weighing two thousand pounds.   The head is

strictly that of the antelope, light, graceful, and bony, with a pair of magnificent straight horns, about two feet in length, spirally ringed, and pointed backwards. A broad and deep dewlap fringed with brown hair reaches to the knee. The color varies considerably with the age, being dun in some, in others an ashy blue with a tinge of ochre; and in many also, sandy grey approaching to white. The flesh is esteemed by all classes in Africa, above that of any other animal; in grain and color it resembles beef, but is better tasted, and more delicate, possessing a pure game flavor, and the quantity of fat with which it is interlarded is surprising, greatly exceeding that of any other game quadruped, with which I am acquainted. The female is smaller and of slighter form, with less ponderous horns. The stoutest of our savage attendants, could with difficulty transport the head of the Eland to the waggons, where one of the Hottentots had just arrived with the carcase of a Sassayby that he had dragged a considerable distance, assisted by upwards of twenty savages. These men were no sooner made acquainted with the occurrences of the morning, than they set off at speed upon the tracks of our horses, and were presently out of sight. About sunset the party returned, gorged to the throats, and groaning under an external load of flesh, which having been unable to consume, they had hung round their necks.

About midnight an unusual commotion caused us to start from our sleep. The whole of the cattle had burst through the thorn fence by which they were surrounded, and panic stricken, were blindly charging, they knew not whither; oxen, horses, and sheep, tumbling headlong over the waggon poles, and over each other, in indescribable confusion. The night was intensely dark, and all the fires had gone out—Cœur de Lion had clambered on to the top of the baggage waggon, and was screaming like a woman, whilst each Hottentot was discharging his gun, loaded with ball, in any direction that the muzzle might happen to have assumed. The horses were the least alarmed, and after floundering about in the dark for some time, we succeeded in recovering all but one; but every endeavour to reclaim the oxen and sheep proving abortive, we retired again to rest, having first ascertained by the light of a candle, that the consternation had been occasioned by three Lions, that had entered the fold and slain two of the sheep.

At day break, both Hottentots and savages were despatched on the tracks of the fugitives. Some of the savages shortly returned with the sheep, several more having, however, been devoured by Lions; but the former did not make their appearance until noon, when they informed us that the oxen had divided into two parties, and being dreadfully alarmed would not stop in all probability until they should reach

the Kuruman; adding, that if we wished to recover
them, each Hottentot must be provided with a horse
and a supply of ammunition. Knowing from sad
experience the fate that awaited our steeds, upon
whose well being our sport entirely depended, we
resisted the application; upon which all but Claas
and Ethaldur, begged to throw up their commissions.
No one had any complaint to allege except April,
who objected to the fatness of the mutton, and Andries, who felt aggrieved by a threat of retribution
extended at Chooi. The latter looked particularly
black, and it was not until after he had been despatched with Cobus on horseback in quest of the
oxen, that we discovered him to have been the insti-
gator of a plot, which had been joined by all, to desert us in the wilderness, and return to the Colony
with the horses and whatever else they could lay
their hands upon.

Apprehensive of another attack from Lions, we
moved in the afternoon to the opposite side of the
river, drawing up the waggons on the top of a hil-
lock, in such a manner as to flank the cattle enclosure—an arrangement which we ever afterwards
observed. Our friends the Batlapi returned about
sunset with the oxen, which they had found twelve
miles off, a piece of service for which according to
agreement, they were rewarded with a yard of tobacco and a tinder box. Cobus and Andries also

came back during the night, having galled the backs
of both the horses, without obtaining any tidings of
the lost one.   The whole of the following day was
passed in fruitless endeavours to recover the truant, and it was not until six months afterwards, that
we ascertained he had returned to the farm on which
he had been bred in the Hantam, a distance of five
hundred miles.

CHAPTER X.

CONTINUING our journey on the 14th October, twenty-eight miles, through a beautiful country abounding with trees and grass, we reached the Lotlokane, the shallow channel of a periodical river, said in the rainy season to contribute its mite to the Molopo, which it joins at some distance to the Westward. At this season it was perfectly dry; but we had fortunately found a small pool of water on the road, at which we breakfasted, after killing several Hartebeests and Sassaybys. The skins of both these animals, and especially of the latter, are in great demand amongst the savages, for *Kobos*, or fur cloaks— both on account of their brilliant color and their supple nature. They are cured by means of continual rubbing, stretching, and scraping ; and for this purpose are constantly carried about, and referred to as an amusement in moments of leisure. The operation is rendered less tedious by the constant addition of grease : and less irksome, by savage howlings and gruntings, intended to pass current for singing.

The Sassayby or crescent horned Antelope, and the

11

Caama or Hartebeest, are members of the same subgenus, and are both remarkable for their elevated
withers, drooping hind quarters, and triangular form.
The color of the former is purple violet, and of the
latter bright orange; their legs and faces being eccentrically marked, as if with the brush of a sign
painter; and their horns placed on the very summit
of the head, upon a prolongation of the frontal bone,
instead of above the eyes as in most other Antelopes.
Their brain, as well as that of the Gnoo, is filled with
large white maggots—a phenomenon, of which, until
I had received ocular evidence, I could not help
being sceptical.

In the morning four savages volunteered to show
us a Rhinoceros. We accompanied them amongst
ruined stone kraals of great extent, situated to the
left of the road, and so overgrown with thorn bushes,
that we were not unfrequently obliged to exchange
an erect for a stooping posture, and at times even to
travel on our hands and knees. We found nothing,
however, but a pack of wild dogs * that had just
hunted down a Hartebeest. Like the wild dogs of
India, these animals take the field in organized packs,
and by their perseverance seldom fail to weary out
the swiftest Antelope. Of a slender form, the general
color is ochreous yellow, blotched and brindled with

* *Hyæna œnatica.*

dingy black. The ears are large and semicircular :
the muzzle and face black, and the tail bushy like that
of a fox.

During the day we passed another extensive stone
town, which once contained its " busy thousands,"
but now presents a heap of ruins. The walls extend
more than a mile on each side of the road; and the
plain on which it is constructed, is thickly covered
with a species of wild basil, yielding an aromatic scent,
when crushed under the foot. We had scarcely passed this, when the lightning began to flash, and tremendous peals of thunder burst over our heads. A
black cloud that had suddenly formed, then emptied
its contents upon us ; the rain pouring down like
a sluice for five minutes, and obliging us to seek shelter in the waggons. Ceasing as abruptly as it commenced, we passed on at once to parched and dusty
land, from a tract which had in an instant become
covered with pools of water.

It was nearly dark when we reached the Molopo,
a few miles below its source. This river, which
forms the Western boundary of Moselekatse's territory, exhibits a broad shallow bed, covered with turf,
traversed by a deep stream about ten yards wide,
completely overgrown with high reeds. The soil on
both sides is black, spread with luxuriant grass, and
detached clumps of acacia. We crossed, and encamped on the Northern bank, under a solitary tree,

around which was a ready made fence for the cattle. During the night, the obtrusive visit of a Hippopotamus, of which amphibious animals there are abundance in the river—caused great consternation : Richard screaming, and the Hottentots expending their ball cartridge as usual.

The two following days were spent in hunting the Eland and Gemsbok.* The latter, which is doubtless the animal from which the delineations of the fabulous Unicorn have descended, is one of the most magnificent Antelopes in the universe. Although common in Namaqua-land, it is rare in this part of the country, and we were fortunate in finding three, one of which I succeeded in riding down : nearly, however, sacrificing my best horse in the arduous achievement. The Oryx is about the size of an ass, and nearly of the same ground color, with a black list stripe down the back, and on each flank; white legs, variegated with black bands: and a white face, marked with the figure of a black nose-band and head-stall. Its copious black tail literally sweeps the ground : a mane reversed, and a tuft of flowing black hair on the breast, with a pair of straight slender horns, (common to both sexes,) three feet in length, and ringed at the base, completing the portrait. During the chase, I passed under the noses of three Rhinoceroses, which,

---

* *Oryx Capensis.* Delineated in the African views.

on my return, I was unable to find. Richardson had
fallen in with a troop of five Lions, one of which he
wounded, but being deserted by the Hottentots, was
unable to follow among the brushwood; and my
horse was so completely exhausted, that I was
obliged to drag him home, carrying the saddle myself.

The night of the 17th was rainy and tempestuous.
Whilst the wind howled against the unsheltered
waggons with a violence that bid fair to overturn
them, the Lions, which never failed to take advantage of such an opportunity, prowled round the camp;
and roaring in concert with the sighing of the reeds,
so alarmed the cattle that they thrice broke loose
and were recovered with difficulty. There was nothing however, to prevent our resuming our journey in
the morning, the thirsty earth having completely absorbed the deluge that had fallen. Our road lay
across a plain, with isolated groves of acacia, and we
frequently passed over a solid pavement of granite.
Searching amongst a low belt of wooded hillocks,
which skirted a part of the road, I found a fine fat
Eland, which I drove into the plain, and assisted by
Richardson, brought up to the waggons, and then
despatched, the caravan being immediately halted.
We frequently afterwards adopted this plan, which
saved the trouble of carrying the meat from a distance; and the unfortunate animal once blown, was
much more manageable than a Smithfield ox.

Andries having donned his best apparel, here proposed to proceed on horse-back to Mosega, in order to apprize the King of our approach—an offer which we gladly accepted. The fears of the rest of our followers, and of Cœur de Lion in particular, increased in the ratio of our advance: he wept almost incessantly, saying that it mattered little where he laid his bones. From this point, the summits of distant ranges of hills could be distinguished, across extensive plains covered with grass waving to the breeze, which stretched away to the Northward and Eastward, far as the eye could reach. On the left, the low range of hillocks already noticed, terminated at some distance in several detached hills—some conical, others table topped—the white slabs on the sides of these strongly contrasting with the black charred bushes which grew amongst the crevices. A large portion of the country had been set on fire a few weeks before, in order to clear off the withered grass, and the bountiful thunder clouds having caused the young green blades to make their appearance, large herds of game had been attracted to the spot. At the gorge of these hills, was an extensive line of pit falls, into one of which a Hartebeest, whose leg I had broken, fell as I was riding him down—my horse only narrowly escaping being ingulfed in a second, at the same moment. During the day I killed another Impoofo, which actually measured nineteen hands two inches at the shoulder.

Our road was now sometimes over a rocky pavement, at others, over ground which threatened the destruction of the waggons. Large stones more than a foot in height, offering sharp sides and projecting points, were firmly fixed in the ground : and, added to careless driving, threw the vehicles from side to side, with a violence that shook every spoke. About 4 o'clock we halted at the Mimori river, only five miles from Mosega. A chain of lakes to the left of our camp, contained a herd of wild Buffaloes,* whose formidable heads, resembling masses of rock, were protruded from the water amid waving sedges, the whole of their bodies being immerged. I wounded one, which I attempted to ride down; but the sharp pointed stones cutting the shoeless feet of my horse to pieces, I brought him back to the waggons dead lame.

Four Matabili warriors arrived from Mosega in the evening, bringing a civil message from the Deputy Governor, who, in the absence of Moselekatse, and of his prime minister Kalipi, had been apprized by Andries of our advent. Tall, straight, well proportioned, and of regular features, these men, although of very dark complexion, were far superior in appearance

---

* *Bubalus Caffer*, Delineated in the African views.

to any tribe that we had hitherto seen. Their heads
were shaven, and surmounted by an oval ring attached
to the scalp; a large perforation in the lobe of one ear,
receiving a small gourd snuff-box. Their dress consisted of a leathern girdle, with a few strips of cat-skin
attached to the front and rear; and each was armed with
two short javelins, and a knobbed stick used for throwing. We made them heartily welcome to our fire-
side—filled their stomachs with beef, and their boxes
with snuff, and left them making their nests among
the sheltered bushes on the river bank. A strong
disagreeable wind setting in, completely destroyed
the fire; and after we had retired, it increased to such
a perfect hurricane that sleep was out of the question. One waggon was carefully closed and drawn
up under the shelter of a superb grove of trees; yet
the bitter blast that howled without, cut so keenly
through the blankets, that it penetrated even to the
narrow of our bones. I wrapped my sheep skin
coverlet closer about me, without any sensible advantage; and my companion, after successively in-
ducting himself into every article of wearing apparel upon which he could put his hand, still declared
himself as cold as ice.

   At day break the mercury in Farenheits thermometer stood at forty-four degrees, yet to the bodily
feelings, the air was still much colder than we had
felt it, when down to eighteen degrees. We crossed

the deep sedgy stream of the Mimori, and ascending to a higher level, were presently met by His Excellency the Deputy Governor, a tall athletic savage
of commanding appearance, blind of the left eye.
His attire was of the nature already described, and,
saving that he was unarmed, differed in no respect
from that of his attendants.　A general greeting and
hand shaking ensued—the snuff-box circulated briskly, and we all became capital friends.

Smoking is not a fashionable vice amongst the
Matabili, but all classes are passionately addicted to
snuffing—indeed the sharing the contents of your box
with a stranger, is the greatest compliment that can
be paid him.　The mode of taking it is not unworthy
of notice.　One half of the powder having been transferred to the palm of the hand, by means of a small
ivory spoon, which is usually hung round the neck,
the recipient leisurely seats himself under a convenient bush: drawing every grain into his nostrils at once,
with an eagerness, which although followed by a
copious flood of tears, proves the extent of the enjoyment afforded.　Worse than barbarian would that
man be esteemed, who would wantonly interrupt a
social party so employed.

After travelling about five miles, over undulating
downs, covered with luxuriant grass, we descended
into a lovely and fertile valley, in form resembling
a basin of ten or twelve miles in circumference,

12

bounded on the North and Northeast by the Kurrichane range of mountains, and containing the sources of the Mariqua river. Prior to the occupancy
of this valley by the Matabili, it formed the principal residence of the Baharootzi tribe. It is now
extensively cultivated, and contains the military town
of Mosega, and fifteen other of Moselekatse's principal kraals. On our way to the houses of the
American Missionaries, we passed several of these,
to the no small delight of their inhabitants, who,
principally women and children, flocked round the
waggons in great numbers, offering their greasy
hands without compunction: at every step the crowd
increased—both sexes were to be seen working in
the fields, but they all quitted their occupation as
they saw us, and adding themselves to the group,
escorted us to the halting ground. We received a
hearty welcome from Dr. Wilson, one of the American fraternity, from whom we learned, on delivering
a letter from Mr. Moffat, that he had had the misfortune to lose his wife a few days before; and that the
rest of the party were likewise dangerously ill with
fever, contracted from having slept in their newly built
house before the floors were dry. This gentleman
likewise gave us accounts of the capture of several waggons, the property of a farmer named Erasmus, who
was hunting on the Vaal river. This was the event
to which Captain Sutton had referred, but Dr. Wil-

son further informed us, that a very large Commando*
under Kalipi, the Minister and Governor of Mosega,
had already been some days gone to the river Vaal, to
complete the destruction of the emigrant farmers
—concluding by strongly advising us not to visit the
King at such a conjuncture. Having come thus
far however, we resolved to proceed, and with that
view immediately despatched messengers to his Majesty, with a present of beads, and a request that we
might be suffered to pay our respects. These men
received a bunch of beads weighing one pound, and
the promise of another if they returned on the third
day—Moselekatse was reported to be at a kraal
fifty miles to the North-ward, at which he had resided ever since the establishment of the Missionaries
at Mosega his head quarters.

It rained during the whole of the night; and
during the whole of the following day, we were surrounded without a moment's respite, by a crowd of
people importuning for tobacco. They entered the
tent, and clambered into the waggon without ceremony, leaving a host of vermin behind them, and
becoming at length so troublesome, that we were
compelled, in self defence, to drive them away with
the waggon whips. A long line of women and girls,

* Commando is the Colonial term for every expedition of
a Military nature.

however, still continued to stand at a distance on
tiptoe, attempting to gratify their curiosity, by peeping in at the back of the waggon; whilst others sat
and loitered about as if their time were valueless.
The Governor invited himself to dinner in the evening, and as it rained again, sat so late, that we were
at last obliged to send the Parsee outside to start
him, which he did by poking a stick under his person from below the walls of the tent, a hint which
he good naturedly took, and departed.

We embraced an early opportunity of mentioning
to the Missionaries, our intention of leaving the country
by the Vaal river; a scheme which they discounte-
nanced as fraught with peril. But whilst they felt sure
that Moselekatse would never listen to such an arrangement, they obligingly consented to allow one of their
domestics, Baba, a converted Bechuana who had accompanied Dr. Smith's expedition as interpreter, to
attend us as far as the King's residence, in the like
capacity.

The next morning we rode through a pass in the
hills behind the Mission houses, towards the Mimori
lakes, in order to obtain food for the people; it being
an object to husband our resources, as far as possible,
against our return. The plains here are broken by
low ranges of stony hills, with clumps of acacia. A
large herd of Buffaloes on being pursued took to the
lakes, into which we followed them, the water reach-

ing up to the horse's girths, and the reeds far above
our own heads. We could hear the animals forcing
their way through, immediately in front of us; but
after several hours severe labour, could only succeed in
driving out one, which breaking at the opposite side
of one lake, had gained another before we could
overtake him. A general skirmish then commenced,
some of the followers wading up to their middles,
whilst others fired from the banks, whenever a glimpse
of the Buffaloes could be obtained. Several were
wounded, and Piet, in attempting to despatch one,
was charged and knocked over by another. Capless
and disarmed, we could see him through a telescope,
lying beneath a shady Karra tree, which reared its
venerable head in the middle of the lake, holding his
hands to his stomach as if mortally wounded; his
adversary drooping near him, the blood streaming
from its nostrils, and the moment of dissolution approaching. A broad deep stream, tangled over with
sedge, encircling this spot on three sides, defied approach either on horse-back or on foot, without incurring the certainty of drowning; and compelled us to
ride three miles round, before we could arrive to the
rescue. By that time the Buffaloe was dead, and Piet
appearing more frightened than hurt, we removed his
leathern doublet, which was much torn, and ascertained that there were no holes in his skin. A laborious
search among the reeds brought his cap and gun to

light, and the wounded man being borne out by the savages, was placed upon a horse and conducted to Mosega, where he enjoyed the advantage of Dr. Wilson's professional aid.

On our return, Mr. Lindley, one of the Missionaries, still very weak, though slowly recovering from fever, came to apprise us of the return of the messengers from Kapain with a pressing invitation from the King, who declared that we were "his own white men," and must hasten our advance as much as possible, so as to arrive on the third day. These men had used extraordinary expedition, and allured by the promise of beads, had performed one hundred miles in less than thirty-six hours. Seeing us determined to continue our journey the next morning, Mr. Lindley and the Doctor again endeavoured by every argument in their power, to dissuade us from our intention of forcing our way out by the Vaal river, which we were bent upon doing, whether Moselekatse permitted it or not; but we at the same time expressed our conviction, that we had in the waggons, that which would bribe his majesty to accede to our wishes. Without the least anticipating the success of our project, Dr. Wilson then entrusted us with a letter, announcing to his family the heavy loss he had recently sustained.

The accounts given by these Gentlemen were not calculated to raise our spirits, or give us a favorable impression of the treatment we should experience from the despot, of whose inhuman executions and horrible butcheries, they could never speak with patience; representing him to be treacherous, oppressive, cruel, and capricious in an extraordinary degree, and to exact from his subjects an abject deference, little according with American notions of tolerance. Amongst his more recent enormities, they adduced the murder of a trader, named Gibson, with the whole of his followers, and of two servants, belonging to Captains Sutton and Moultry, the particulars of which shall hereafter be given. Although the tyrant had not opposed the establishment of the Mission, its presence was far from agreeable to him; and not only had he entirely withdrawn himself from Mosega, but he had also given great annoyance, by interdicting his people from entering the service of its members, alleging that they were capable of taking care of themselves. Under so despotic a Government, it is not probable that the Matabili will ever derive much advantage from the exhortations of Ministers of the Gospel, were they even better disposed to receive them. In lieu of the reverence to which these worthy men were entitled, and which they would have received from other savage tribes, we not unfrequently observed groups of both sexes, gazing in at the windows of the Mission houses as at wild beasts in a menagerie, with every demonstration of merriment at the expence of their inmates—behaviour, which the proceedings on the part of the King, could not fail to induce on that of his subjects.

CHAPTER XI.

FROM MOSEGA TO THE KURRICHANE MOUNTAINS.

LEAVING the Mission house on the 22d October, and repassing the town of Mosega, within the fence of which we saw Erasmus's captured waggons, our road wound for some distance, in a North-westerly direction, amongst numerous Matabili villages, having all the same form and appearance, though varying considerably in size and extent. A circular thorn fence, six or eight feet in height, with only one entrance, encloses a sloping area; around the circumference of which the dwellings or huts are constructed. The cattle are kept during the night in the space so surrounded. The domiciles are paltry low huts, of a circular form, having one small doorway directed towards the centre; it is of very narrow dimensions, barely affording space for a man to crawl through upon his hands and knees. Crowds of women and children poured down from each kraal as we passed, holding out their hands, and then placing their noses in the hollow of the palm, snuffing and sneezing violently, as a hint that they required *Qui* or snuff, for which, to them the greatest of all luxuries, they became as usual extremely clamorous.

We saw comparatively few men, the larger proportion of the able bodied being absent with Kalipi on the Commando against the emigrant farmers. The Missionaries estimated this force to consist of near five thousand warriors.

On the North and North-east, the Kurrichane range of mountains rose in majestic grandeur, a great treat to us after the extensive unvaried flats over which we had travelled since leaving Kuruman, and indeed almost ever since passing the Sneuwbergen. The cultivated land in all parts of the basin was extensive; and countless herds of sleek oxen were grazing on the slopes. Our one eyed friend, the Deputy Governor, who was exceedingly reluctant to leave such amiable society, had taken his seat on the fore chest of the leading waggon, having first paid Cœur de Lion the compliment of removing his camlet cloak, and enveloping his own greasy person therein as a protection against the cold, which was far from moderate. The old man's elliptically crowned bald pate protruded above the high collar, contrasted with the grotesque solemnity of his deportment, had a sufficiently ludicrous appearance. Baba, the interpreter, had brought two horses one of which he rode. Piet, who fancied himself at the point of death, had composed himself upon my cot, of which he held the monopoly for several days, and the two savages who had announced our advent to the King, accompanied

13

us as guides, or more correctly speaking, as spies. These fellows rendered themselve particularly obnoxious during the whole journey, by their peremptory interference in our affairs, as well as by their offensive familiarity.   They often clambered into our beds without ceremony, and obtruded themselves stark naked when least required.

We unyoked for breakfast on the bank of one the numerous streams, that here form the source of the Mariqua, a river of which I shall have occasion frequently to speak.   A spacious and level valley, hemmed in on three sides by the skirting hills of the Kurrichane range, was intersected by three or four of these rivulets, whose serpentine course could be traced by the sedges that rose high above their banks. As soon as the Governor had completed his breakfast, and the waggons were ready to proceed, the extension of his Excellency's greasy hand, announced his intention of leaving us and returning to Mosega. A severe *pump handling*, and the presentation of two bunches of beads to himself, and a brass wire collar to his little son, whilst it firmly cemented our friendship, terminated our acquaintance for ever under a parting assurance, that he had made a favorable report of us to his royal master, who was, he said, *"Monanti, Monanti, Monanti,"* or in plain English, the most gracious of sovereigns.

As the waggons proceeded, we turned off the road

in search of a Rhinoceros, and speedily became so
entangled in a labyrinth of thorn fences, newly constructed to entrap game, that we had great difficulty in extricating ourselves. Stiff thorn branches,
too high to be surmounted, were firmly fixed in the
ground, and so entwined amidst a dense grove of mimosas, that after fruitless endeavours to force a passage in various places, we found that we had ridden
completely round the enclosure, to the point at which
we had first entered.

In the course of two hours the waggons had reached the termination of the plain, and were beginning
to ascend the ridge which bounds the valley of Mosega. We shortly afterwards entered a pass or gap,
which conducted us between two ranges of the Kurrichane hills; the slopes on either side were covered
with stately trees, from which depended clusters of
moss and festoons of various parasitic plants. The
ground was broken and stony, and in parts abounded with deep holes. In the act of killing a Sassayby,
my horse put his feet into one of these, and came
down with frightful violence, cutting my knees and
elbows to the bone, breaking his own nose, and,
what was a far greater misfortune, and one that I
had long anticipated, fracturing the stock of my
only and especially favorite rifle. I could have wept,
if the doing so would have availed any thing. A
strip of the Sassayby's hide rectified the damage for

the present at least; and having packed the flesh in the waggon, we continued winding among the hills, constantly assured by the guides, that the kraal at which they had resolved we should pass the night, was close at hand, but still not reaching it until we had travelled full thirty miles from Mosega, by which time it was fairly dark. At last we perceived fires in the valley beneath us, and soon drew up under the fence of a little village, constructed as usual on a slope.

Scarcely were the oxen unyoked when the clouds, which had been collecting for some hours, burst at once upon our devoted heads. Deafening claps of thunder pealed above us, preceded by forked and vivid lightning, which cast upon the surrounding landscape, a lurid and almost incessant glare. The windows of heaven were literally opened, and a pelting pitiless deluge descended, which in an instant extinguished the fire and put an end to all culinary operations. We, however, succeeded in obtaining a little milk from the village, and in a few minutes Morpheus strewing his poppies over us, we ceased to trouble our heads about the state of the weather, or our soaking supperless condition.

A tranquil morning succeeded the most tempestuous of nights. The inhabitants of the kraal were anxious that we should shoot a Rhinoceros, which they pretended to have seen at no great distance—

but although we sacrificed one half of our raiment
in the attempt to oblige them, the animal was no
where to be found.   The road still wound among
the mountains; three hours travelling brought us to
a kraal at no great distance from the ancient town
of Kurrichane, in which Mr. Campbell found the
Baharootzis about ten years ago.   This once populous city was destroyed by Moselekatse, and the
inhabitants scattered in various directions.   Here
the guides declared it was the King's command that
we should tarry until the following day when he
expected to see us.   But as the royal lodge was still
far distant, we obstinately insisted upon continuing
our journey after breakfast, so as to get clear of the
hills in the course of the day; and were accordingly
preparing to start, when a herald, called in the Matabili language *Imbongo*, a proclaimer of the King's
titles, suddenly made his appearance outside the
kraal, to give us a little insight into his majesty's biography.   Advancing slowly towards the waggons
he opened the exhibition by roaring and charging,
in frantic imitation of the king of beasts—then placing his arm before his mouth and swinging it rapidly
in pantomimic representation of the Elephant, he
threw his trunk above his head and shrilly trumpeted.
He next ran on tiptoe imitating the Ostrich, and
lastly humbling himself in the dust, wept like an in-
fant.   At each interval of the scene, he recounted
the matchless prowess and mighty conquests of his

illustrious monarch, and made the hills re-echo with his praise. He was a brawny athletic savage, upwards of six feet in height, naked as he was born. Frenzied by his energetic gesticulations, the perspiration trickled from his greasy brow, and white foam descended in flakes from his distorted mouth, whilst his eye glared with excitement.

The road now became almost impracticable—large trees overhung the way, and threatened the destruction of the waggon tents; we proceeded very slowly, and narrowly escaped being upset, the jungle becoming more and more intricate as we advanced. Game traps and pit fall were to be sseen through every avenue, many of the thorn fences extending across the path, and impeding the waggons until cut away with the hatchet. A party of six natives had followed our tracks and volunteered to show a Giraffe.* I emerged under their guidance from the forest we were threading, into a wide plain, on which I saw, for the first time, the footsteps of four of these gigantic quadrupeds, but no living objects save a few Sassaybys, one of which I foolishly shot, when four of my savages immediately slunk behind to eat him. I was much struck with the *spoor* or track of the Cameleopard—it was different from every thing I had seen or imagined it would resemble. The larg-

---

* *Cameleopardalis Giraffa,* Delineated in the African Views.

est impression was eleven inches in length, of parallelogramatic form, tapered at the toe, and rounded at the heel. I felt singular satisfaction in finding myself at length treading on ground imprinted with the recent foot steps of that extraordinary animal.

I had by this time ridden far in advance of the waggons, and as night was fast closing around, I began to be apprehensive that I should have to bivouac in the bush. The savages appeared to contemplate the same contingency, and evinced a vast longing to join their companions, who had wisely remained with the flesh pots. I gave them by signs to understand that I disapproved of such a measure, and we all pushed on as briskly as possible. A contumacious Rhinoceros * was standing directly in our path, and although hailed repeatedly refused to make way. There was just light sufficient to admit of my discharging both barrels of my rifle into his unweildy sides. Sneezing violently and wheezing he ran off in the direction we were taking, and presently subsided in the path. We approached him with caution, but he was dead. At the same moment a discharge of musquetry, and a bright beacon fire bursting forth, directed our benighted steps to the encampment. It was at the termination of the forest, and not more than two hours journey from the residence of the King.

* *Rhinoceros Africanus.* Delineated in the African Views.

CHAPTER XII.

ARRIVAL AT KAPAIN, AND VISIT FROM THE CHIEF
MOSELEKATSE.

THE absence of water, added to our anxiety to
kiss the hand of his Majesty, induced us to yoke the
oxen much earlier than usual on the 24th. The
Hottentots were all in high spirits, their timidity having actually left them for a season. It seemed as if
some new and exciting emotion were felt at our near
approach to the King, which they considered as a
crisis in their fate. Even Cœur de Lion was resigned to his doom—he had dried his eyes, and went like
a lamb to the slaughter. Five miles travelling over
a fertile plain, broken occasionally by isolated hills
of inconsiderable altitude—and covered with large
herds of oxen, brought us within a short distance of
three conical mountains, disposed in a triangular
form, within the area enclosed by which we were
told that the royal kraal would be found. As our
approach was discovered, the tops of the hills became lined with natives, some of whom ran down
at intervals to report our progress, but it was not
until we had actually entered the gorge, that a miserable hamlet was perceived, which Baba immediately pointed out as the imperial residence.

Piet and the Parsee now guided the waggons:
Cœur de Lion, not wishing to find himself in the
front of the battle, volunteered to drive the cattle in
the rear, and the other six Hottentots proceeded in
advance with solemn step, saluting the King with
repeated discharges of musquetry, as a complimentary mode of announcing our arrival.   Several of
the subordinate chieftains, who were standing near
the gateway of the kraal then advanced, and as the
waggons ascended the acclivity, took the hand of
each of our party in succession, repeating the word,
fellow! fellow! fellow! several times.   The principal
of these men was Um'Nombate, a peer of the realm.
He was an elderly man of slight figure, benevolent
aspect, and mild but dignified demeanor.   He wore
the usual tails, consisting of a few strips of wild cat
and monkey skin dangling in front, and some larger
and more widely apart behind.   The elliptical ring
or *issigoko,* was surmounted by the inflated gall blad-
der of a sheep.   Andries, Piet, and April, were old
acquaintances, and he appeared glad to see them.
In reply to our enquiries respecting the health of
the King, and whether it was the royal pleasure that
we should visit him, he observed that his Majesty
was very glad we had arrived, and would come to
the waggons anon, at the same time directing them
to be drawn up outside the gate.   The next in rank
was a chief of mean and contemptible exterior, whose

14

repulsive manners were but too exactly indicated by his scowling profile. He was deeply scarred with small pox; and excepting a necklace of Lions' claws, three inflated gall bladders on his pate, and a goodly coat of grease upon his hide, was perfectly naked. I saw nothing remarkable about any of the others. They all carried snuff-boxes stuck in their ears; a collection of skin streamers like the tails of a lady's boa attached to a thin waistcord, being the nearest approach to an habiliment amongst them. All their heads were shaven, sufficient hair only being left to attach the *issigoko*, which is composed of sinews sewn to the hair and blackened with grease.

Shortly after the oxen were unyoked, and the tent erected, Mohanycom, the King's page, came forth from the kraal bearing the congratulations of his Majesty. He too was unincumbered with raiment of any sort; but wore a red feather from the long tailed Finch in his hair, which, unlike that of the rest, was unshorn, and destitute of the issigoko. The dimensions of his mouth were calculated to excite the astonishment of every beholder; that feature literally extending from ear to ear. An inspection of our property then took place. Not a word was spoken: neither did any of the party betray the smallest symptom either of surprise or even of gratification. An imperturbable gravity pervaded the countenance of every one, and as soon as they had

sufficiently scrutinized, they retired to report to the
Chieftain the result of their observations.

It was some hours before we could obtain any
breakfast, the nearest water being three miles from
the kraal. We felt quite certain that the King must
be dying with impatience to obtain possession of the
various presents we had brought for him, but he
thought it dignified to affect indifference, and prosecuted his ideas of propriety so rigorously, that his
non-appearance became at length alarming. We
therefore despatched Baba to say that every thing
was prepared for his reception, and that we were
extremely anxious to pay our respects. In the
course of a few minutes, loud shouting and yelling
announced his approach. He was attended by the
spies that had accompanied us from Mosega, several
of his Chiefs, and most of the warriors who were
not absent on the expedition I have alluded to, armed with shields and assagais. As he advanced
others rushed up with a shout, brandishing their
sticks. A number of women followed with calabashes of beer on their heads; and two pursuivants
cleared the way, by roaring, charging, prancing, and
caricoling as already described, flourishing their
short sticks in a most furious manner, and proclaim-
ing the royal titles in a string of unbroken senten-
ces. As we advanced to meet him, several of the
crowd exclaimed " *Haiyah! Haiyah!* " a shout of

congratulation and triumph. Having shaken hands, we led him into the tent, and seated him on a chair; the courtiers and great men squatting themselves on their hams on the ground in semicircular order on either side. He was particularly glad to see Andries, and shook him by the hand several times.

The expression of the despot's features, though singularly cunning, wily, and suspicious, is not altogether disagreeable. His figure is rather tall, well turned and active, but leaning to corpulency. Of dignified and reserved manners, the searching quickness of his eye, the point of his questions, and the extreme caution of his replies, stamp him at once as a man capable of ruling the wild and sanguinary spirits by which he is surrounded. He appeared about forty years of age, but being totally beardless, it was difficult to form a correct estimate of the years he had numbered. The elliptical ring on his closely shorn scalp, was decorated with three green feathers, from the tail of the Paroquet, placed horizontally, two behind and one in front. A single string of small blue beads, encircled his neck; a bunch of twisted sinews encompassed his left ankle, and the usual girdle dangling before and behind with leopards' tails completed his costume.

The interpreters, three in number, were ranged in front. After a long interval of silence, during which the chieftain's eyes were far from inactive, he

opened the conversation by saying he rejoiced we
had come to bring him news from his friends the
white people. Mohanycom put this speech into Bechuana, Baba translated it into Dutch, and Andries
endeavoured to render the meaning intelligible in
English. To this we replied, that having heard of
the King's fame in a distant land, we had come three
moons across the great water to see him, and had
brought for his acceptance a few trifles from our
country, which we thought would prove agreeable.
He smiled condescendingly, and the Parsee immediately placed at his august feet the *Duffel* great coat
which I have already described, as being lined and
trimmed with scarlet shalloon; a coil of brass wire
weighing fifty pounds; a mirror two feet square; two
pounds of Irish *blackguard* snuff, and fifty pounds
weight of blood red beads. Hitherto the King had
considered it beneath his dignity to evince the slightest symptom of astonishment—his manner had been
particularly guarded and sedate—but the sight of
so many fine things at once threw his decorum off
the balance, and caused him for the moment to forget what he owed to himself in the presence of so
large an assembly. Putting his thumb between his
teeth, and opening his eyes to their utmost limits, he
grinned like a school boy at the sight of ginger-
bread, patting his breast, and exclaiming repeatedly,

*"Monanti, monanti, monanti; tanta, tanta, tan-
ta!"** Having particularly brought to his notice that
the device of an uplifted arm grasping a javelin, on
the clasp of the great coat, referred to his extensive
conquests,of which all the world had heard; we placed before him a suit of tartan sent by Mrs. Moffat,
with a note which he requested me to read; and hearing his own name, coupled with that of Ma Mary,
as he termed that lady, and the word *tumerisho* (compliments) he grinned again, clapped me familiarly on
the back, and exclaiming as before *"tanta, tanta,
tanta!"* He now rose abruptly, big with some great
conception, and made signs to the Parsee to approach
and assist him on with the coat; habited in which
he strutted several times up and down, viewing his
grotesque figure in the glass with evident self-ap-
plause.   He then desired Mohanycom to put it on
and turn about, that he might see if it fitted behind;
and this knotty point settled to his unqualified satisfaction, he suddenly cast off his tails, and appearing
in puris naturalibus, commanded all hands to assist in the difficult undertaking of shaking him into
the tartan trowsers.   It was indeed no easy work
to perform—but once accomplished, his Majesty cut
a noble figure.   The Parsee wore a pair of red silk
braces, which he presently demanded, observing that

* Good, good, good; bravo, bravo, bravo !

they would supply the place of those that Mrs. Moffat *had forgotten* to send. Shortly after this, he directed an attendant, who was crouching at his feet, to take every thing to his kraal; and resuming his solemnity and his seat, tea was brought in. A number of gourds filled with *outchualla* or beer, were placed by the King's orders before the assembly, who, passing them from one to the other emptied them on the spot. Richardson and myself drank tea out of two battered plated goblets, whilst the King's mess was served in a flowered china bowl, as being a more attractive vessel, and less likely to retain the heat; but having eyed the different drinking cups for some time suspiciously, he handed his own to his attendants, and then extending his arm abruptly seized upon my goblet, and greedily drained the contents. It is well known that savages, however debased they may be in the scale of humanity, are keenly susceptible of indignity; and he either considered himself slighted, or had prudently determined, until we should become better acquainted, to taste nothing of which we had not in the first instance partaken ourselves.

It was now time to allude to our affairs, and having repeated that our principal object in coming into his country, was to make his acquaintance, we proceeded to ask permission to hunt Elephants. This request was readily granted: but on stating that we had little time, and should wish to return to the colony by a nearer route than the one we had come, he shook his head and gravely remarked that there was no other road. As this reply passed through Andries, he became dreadfully agitated, and opening both eyes, he stuttered forth with a vehemence of manner, which drew upon him the attention of the whole assembly, that the King never would consent to let any person depart by the Vaal river, and that we should all have our throats cut if we hinted further at such an arrangement! At this moment however the opportune return of a messenger, gave a fortunate turn to the conversation. The King had sent for his dress of state, that we might have an opportunity of admiring the matchless taste with which he had arranged some materials that had been presented to him, by Sir Benjamin D'Urban. It was an apron composed of black goat skin streamers, loaded with beads of every size and color, and with a profusion of brass chains and ornaments disposed in an endless variety of patterns that did ample honor to his inventive genius.

The production of this article led the King to enquire after the health of our most gracious Sovereign, of whom he said he had heard, and whom he declared to be next to himself the greatest monarch in the universe, adding that the white King's nation was undoubtedly second to his own in power. The dialogue proceeded very slowly, in consequence of the necessity of its being conducted through the tiresome medium of four different languages. Andries did not perform *his* duties with much regularity, and seemed to consider, that the colloquy was intended for his own instead of for our edification. Under this delusion, he fancied that he had accquitted himself of the obligation we had imposed, if he favored us with an occasional scrap. The King sometimes understood what Baba said in Bechuana to Mohanycom, nodding his head graciously, smiling, and repeating "tanta tanta tanta." At length the conversation flagged. Directing a sheep and sundry calabashes of beer to be placed before us, the despot arose, and abruptly without the slightest compliment, made his exit amid the congratulations of his loyal subjects. The heralds preceding him as before, rent the air with shouts and acclamations, until "the great black one" had re-entered his kraal.

During this serious yet laughable interview, we were not a little surprised to observe that the guides, who had by their freedom rendered themselves so highly offensive to us, continued bruising and snuffing tobacco, without appearing the least abashed in the royal presence. Whilst every one else cringed beneath the tyrant's glance with obsequious humility, they alone appeared at ease, nor were we able to account for this behaviour, otherwise than by

15

conjecturing that their too palpable office of spies upon our actions admitted them to these liberties. They
had never quitted the waggons for a single instant
since we left Mosega, had watched all our actions
with the most provoking attention, and on our arrival at Kapain, had doubtless reported to the King
every, the most minute, circumstance that had transpired.

CHAPTER XIII.

RESIDENCE AT KAPAIN.

WE were shortly afterwards visited by the King without either pageant or ceremony. This he considered a confidential interview, and said he had come "to see what we had got for him." The weather being cold, he was attired in a handsome black leathern mantle; its ample folds reaching to his heels, well became his tall and manly person; and he looked the very *beau ideal* of an African Chief. He had completely thrown aside that reserve and gravity, which in a public assembly he had conceived most becoming, and now appeared in high good humour, joking, laughing, and familiarly pulling our beards, of which the luxuriant growth elicited his admiration and surprise. He frequently asked us how many wives we had, and whether they also had beards. We thought this an auspicious moment, in which to revert to the subject of our desired exit by the Vaal river, but took especial care to exclude Andries from the conference. Besides being a bad interpreter, we had seen that he was personally opposed to the measure, and we consequently preferred Richard, who had now recovered his self possession, and was a much more impartial dragoman.

Arrowsmith's map of Africa having been produced, we placed a finger upon Graaff Reinet, Kuruman, and Mosega, explaining to the King, how many days journey would be saved, if we were to return to the Colony by the Vaal river. He shook his head as before, and petulantly observed, that he had already said there was no road through that country. We laughed, and expressed a wish to look for one; but he rejoined that his anxiety for our safety would not allow him to hear of our travelling in that direction, —that should any accident befal us, the white King would undoubtedly attribute blame to him, and he therefore, must insist upon our giving up the intention. Through this flimsy veil however, we could distinguish motives that were in no way connected with our safety. The Chieftain was naturally desirous of concealing, as far as possible, the havoc that his people had made amongst the Emigrant Farmers; and he was above all things, anxious to obtain further presents on our return from the interior. We saw the necessity of waiving the subject for the present, but secretly determined to attack him anon with his own weapons.

He soon became extremely eager to have a sight of our various wares, but we steadily resisted his teasing importunities to examine the contents of the boxes. Knowing that all savages possess the sordid passion of avarice in an extraordinary degree, and have the insatiate desire of accumulating property for the mere pleasure of possessing it, we had omitted no precaution to keep His Majesty in profound ignorance of the nature and extent of our supplies. To have permitted him to see the contents of the waggons, would most assuredly have tempted him to practise every unfair and extortionate stratagem to obtain possession of them. We only therefore placed in his way, as baits, those trinkets that we designed he should take, and these as well as every thing else that met his eye, he never failed to appropriate. A pair of my shoes having been casually exposed, though much too small, were instantly seized and donned, and the operation of trying them on was highly diverting. A silken waist cord was quickly transferred from my Indian sleeping drawers to his own neck, the tassels dangling in front; a red woollen night cap was drawn over his bald pate, and a comforter over his shoulders, and he repeatedly desired the interpreters to explain that "he liked all and every thing!" He crawled through the waggons, and diligently rummaged in every corner for beads, of which he frequently spoke. On this most important topic with all savages, he was particularly urgent; he said he liked every color and size, sending at the same time

to his seraglio for a vast variety, that we might distinctly comprehend his wishes on the subject. With
the greatest reluctance, he at last prevailed upon
himself to part with a single grain of each color,
as a sample to guide our selection when we should
next visit him, and having gained this victory over
his niggard nature, he repeated several times signi-
ficantly, that we " now knew exactly what he wanted." The visit was a very long one: the King
begged that we would publish to the traders in the
Colony, his anxiety to obtain musquets and ammunition in barter for Elephants teeth. He spoke also
on various subjects that interested him, particularly
respecting the productions of the white men's country.
His eyes had repeatedly wandered towards, and lat-
terly been rivetted upon a coil of brass wire, a portion of which protruded from the waggon, and before quitting us he darted suddenly upon it, grinning
with triumph, and bearing it along with him, with
the greatest exultation.

In the evening, as his numerous herds of cattle
were returning from pasture, the King gave us a
proof of the munificence of his nature, by selecting
two of the worst oxen and a toothless cow, of which
he begged our acceptance. We had repeatedly introduced the subject of cattle, bringing to his notice, the miserable condition of our own teams, and
hinting an expectation that he would recruit them.

He had always replied with great readiness that they would soon get fat, as there was abundance of grass and water in the country to which we were journeying; but we were certainly not prepared for so unequivocal a specimen of the Royal bounty. About dark he sent to *borrow* some wax candles, at the same time sending by Um'Nombate the stewed breast of an ox, and a supply of beer. We requested the old man to honor us with his company, which he readily did, emptying his plate faster than we could fill it, and swallowing at a draught the contents of a whole calabash of the native malt liquor. This detestable beverage, which is denominated *outchualla*, is of a whitish color, frothy, and produced from fermented Kafir corn. Moselekatse avowed himself an ardent admirer of it, and we understood frequently drank it to intoxication. Out of compliment to him I partook of it, but found it very unpalatable. The Hottentots averred that it was not stronger than water, but they invariably talked more at length and louder after drinking it, and Claas was lying the whole day under a bush, sealed in a torpor induced by the potations of it he had swallowed. Long files of women, singing as they walked, were constantly to be seen arriving from the adjacent kraals, with bowls of this nectar upon their heads; and our guides were ready recipients for any quantity that might be sent for our consumption, loudly in their cups shouting the praises of the King.

The full moon rose in cloudless beauty, rendering the night nearly as light as day, We had been a short time in bed when Um'Nombate aroused me stealthily, offering me an Elephant's tooth in exchange for beads, and assuring me that the King should never know of the transaction. We were too well acquainted with Moselekatse's character to be lured by Um'Nombate's proposal, and never doubting that he was a mere tool in the hands of the King, dismissed him without ceremony, apprizing him that we could make no exchange, except by His Majesty's order. The courtier retired discomfited, and the result proved that we were not wrong in our conjecture.

Shortly after day break, and almost before we had dressed, the despot himself was seen approaching with solemn step, accompanied by Um'Nombate, and a man bearing the identical Elephant's tusk on his shoulder. He was instantly surrounded by ten or twelve persons, who ran from a distance and crouched before him. All this looked exceedingly ominous. We had heard of the execution of two culprits some time before, in presence of a trader, and were half afraid, that the old man having been detected in his delinquency by some of the spies about the waggons, was about to suffer condign punishment. The king seated himself upon a chair and looked mysterious; Um'Nombate squatted himself upon the ground with the dejected air of a criminal, and the rascally tooth was placed before them.   We felt very uneasy, but pretended not to notice it, until His Majesty himself drew our attention to it, by kicking it with his foot, and observing that Um'Nombate wished to receive some beads in exchange for it.   This speech, although bearing more the character of a demand than a request, relieved our anxiety, but we replied that ivory was of no use to us, our oxen being quite unable to transport so heavy a commodity—that we were ready to barter beads, or indeed any thing we possessed for fat oxen, adding that if the King wished, we would gladly present a few beads to our friend Um-'Nombate, but begged to decline accepting the ivory. The King did wish this very particularly, and the beads were accordingly given, the tusk being, however left on the ground, to give to the transaction the color of an equitable exchange.

We very justly took credit to ourselves for the way in which we had brought this affair to so amicable a conclusion.   It was now evident that Moselekatse, as we suspected, had been privy to the whole transaction, and had availed himself of this pitiful stratagem to gratify his insatiate appetite for beads, and if possible to ascertain the extent of our resources.   The villain Andries was clearly in the King's confidence, and had doubtless given him all the information in his power, and it is more than probable,

16

that the realization of half a dozen bunches of beads,
by this paltry contemptible scheme, had afforded His
Majesty infinitely greater gratification than he had
been capable of deriving from the receipt of our
liberal, and in his judgment no doubt, princely presents.

But we had soon an opportunity of turning this
greediness to account, and dealing with the King in
his own fashion. In order to avoid creating suspicion as to the object of our desired return by the Vaal
river, we lost no opportunity of impressing upon him
that our leave was limited, that we were not Colonial subjects, but that we had come in a ship from a
far country of which the Parsee was a native. His
Majesty frequently expressed amusemeut at his dress,
remarking that he was a fine fellow to come so great
a distance, and must not forget to make his *tumerisho* to the Parsee King, enquiring if that Potentate
too had a black beard, and wore a high turban—how
many wives he had, &c. He even paid Nesserwanjee the compliment of desiring to inspect his pocket
knife with six blades, nippers, picker, and corkscrew
complete, which, however, he forgot to return. We
ever carefully abstained from making any allusion to
the capture of Erasmus' waggons, or to the military
proceedings against the emigrant Farmers.

This morning messengers were seen running
breathless with haste to acquaint the King with the

success of Kalipi's attack. There was an unusual
stir in consequence, and warriors were continually
coming and going during the greater part of the day.
The King appeared in high glee, but we carefully
affected ignorance of all that was passing, and were
thus gradually securing his confidence in the honor-
able nature of our intentions, regarding which he had
evidently been distrustful. In spite, however, of all
we could do, our Hottentots were perpetually prying
round the imperial kraal, and putting impertinent
questions to persons about the waggons; all which
being scrupulously reported, had an exceedingly mischievous tendency, and caused us constant annoyance
and anxiety.

CHAPTER XIV.

RESIDENCE AT KAPAIN, CONTINUED.

A DESIRE to see something of the King's domestic economy, induced us repeatedly to ask permission to visit him, but he invariably replied that he had no place in which to receive us, and indeed he passed the greater part of his time in lounging on our beds, or in the tent.   To day, 25th October, he was in unusual spirits, in consequence of the success of his arms against the emigrants. We affected to be alarmed at the possibility of an attack from Dingaan whilst hunting elephants to the Eastward, but he ridiculed the idea, adding bitterly that Dingaan was a cowardly rascal and not fit to live.   We had observed him for some minutes plucking blades of grass from below his chair, apparently lost in thought, and at times scanning our countenances with great intenseness; when all of a sudden he exclaimed that he wanted our tent.   This was the very opportunity we had been looking for; we had foreseen that he would become enamoured of it, and had determined to make it the stepping stone to the attainment of our wishes. With affected indifference we accordingly replied, that if he had determined that we should return by the circuitons route of Kuruman, we could not dispense with the accommodation the tent afforded; but that if we could proceed by the Vaal river, it should be sent to him as soon as the hunting was over. The high road to his heart was gained; his eyes twinkled, and after a moment's hesitation, he said that he had been thinking the matter over, and that we were at liberty to go wherever we pleased! Having made this gratifying announcement, the King withdrew.

Our object was now accomplished, but the miscreant Andries no sooner heard that his predictions had been falsified, than he industriously circulated a report that the Bushmen across the Vaal were so cruel and vindictive, that there was not the most remote probability of our regaining the Colony by that route; and from that moment the fear of death by poisoned arrows, took the place of the dastardly dread of the "great black one," whom our followers now pronounced to be a "very fine gentleman." I need scarcely add that the despot's beer had no small effect in producing this revolution of sentiment. In about half an hour the King sent for the tent. This we had anticipated in the natural train of events, but in order to enhance the value of the bribe, we took the liberty of reminding him of the terms of the agreement, and declined to part

with it until the hunting should be over, inwardly
hoping that this *ruse* would hasten our dismissal, for
which we were hourly becoming more anxious.

The wealth of this barbarous sovereign may be
said almost to consist in his innumerable droves of
horned cattle.   These are herded in various parts of
the country, and furnish employment to a considerable portion of his lieges, who are precariously maintained by his bounty, but depend chiefly for support
upon their success in hunting.   The deaths and
casualties which occur amongst the oxen at different out stations are regularly reported, and we had
an opportunity of seeing this frequently done during
our visit.   Running with all speed to within about
fifty yards of the King, a warrior places his arms
upon the ground, and assuming a subdued posture,
with his head bowed to the dust, crawls within ear
shot, when all those about the Royal person exclaim
Haiyah! Haiyah! and the report is made in a raised tone.   This done, the soldier remains crouched a
few seconds, his eyes bent on the ground, and if the
King has no questions to ask, suddenly springs on
his feet, exclaiming *Haiyah!* and runs back to his
arms.

Moselekatse frequently enquired about King William's flocks and herds, asking if they were very
extensive, a subject on which we could not enlighten
him.   He also spoke of our Sovereign's armies.   The

King's own warriors, who were present, we could not
but admire, although the despot described them as
young unfleshed soldiers, who had not yet gained a
name in arms.   They were, generally speaking, tall
and handsome; clad with the usual tails, and the addition of two long red feathers in the hair when it
was unshorn, or a cluster of variegated white and
black feathers from the Kingsfisher or Jay, falling
gracefully so as to obscure one eye.   They carried a
short thrusting spear—a club of Rhinoceros horn,
which is thrown with unerring precision—and an
elongated elliptical shield of ox hide, with the hair
displayed.   The size of this buckler is regulated by the
stature of the warrior, reaching in all cases from the
ground to his chin.   A stick variously decorated
at the ends is secured on the inner side, and two
parallel strips of hide, differing in color from the
shield are so interlaced as to traverse its whole length,
imparting a striking effect to the accoutred warrior.

Excepting those individuals of distinction by whom
he was generally attended, no subjects, or "dogs"
as he termed them, ever passed the Royal person
without bending their bodies almost double, preserving that obsequious posture several paces before and
after passing.   The King seldom moved without half
a dozen Magnates in his train, the heralds howling
at intervals, leaping about in imitation of some wild
beast, and loudly praising "the noble Elephant."

The usual answer to an order was "*ya bo ba*," "yes my father," and no one quitting or approaching the Presence, omitted to exclaim *Haiyah!* Any attempt to have taken the King's portrait openly, would probably have been attended with disastrous consequences, drawing being supposed to be connected with witchcraft, but I seized the first opportunity of giving His Majesty a sitting unobserved. I exhibited several drawings of animals, and was surprised to find him so quick of apprehension. He instantly recognized them all, repeating the Matabili name. He enquired if we did not wish to visit the great lake in the interior, which he said we might easily do, as there had been plenty of rain, and he would send a Commando to take care of us. This was a very tempting offer, but we replied we were sadly pushed for time, and were afraid of displeasing the white King by overstaying our leave. He rejoined that he would take care and prevent any unpleasant consequences by sending the white King a message about us.

This afternoon he was reclining on Richardson's bed, when the well known sound of a box, which had imprudently been opened by the Parsee, drew his attention to the baggage waggon. He pricked his ears, hastily sprung from the bed, and, before the alarm could be given, had plunged both arms into the bead chest. Never shall I forget the triumphant expression of his face at that moment. The lid having been closed upon his arms, his idols were hidden from his sight, but he consoled himself by feeling them, and conjecturing their color, grinning the while with exstacy, and, if so mild a term can express his manner of asking, *requesting* to have them all.   We said that they were all we had left, and that they were brought expressly for him; but that we must be allowed to keep them until he granted us permission to depart, it being in our country the custom to make a present on taking leave of a great man.   Looking eagerly at the beads, he exclaimed *mooe, mooe! monanti, monanti! tanta, tanta, tanta!* and added that although he deplored our departure yet trustworthy guides should be provided to conduct us on our journey early the following morning, pointing at the same time to the eastern horizon.   This bargain being fully settled, His Majesty marched off in triumph, a man before him carrying the box containing thirty pounds of blue and white beads.

We were a little surprised at his having so readily consented to part with us, and were half afraid he might alter his mind before the morning.   The desire of obtaining immediate possession of the beads without infringing appearances, had of course due weight with him; and there can be no doubt that he felt considerable uneasiness at our presence, now

17

that the return of Kalipi's Commando from the Vaal river drew so near. His anxiety to get rid of ourselves therefore overcame the reluctance he felt at parting with the small remnant of our property which had escaped his too successful forays. It was the expected return of the Commando too, that rendered him so anxious to send us to the great Lake, or indeed in any direction but that in which we were bent on proceeding. We had every inclination to avail ourselves of this most tempting offer, but our leave from India being limited, it would have been imprudent to have undertaken this journey, which might have detained us beyond the desert until the next rainy season. And although every other circumstance conspired to favor the project, and by smoothing the path to render it probable that two "poor Indian gentlemen" could have achieved so desirable and arduous an undertaking, we were yet compelled to sacrifice to circumstances our thirst for geographical discovery beyond the tropic of Capricorn.

In order that there might be no excuse for delaying our departure, we sent Baba in the afternoon, to ask the King's permission to pitch the "house" in his kraal. He was taking a siesta in Mr. Bain's waggon, but came out immediately in high spirits, and pointed out the spot upon which he had determined that it should be erected. Whilst this was being done, I had an opportunity of leisurely examin-

ing the imperial kraal. The plan of the enclosure
was circular, a thick and high thorn fence surrounding an area which was strewed with the sculls, paws,
and tails of Lions, some of them quite fresh, others
bleached by long exposure to the sun. Below the
waggon I observed a file of old muskets, probably
some that had been taken on the defeat of Barend's
Griquas in 1831. The Royal lodge, and the apart-
ments of the ladies, were shut off by a rough irregular palisade; and a portion of this enclosure was surrounded by a very closely woven wattle fence, having only one aperture of barely sufficient dimensions
to admit the King's portly person upon all fours. The
space was smeared with a mixture of mud and cow
dung, resembling that used in all parts of India for
similar purposes. In the centre stood a circular,
plumpudding shaped hut, about twelve feet in diameter, and perhaps four in length, substantially thatched
with rush matting. A low step led up to the entrance,
which was very confined and provided with a slid-
ing wicket. The floor was sunk to the depth of
three feet below the surface of the ground, and two
more steps led down to it. The furniture consisted
exclusively of calabashes of beer ranged round the
wall.

Thirty ladies only of the imperial seraglio were
present on this eventful occasion, and they remained
standing round the King who was seated in the open

air. They were generally swarthy and somewhat
en-bon-point. Many were even obese, with enormous pendant bosoms, and their heads were shaved,
a small tuft of hair only being left on the crown,
which was decorated with feathers.   Their dresses
consisted of short black kilts of leather, the fur worn
inside, and the outside rubbed with some hard substance and charcoal until it had acquired the appearance of black clotted wool.   These were studded with brass ornaments and a profusion of beads
of divers colors; they had besides a vast accumulation of these ornaments upon their bodies.   Some
wore blue from top to toe, others were enveloped in
one. mass of red, the endless variety of patterns in
which they were disposed, having doubtless emanated
from the inventive brain and prolific fancy of His
Majesty, a large portion of whose valuable time is
passed in devising and superintending the construction of ornaments for the *Harem*.

Amongst the ladies, I observed a captive Griqua, called Truëy.   This is the familiar name for
Gertrude.   She is the unfortunate daughter of Peter
Davids, Chief of the Bechuana Bastards, and successor to Barend Barends.   This Chief had, about three
years before, undertaken a hunting expedition to the
Vaal river, and in the natural course of events was
attacked by a party of Moselekatse's warriors who
were scouring the country in that direction; he

narrowly escaped with his life, but the whole of his property was carried off, and his nephew and daughter were taken prisoners.

When the tent was nearly pitched, the King suddenly changed his mind, and resolved to have it immediately in front of the palace door. In order to accomplish this, it became necessary to remove a portion of the wattle fence—a work of considerable labour, in the progress of which *outchualla* was liberally circulated to the perspiring Hottentots. It was about three o'clock and the pavilion had reared its head a second time. A bright thought then suddenly crossed the Royal mind. Investing himself with the *duffel* great coat, placing a red night cap on his head, and commanding two wax candles to be lighted and placed before him, he seated himself with a dignified deportment upon an inverted calabash, the contents of which he had previously swallowed, and became totally absorbed in the contemplation of his surpassing importance. It was with difficulty that I preserved my gravity, and having hastily complimented the King on his accession of property, and reminded him of our wish to leave the following day, I left him to his domestic enjoyments.

In the evening Truëy brought a dish of stewed beef from the King. Despite of our assertions to the contrary he could not help suspecting that we still had beads in our possession, and thought that the

Griqua maid might find means of inducing us to
part with some more before we departed.   The poor
girl shed tears when she heard spoken the language
of her tribe, and begged us to convey to her father,
should we see him, the intelligence of her safety and
that of her cousin Wilhelm, who had been sent to a
distant kraal, the day before our arrival, in charge
of a waggon containing two Dutch girls, prisoners
of war, of whose presence the King was anxious
that we should if possible be kept in ignorance.   She
had herself resided for some time at the kraal in
question with the King, who is in the habit of passing several months of the year there with one hundred of his wives, all of whom are decorated with bead
dresses of the nature I have described.   Every female married or single is at his command; his subjects not having it in their power to call even their
wives their own.   The King alone is rich—his subjects are all equally poor, and can be said to possess
nothing in the shape of property beyond the skins
with which nature has clothed them,—

> " And that small model of the barren earth
>   Which serves as paste and cover to their bones."

CHAPTER XV.

WE had been some time ready to depart on the morning of the 26th October, ere the King made his appearance. This he at length did, limping, and attended by the whole of his court. Andries, ever ready to create mischief, lost no time in spreading a report, that he had overheard the discussions at a council held the preceding evening, when it had been determined to revoke the permission granted us to depart by the Vaal river—a measure to which ministers were very averse. The chairs having been put away in the waggons, we conducted the King to his old seat on Richardson's bed. In the act of ascending to this post of honor, having to climb over the chest which contained my wardrobe, he opened it eagerly, and darting his hand into the medley, triumphantly clawed up a pair of thick shooting shoes, which, unfortunately fitting him exactly, I was compelled to make a sacrifice of at the risk of returning bare footed to the Colony. He now stated for our information, that his lameness had been occasioned by the tightness of the shoes he had taken the preceding day, and obstinately worn until they had raised large blisters on the Royal heels. Having desired an attendant to advance with a very handsome Weasel skin cloak, which I had seen him wearing the day before in the kraal, he invested me with the greasy robe, saying that I looked very cold, and must keep it as a token of his friendship. A similar speech to Richardson was accompanied with a Leopard skin girdle. Determined not to be out-done in generosity, we presented him in return with a rich Persian carpet, which had formed the basis of my bedding. This being spread on the ground, had the desired effect of enticing him down from his seat, with the design of inspecting it narrowly, and we instantly gave orders to yoke the oxen, which had purposely been kept close to the waggons.

Having informed his Majesty that we were ready to start, and the whips being cracked, he accompanied us a considerable distance—at last stopping, and extending his hand when a general leave-taking took place, the word *fellow! fellow! fellow!* being repeated as before by each great man, the bystanders shouting *Haiyah!* He desired us to convey his *tumerisho* to the white King—to Sir Benjamin D'Urban, to whom he sent a special message—and to Dr. Smith, adding that Mohanycom would accompany us to the Vaal river—but that we must make haste back to the Colony, lest the Governor

should think that he had slain us.   Upon my repeating that I should shortly come again bringing for
him a double poled tent, he replied that that was
*mooe, mooe, mooe! monanti, monanti, monanti!
tanta, tanta, tanta!* that we must bring him
"every thing," and take care to visit him via Mr.
Moffat's station, and not by the Vaal river, lest mischief should befal us by the way.

We now paid and dismissed the interpreter, with
a supply of provision for the road, and a note to Dr.
Wilson thanking him for Baba's services, and informing him of the complete success of our negocia-
tions with the King.   Upon this point we had certainly good reason to congratulate ourselves.   Visiting this capricious savage as we had done, at an in-
auspicious juncture, when he was embroiled with
white men, and might not unreasonably have regard-
ed us in the light of spies upon his land—a suspicion
which the pusillanimous conduct of our Hottentots,
and of Andries in particular, was calculated to inspire and confirm—we had had throughout a difficult and somewhat hazardous part to perform.   The
probabilities were in favor of our being detained,
and were certainly greatly against our obtaining permission to make our exit by the hitherto proscribed
route of the Vaal river, conducting as it would, directly through the scene of his operations against
the migratory Farmers; but by closing our eyes

18

upon passing events, and preserving throughout our intercourse with the despot, a firm, conciliatory, and confiding demeanor—not only had we succeeded in convincing him of the honesty of our intentions— but now pursued our journey with every reason to believe in the good faith of his professions towards ourselves.

As we were now considered to be on terms of close intimacy with His Majesty, we had no danger whatever to apprehend from any of the native tribes, through whose territories we might have occasion to pass. All those that inhabit the country between the Vaal river and the tropic of Capricorn, were his tributaries, and the terror of his name filled the surrounding nations. None of his own subjects indeed would dare to refuse us assistance, without incurring the certainty of his summary vengeance.

Our course, in order to reach the Cashan range of mountains, where it had been resolved that our operations against the Elephants should commence, was for the first three days a little to the Southward of East. Mohanycom, now armed to the teeth, had relinquished his appointment in the imperial household for that of guide. He had received in our presence, more than once, the most positive injunctions to accompany us wherever we pleased to go within the King's dominions, and not to return until he had safely conducted us to the Vaal river; and he had been further directed to obtain from one of the kraals on our route a subordinate Captain named Lingap, to assist in protecting us. Mohanycom having accompanied Um'Nombate, when that minister visited the Colony under Dr. Smith's escort, (for the purpose of forming an alliance on the part of His Majesty with the Cape Government,) could understand the general tenor of conversation held in Dutch, and could even express himself intelligibly. Andries could stutter tolerably in Bechuana, and possessed a smattering of Zooloo, and we thus hoped to be able to proceed without the aid of a sworn interpreter.

Owing to our unlooked for detention in the morning, we were glad to halt for breakfast after an hour's travel. Our long and wearisome marches through a parched and sterile country, in the course of which, as will have been remarked, our cattle were frequently deprived of all sustenance for many hours, had so reduced them in condition, that they could hardly support the weight of their own emaciated bodies. The last feed of corn was here divided amongst three of the horses that appeared most in need of it, the other half-starved wretches thrusting in their noses for a share, at a loss to understand why they should be excluded from so rare a feast.

Shortly after leaving Kapain, we observed a dog with neatly trimmed ears and tail, following

Mohanycom, who repeatedly endeavoured to drive him away, saying that he was the King's dog, and had been captured with Mr. Bain's waggons. Two messengers were speedily sent to bring back this pet, and His Majesty, unwilling to let slip so good an opportunity of asking for something, had desired them on no account to return without a fresh supply of wax candles. Conceiving, however, that our compliance with this unreasonable request, would but lead to further exactions, we excused ourselves, sending in lieu a tin mould and a bundle of cotton wicks, with abundant compliments, and brief instructions in the art of manufacturing "tallows" from the fat of the Eland.

Having thus freed ourselves from the duns, it was discovered that the oxen had gone off in search of water—not one of the Hottentots having thought proper to remain with them, although positively enjoined to do so. Three hours elapsed ere they were recovered, and before we had proceeded many miles, the sheep were missed. Andries being immediately sent back upon horseback, found Frederick lying under a bush in a state of stupefaction, the consequence of his frequent libations to the jolly god. The sheep as might have been expected, had availed themselves of his drowsiness to *levant*, but were traced up and recovered.

In spite of all these provoking delays, we contrived

early in the afternoon, to reach the Moriqua about
thirty miles below the point whence it issues from
the mountain chain. The approach to this small,
but beautiful river, is picturesque in the highest
degree. Emerging suddenly from an extensive wood
of magnificent thorn trees, we passed a village surrounded by green corn fields, and then descended by
a winding path into a lawn covered with a thick and
verdant carpet of the richest grass, bounded by a
deep and shady belt of the many stemmed acacia,
which margined the river on either hand far as the
view extended—and clothed with a vest of golden
blossoms, diffusing a delicious and grateful odour
around. Single Mokaalas, and detached clumps of
slender Mimosas, hung with festoons of flowering
creepers, heightened the effect, screening with their
soft and feathery foliage considerable portions of
the refreshing sward, across which troops of queru-
lous Pintadoes and herds of graceful Pallahs * were
to be seen hurrying from our approach.

As we threaded the mazes of the parasol-topped
acacias, which completely excluded the sun's rays,
a peep of the river itself was unexpectedly obtained.
A deep and shaded channel about twenty yards in
breadth, with precipitous banks overgrown with
reeds, was lined with an unbroken tier of willows.
These extended their drooping branches so as nearly

* *Antilope Melampus.* Delineated in the African Views.

to entwine, had they not been forbidden by the force
of the crystal current, which swayed them with
it as it foamed and bubbled over the pebbly bottom.
A plain on the opposite side, bounded by a low range
of blue hills, was dotted over with Mokaala trees,
beneath which troops of Gnoos, Sassaybys, and
Hartebeests, were reposing.

We drew up the waggons on a verdant spot on
the river bank, at a convenient distance from an extensive kraal constructed on the slope. Although
the sun shone, the cold occasioned by a dry cutting
wind, was scarcely to be endured even with the assistance of a great coat ; and the inhabitants being
clamorous for food, I readily placed myself under
the guidance of their chief with ten of his men, and
diving into the heart of the extensive groves, soon
furnished them with the carcase of a black Rhinoceros upon which to whet their appetites. This huge
beast, which shall be hereafter described, crossed the
river twice after being mortally wounded at duelling
distance: and I was compelled, cold as it was, to
wade after him, through water reaching to my middle—following his trail by the blood, until from single drops, the traces became splashes of frothy crimson. Struggling to force his tottering frame through
the tangled cover, the wounded monster at length
sank upon his knees, another bullet from the grooved bore ending his giant struggles, while he was
yet tearing up the ground with his ponderous horn.

CHAPTER XVI.

FROM THE MORIQUA RIVER TO TOLAAN, THE RESI-
DENCE OF MOSELEKATSE'S SON.

A t day break the following morning, a large party
of hungry savages, with four of the Hottentots on
horseback, accompanied us across the river in search
of Elands, which were reported to be numerous
in the neighbourhood. We formed a long line,
and having passed over a great extent of country,
divided into two parties; Richardson keeping to
the right, and myself to the left. Beginning to despair of success, I had shot a Hartebeest for the savages, when an object which had repeatedly attracted
my eye—but which I had as often persuaded myself
was nothing more than the branchless stump of
some withered tree, suddenly shifted its position, and
the next moment I distinctly perceived that singular
form, of which, the apparition had ofttimes visited my
slumbers—but upon whose reality I now gazed for
the first time. It passed rapidly among the trees,
above the topmost branches of many of which its
graceful head nodded like some lofty pine—it was
the stately, the long sought Giraffe. Putting spurs
to my horse, and directing the Hottentots to follow,

I presently found myself half choked with excitement, rattling at the heels of the tallest of all the
Mammiferes, whom thus to meet, free on his native
plains, has fallen.to the lot of few of the votaries of
the chase. Sailing before me with incredible velocity, his long swan-like neck keeping time to the
eccentric motion of his stilt like legs—his ample
black tail curled above his back, and whisking in
ludicrous concert with the rocking of his disproportioned frame, he glided gallantly along "like some
tall ship upon the ocean's bosom," and seemed to
leave whole leagues behind him at each stride. The
ground was of the most treacherous description; a
rotten black soil overgrown with long coarse grass,
which concealed from view innumerable cracks and
fissures that momentarily threatened to throw down
my horse. For the first five minutes I rather lost
than gained ground, and despairing, over such a
country, of ever diminishing the distance, or improving my acquaintance with this ogre in seven league
boots, I dismounted, and had the satisfaction of hearing two balls tell roundly upon his plank-like stern.
But I might as well have fired at a wall: he neither
swerved from his course, nor slackened his pace, and
had pushed on so far a head during the time I was
reloading, that after remounting, I had some difficulty in even keeping sight of him amongst the trees.
Closing again, however, I repeated the dose on the

other quarter, and spurred along my horse, ever and
anon sinking to his fetlock; the Giraffe now flagging
at each stride, until, as I was coming up hand over
hand, and success seemed certain, down I came
headlong—my horse having fallen into a pit, and
lodged, me close to an ostriches' nest, in which the
old birds were sitting.

There were no bones broken, but the violence of
the shock had caused the lashings of my rifle to give
way, and had doubled it in half—the barrels only
now hanging to the stock by the trigger guard. Nothing dismayed by this heavy calamity, I remounted
my jaded beast, and one more effort brought me
ahead of my wearied victim, which stood still and allowed me to approach. In vain I attempted to bind
my fractured rifle with a pocket handkerchief, in order to admit of my administering the *coup de grace*
— it was so bent that the hammer could not by any
means be brought down upon the nipple. In vain I
looked around for a stone, and sought in every pocket for my knife, with which to strike the copper cap,
and bring about ignition, or hamstring the colossal
but harmless animal, by whose side I appeared the
veriest pigmy in the creation—alas, I had lent it to
the Hottentots to cut off the head of the Hartebeest.
Vainly did I wait for the tardy and rebellious villains
to come to my assistance, making the air ring, and
my throat tingle, with reiterated shouts—not a soul

19

appeared—and, in few minutes, the Giraffe having recovered his wind, and being only slightly wounded in the hind quarters, shuffled his long legs—twisted his tail over his back—walked a few steps—then broke into a gallop, and diving into the mazes of the forest disappeared from my sight. Disappointed and annoyed, I returned towards the waggons, now eight miles distant, and on my way overtook the Hottentots, who, smoking their pipes, were leisurely returning, having come to the conclusion that "Sir could not catch the Cameel," for which reason they did not think it worth while to follow as I had directed.

My defeat did not cause me to lose sight of the flesh pots. Any change from the monotony of an unvaried bread and meat diet being highly agreeable, I went back to the nest of the ostrich with a view of obtaining the eggs. So alarmed were the old birds by my unceremonious intrusion in the morning, that they had not returned. Twenty-three gigantic eggs were laid on the bare ground without either bush or grass to conceal them, or any attempt at a nest beyond a shallow concavity which had been scraped out with the feet. Having broken one, to ascertain if they were worth carrying home, a Hottentot took off his trowsers, in which, (the legs being first tied at the lower end,) the eggs were securely packed, and placed on the saddle. Although each of these enormous eggs are equivalent to twenty-

four of the domestic fowls', many of our followers
could devour two at a single meal, first mixing the
contents, and then broiling them in the shell.   When
dressed in more orthodox manner, we found them a
highly palatable omelette.

Richardson shortly returned, having been engaged
in close conflict with a Rhinoceros.   Aroused from a
siesta by the smarting of a gun shot wound, the infuriated animal had pursued his assailant so closely
that it became necessary to discharge the second barrel into his mouth, an operation by which the stock
was much disfigured.   I employed the rest of the
day in repairing my own weapon with the iron clamp
of a box, binding it with a strip of green hide from
the carcase of an Eland.

There being no practicable road across the Mariqua within several miles of our position, we were
compelled on the 28th, to make one by paring down
the steep banks: and even then, experienced great
difficulty in towing our heavy vans to the opposite
side by the united strength of the teams.   The descent was almost perpendicular, requiring both wheels
to be locked: the bed of the river, covered with
loose stones, was too confined to admit of the oxen
acting in concert:—and the current, straightened by
the narrowness of the channel, was rapid and rose
to the floors of the waggons.

Shortly after we had crossed, a large mixed herd

of Sassaybys and Quaggas, alarmed by the sudden
appearance of our cavalcade, charged past me so
close, that one of the latter fell at my feet at each
discharge of the rifle.   Several savages had followed
us to obtain a supply of dried meat and assist in hunting; but although they were greatly delighted at this
performance, it was not until an unwieldy white
Rhinoceros * had bit the dust, that they were perfectly satisfied.   Smacking their thick lips, patting their
stomachs, and repeatedly exclaiming *Chikore, Chick-
ore*, they pointed out this huge beast standing stupidly
under the shade of a spreading acacia.   I crept within thirty yards before firing, but it was not until he
had received six two-ounce bullets behind the shoulder that he yielded up the ghost—charging repeatedly
with his snout almost touching the ground, in so
clumsy a manner, that it was only necessary to step
on one side to be perfectly safe.

This grotesque looking animal, which in many
points bears a ridiculous resemblance to the Elephant, is upwards of six feet high at the shoulder,
its shapeless head exceeding four feet in length.   It
is the larger but less ferocious of the two species of
African Rhinoceros, neither of which is clad in shell
armour like their Asiatic brethren: they have in lieu,
tough hides an inch and a half in thickness, of
which the whips known at the Cape under the de-

* *Rhinoceros Sinusus.*   Delineated in the African Views.

nomination of *Sjamboks*, are usually manufactured. Both have double horns: those of the black species are short, and sometimes nearly of equal length— whilst the anterior horn of the white Rhinoceros is upwards of three feet in length, the second being a mere excrescence. These animals may be readily approached within a few yards, against the wind, and being heavy and inert, their attacks are easily avoided.

Rejoining the waggons to breakfast, we found many savages assembled from neighbouring kraals, clamorous for snuff. One old lady inhaled it in large quantities and without wasting a single grain, by means of a long tube of wood, the ends of which were respectively applied to her nose and to the back of her hand on which the powder was placed.

The country through which we passed this day was more thickly wooded than any we had seen since leaving Kurrichane : and I for the first time observed several pit falls constructed purposely for taking the Rhinoceros. They differed from others in being dug singly instead of in groups—very deep and large— at the extremity of a narrow path cut through the bushes, and fenced outside with thorns—a sharp turn leading directly upon the trap, so that an unweildy animal being driven furiously down the avenue could have no chance of avoiding the snare. Many skulls and bones of these huge beasts were lying at the bottom of the sepulchres that had swallowed them up alive.

After travelling upwards of fifteen miles, and passing three or four very large kraals, we arrived at the
Tolaan river, a deep, narrow, and rocky channel,
containing several extensive pools—the hollowed
banks bearing testimony to the depth and rapidity of
the current at certain seasons. The bed was perfectly dry where we crossed, but covered with huge
fragments of granite, which threw the waggons
from side to side with frightful violence—and, added
to the almost perpendicular character of the banks,
rendered to passage extremely perilous. We
halted on an isthmus, formed by a double bend
of the river; a grove of large acacia trees proving
an agreeable shelter, and rendering the spot delightful. Here we were visited by Moselekatse's son, an
aristocratic and intelligent lad, fourteen or fifteen
years of age. His dress consisted of the usual girdle with long fur streamers—and a chaplet of white
beads bound about his forehead, to which were attached three tufts of clipped quills, resembling in
size and shape the flower of the African marigold.
A lad of his own age attended him. The blood of
the despotic sire flowing in the veins of the heir apparent to the throne of the Matabili, his first step
was to deprive Mohanycom of a clasp knife that we
had given him, which he immediately hung about his
own neck, with a look of absolute superiority hardly
to be expected from such a youth.

CHAPTER XVII.

THE MATABILI DESCRIBED — ARRIVAL AT THE RIVER
SIMALAKATE.

THE history of the assassination of one of the
Hottentot followers of Captains Sutton and Moultry,
to which allusion was made in a former part of this
narrative, is brief. Like most of his tribe, being unable to keep his hands from picking and stealing, he
purloined a musquet from the King's kraal; and,
presuming also to aspire to the affections of Truëy,
Moselekatse's favorite concubine, his body was one
morning picked up pierced with assagais. A boy
belonging also to one of those gentlemen disappeared about the same time, but his fate and his crime
remained equally veiled in obscurity.

The death of the trader Gibson, which formed
one of the reasons adduced by the worthy Missionaries at Mosega to dissuade us from prosecuting our
journey, was caused by the insalubrious climate of the
country bordering on the sea coast. It is the inva-
riable policy of all African Chiefs, to deter travellers
from visiting tribes residing beyond them, by exag-
gerated representations of peril, hoping by these
means to effect a monopoly of traffic. Gibson had

long been engaged in trading speculations, and in hunting Elephants, amongst the tribes in the interior; and tempted by the prospect of gain, penetrated in opposition to the advice of Moselekatse amongst the Babariri considerably to the Northwest of Delagoa Bay. There, the whole party, one Hottentot only excepted, was cut off by fever. The report of this event reaching Moselekatse, who, whatever his vices may be, is yet extremely anxious to produce impressions favorable to himself amongst the white people, he immediately despatched a Commando with directions to bring the survivor, who had taken refuge with a hostile tribe, alive—in order that by his testimony he might clear himself from all suspicion of murder. Ignorant of the intentions of the Commando, and alarmed for his own safety, the Hottentot resisted, and being slain in the attack, his head was laid at the feet of the King. The despot however, far from being pleased with the zeal shown by his warriors, ordered four of the principal of them to be put to death, on the ground that they had merely brought him a lifeless head instead of the living person as he had commanded.

Notwithstanding such acts of cruelty on the part of the tyrant, the devotion of the Matibili warriors to his commands almost exceeds belief. No soldier dares present himself to Moselekatse who has been wounded in an ignoble part, or has failed to execute his duty to the very letter. If a lion attacks his herds, either his death, or that of their guardians invariably ensues. Armed only with assegais and shields, they rush in upon the marauder, and generally at the expense of one or two of their lives, which are held of no account, retire from the conflict, bearing with them his head and feet to their Royal master. These are left to decompose within the fence of the imperial kraal, which, as I have already explained, is strewed with the bones of wild animals. War is the prevailing passion of the Matabili; they burn with an insatiate thirst for the blood of their enemies, of whom they cannot even speak without assuming an aspect of vengeance and fury. They are doubtless the stoutest soldiers in Southern Africa, not excepting the more disciplined troops of the Zooloo tyrant, from whom they deserted, and whose invading armies they have thrice routed in a pitched battle with terrible slaughter.

To be fat is the greatest of all crimes, no person being allowed that privilege but the King. Speaking evil of the King, or alluding to the heir apparent, are considered equivalent to treason, or compassing the death of the Sovereign in Britain. Neglecting his cattle is reckoned a capital crime, the execution following upon the sentence, from which there is no appeal, "quick as the thunderbolt pursues the flash."

20

It is not permitted to a subject to allude to the Elephant in presence of the despot; "The noble Elephant" being one of his titles. When speaking of hunting that animal, Moselekatse frequently urged us to instruct some of his warriors in our method, but as his people can neither ride nor be persuaded to fire a gun, it was impossible to comply with his request. Accustomed from childhood to the use of the assegai or javelin, without which the Matabili never quits his home, they are expert in the destruction of the Elephant; hemming him into a defile, they attack him with great intrepidity, and not unfrequently incur the utmost effects of his rage and fury. Occasionally also, they assail the Rhinoceros, but this inert animal is more usually ensnared in the pitfalls already described, which are generally provided with a sharp stake at the bottom, on which he is impaled.

The Matabili possess no horses; all those that have been from time to time taken from the Griquas and other tribes, with whom they have been engaged in war, have been carried off by the *Distemper*, as it is called, a fatal murrain, which sometimes extends itself to the oxen, over every part of Southern Africa during the early months of the year. The ravages of this disease, which is said to be an affection of the lungs, are supposed to be occasioned by the young grass which springs up after the first rain; and at these seasons, the Colonists who can send their horses into the more elevated districts, are able generally to preserve them.

The attempts of our friends at equitation drill, and horsemanship, were ludicrous and awkward in the extreme. Although active, muscular and agile in a wonderful degree, they tumbled off the horse as fast as they ascended, notwithstanding that the saddle, bridle, mane, and even tail were unceremoniously pressed into the service.

Although a soldier of fortune who has gained all his glory and power in the field, Moselekatse has now ceased to lead his armies to battle; but he still honors with his presence, the great hunting expeditions which frequently take place. On these occasions he is attended by a retinue of several thousand men, who extend themselves in a circle, enclosing many miles of country, and gradually converging so as to bring incredible numbers of wild animals within a small focus. Still advancing, the ring at length becomes a thick and continuous line of men, hemming in the game on all sides, which, in desperate efforts to escape, displays the most daring and dangerous exhibition of sport that can be conceived. As the scene closes, the spears of the warriors deal death around them, affording a picture thrilling to the sportsman, and striking in the extreme.

The dexterity of the Matabili in the use of the knob-stick is also wonderful; they rarely miss a partridge or a guinea fowl on the wing, and knock over hares, cats, and other ground game with equal precision.   In a nation such as I have described, it will be readily conceived that agriculture is not in high repute, and accordingly excepting for the grain used in making beer, I saw little attempt at cultivation. A few melons, rather deserving the name of vegetables, were the only fruit we met with, and these I presume are nurtured chiefly for the gourd, which becomes their calabash or water flagon.   We could hear of no funeral ceremonies amongst them.   High and low, their bodies are thrown forth upon the plain, soon after life departs, a prey to wild beasts; the flap of the Eagle's wing and the howl of the Hyæna being their only death note.   In the Zooloo tribe however, from which Moselekatse has sprung, some respect is shown to the memory of Royalty, and persons of high distinction; the defunct dignitary being interred within the hut where he has expired or been assassinated.   The marriage ceremonies of the Matabili were exceedingly difficult to understand.   Acceptance or non-acceptance of a snuff-box on the part of the lady, indicates the success of her suitor, or the contrary: and it would seem that marriage has sometimes altogether been prohibited amongst the Zooloos, or confined to men in advanced life.   We were informed that the issigoko, or ring, so often alluded to, indicated a married warrior; but to this rule there must be exceptions.   Of the population of Moselekatse's empire, I can form no correct estimate.   The constant wars in which he is engaged, diminish the number of the males, but the women are exceedingly prolific.   His standing army of warriors of his own tribe exceeds five thousand men, but numbers of the conquered nations swell his followers to a large amount, and are chiefly employed as guardians of his cattle, during the intervals of peace.

On the 29th we took the field, accompanied by the whole of the male inhabitants of three kraals, in addition to those that had accompanied us from the Mariqua river.   The country here is generally undulating, extensive mimosa groves occupying all the vallies, as well as the banks of the Tolaan river, which winds amongst them on its way to join the Mariqua.   We had not proceeded many hundred yards before our progress was opposed by a Rhinoceros, who looked defiance, but took the hints we gave him to get out of the way.   Two fat Elands had been pointed out at the edge of the grove the moment before, one of which Richardson disposed of with little difficulty, but the other led me through all the intricacies of the grove to a wide plain on the opposite side, immediately on emerging upon which, the fugitive was prostrate at my feet in the middle of a troop of Giraffes, who stooped their long necks, astounded at the intrusion, and in another moment were sailing away at their utmost speed. To have followed them upon my jaded horse would have been absurd, and I was afterwards unable to find them. Returning to the camp after killing several Elands and Rhinoceroses, besides other game, which the savages quickly took charge of, I was furiously charged by a herd of horned cattle, and my horse being much exhausted, I had no small difficulty in escaping their persecution. Objecting I presume to my garb or complexion, they pertinaciously pursued me through thickets and over ravines, regardless of the loud whistle of the herdsman to which they are usually very obedient. During the night, our camp was thrown into disorder by the intrusion of a Rhinoceros, which actually stood sometime between the waggons.

Several hours diligent search the next day brought us upon a herd of twelve Cameleopards. We pursued them a considerable distance, and repeatedly wounded the largest, a gigantic male, probably eighteen feet in height; but our famished horses falling repeatedly into the numerous holes with which the ground was covered, we at length became convinced of the impossibility of humbling the lofty head of the Giraffe, until our steeds should have improved in condition upon the fine pasturage which now abounded.

The day was sultry and the glare distressing. To the North-eastward, the distant prospect was bounded by a range of blue mountains which we visited some weeks afterwards; the whole of the extensive plain being sprinkled with huge Mokaala trees, mat rushes, and thistles. Large herds of Elands were grazing amongst these, the host of savages by which we were attended quickly clearing away the carcases of those we slew, and then quarrelling for the entrails. I hope my reader has understood that these barbarians generally devour the meat raw, although when at leisure they do not object to its being cooked. They usually seize a piece of the flesh by the teeth, cutting a large mouthfull of it with the assegai close to the lips, before masticating it, which they do with a loud sputter and noise. The meal being finished they never fail to wipe their hands on their bodies, and then being generally gorged they lay themselves down to repose—previously relaxing their leathern girdles, which are so contrived as to be readily expanded according to their girth.

As the sun was setting, our friend the Rhinoceros imprudently appeared upon the bank of the river within pistol shot. Five balls were immediately lodged in his body, with which he retreated, and was picked up the following morning.

Leaving the Tolaan river we passed between two ranges of hills, and travelled nearly Southeast, over a rugged country, strewed with huge loose masses of stone, and thickly covered with low bush. To the right, extensive stone walls marked the site of a once flourishing Bamaliti town, now destroyed. At noon unyoked in a well watered valley, covered with turf and abundantly cultivated. Here 'Unchobe, the Captain of an adjacent Matabili kraal paid us the compliment of climbing into the waggon, and of squatting himself without ceremony upon my bed, inviting his greasy vrow to do the same. The stench of this worthy couple was quite overpowering, but he was evidently considered by his countrymen as a person of consequence, being loaded with a profusion of beads and ornaments, amongst which we remarked a necklace composed of Spanish dollars, and a medal which had been struck in England in honor of the abolition of slavery. His hair, contrary to the custom of the Matabili, was matted with grease and sibilo, and his consort also was decorated with beads of various colors, to the amount of at least thirty pounds weight. A crowd of women and girls assembled round the waggon, clamorous for snuff and tobacco, and afforded us much amusement by their insatiable curiosity and good humour. The looking glass, that never failing source of surprise and delight to uncivilized beings, produced more than its usual effect upon them. Forming a group of merry faces at the end of the waggon, and chattering to each other they gazed incessantly at their reflected images, trying by pressing their hands behind the mirror to discover the cause of such a magical effect; covering their eyes, and peeping askance to see if their double selves imitated the action.   Scarcely a less powerful impression was produced by some of my drawings of wild animals, which I exhibited to them.   In India even educated natives are exceedingly slow in recognizing representations of objects, but these unsophisticated damsels instantly acknowledged the likenesses, by pronouncing the name of the quadruped in an animated manner, drawing the attention of their neighbours to the sight.   The Matabili females are neither prepossessing nor engaging; they shave their heads in the manner already described, and wear a short leathern petticoat, which in most cases is their only covering, although they occasionally also have a flap of leather suspended from the neck.   Their skin from being constantly lubricated with grease and fat, acquires a shining appearance and is of a dark brown color approaching to copper.   Both sexes occasionally employ themselves in sewing skins, an operation which is performed by means of a skewer or awl, by which they pierce a hole, and afterwards introduce a thread composed of an animal's sinew, resembling our fiddle strings.   Of this substance, which is also used to string beads upon, they are generally provided with a large supply suspended from

21

the waist. So far as we remarked, the women appeared little oppressed with sensibility, although affectionate to their children : the latter wander almost in a state of perfect nudity until the age of puberty. All classes are equally devoted to tobacco, taken as snuff; and the plant is so precious that it is never used alone, but invariably adulterated with a due admixture of earth or sand.

Late in the afternoon we halted on the banks of the Simalakate, a deep and tranquil stream, margined by reeds and rushes, affording a ready covert for Lions, those fresh marks were every where visible in the neighbourhood. The day had been very sultry, and our two dogs, nearly blind from thirst, ran down the steep bank to the water's edge, into the very jaws of an enormous Alligator. One of them returned immediately in a state of great alarm. Suddenly a splash was heard, and bubbles of blood rising a minute after, too truly told what had been the fate of his unfortunate companion. Not content with depriving us of our valued fourfooted companion, the Alligators quitted their watery homes during the night, and eat up a portion of the leather of the waggon furniture, besides the shoes of our followers. These scaly monsters are very common in many of the African rivers, and this was not the only occasion on which we suffered from their ravages. We frequently killed some of an immense size.

About sunset an unwieldy white Rhinoceros approached the waggons evidently with hostile intentions. There being neither bush nor hollow to conceal my advance, I crawled towards him amongst the grass, and within forty yards fired two balls into him. He started, looked around for some object on which to wreak his vengeance, and actually charged up with his eye flashing fire to within an arm's length of me. Crouching low, however, I fortunately eluded his vengeance, and he soon afterwards dropped down dead.

Thus far on our journey we had pursued a partially beaten track, dignified by the Hottentots in Colonial phraseology with the name of a road, though since leaving Kurrichane, it had consisted merely of the faint vestiges of the trader's waggons, which "few and far between" had traversed it—and even these could only be discovered by a practised eye. But from our entrance into the hills this morning, all traces had disappeared, nor did we again see the tracks of a waggon for several months, until we had crossed the river Vaal on our return to the Colony. Thus left to ourselves, matters resumed a smoother aspect, and the dread of Moselekatse appeared to have left the Hottentots, leaving behind it like an intermittent fever, an interval of tranquillity, which lasted for some time.

CHAPTER XVIII.

MEETING WITH KALIPI'S COMMANDO, AND ARRIVAL
AT THE CASHAN MOUNTAINS.

THE morning of the 1st November brought to light
several parties of Matabili warriors on the opposite
side of the river, escorting large droves of cattle towards Kapain. They appeared purposely avoiding
us, but although we were unable to hold any communication with them, we felt convinced that they
formed a part of Kalipi's Commando. After skirting the deep sedgy channel of the Simalakate several
miles, in quest of a ford, we arrived at a point where
it takes a sudden bend to the Eastward, and, even at
this season, falls with considerable violence over a
stratum of granite, which forms a rough, but complete pavement. Across this stony drift we effected
a passage, though not without sundry violent con-
cussions, that bid fair to dislocate the joints of our
heavy vehicles, and rendered necessary the precaution of removing the guns, and all brittle wares, during the *trajet.*

We unyoked for breakfast in an extensive Mimosa
grove, which rivalled in beauty all that we had

hitherto seen. The airy parasol-shaped foliage was intertwined above our heads in such a manner as to be perfectly impervious to the sun's rays, the constant and delicious shade it afforded having induced the growth of a luxuriant carpet of grass, spangled with numerous gaudy flowers. Whilst the oxen were revelling in these sweets, I strolled down the river with my rifle in search of Riet Buck,* of which some had been seen in the morning. Here the scenery was beautiful. Three cascades fell over descents of several feet, within a quarter of a mile of each other, flanked by stately timber trees, of splendid growth, and graceful foliage, which leaning their venerable forms over the limpid stream, were reflected on its glassy bosom. Huge isolated masses of rocks reared their stupendous heads at intervals, as though cast there by some giant hand in sportive derision of the current, which foamed and bubbled around them. Upon the tops of these, Cormorants were sunning themselves in hundreds, whilst scaly Alligators were basking on the lower tiers amid flowering bushes and evergreens. Straggling hamlets were scattered along the banks, and near the ford I observed one constructed upon a raised platform, the only instance of attic architecture that occurred during my travels. The number of huts did not

* *Redunca Eleotragus.* Delineated in the African Views.

exceed twenty, and they appeared to have been sometime uninhabited.

We resumed our journey about noon. The route towards an opening in the mountains led us nearly due South, through an exceedingly rich and fruitful part of the country, abounding in verdant savannahs and hamlets, around which large herds of cattle were indulging in luxuriant pasture. These were tended by armed herdsmen, and we were at first surprised to observe the oxen leave their grazing, and flock around our waggons as they proceeded, snorting and exhibiting signs of pleasure, as though in recognition of objects with which they were familiar. The appearance shortly afterwards of several hundred Matabili warriors in their war costume explained the riddle, and we knew that these must be some of the cattle taken from the unfortunate emigrants. Shortly before this, Mohanycom, our guide, had left the waggons, and proceeded to a kraal at some distance, for the purpose of communicating to 'Lingap, the subordinate Captain of whom I have before spoken, and who resided there, the King's orders that he should attach himself to our suite. The consequence of this ill judged proceeding was, that we were deprived of his services at the very moment when they were most required. The warriors not perceiving any of their own tribe with our party, and having had their hands so lately imbrued with the blood of white men, could think of nothing but war and plunder. Suspecting, or rather hoping, that we had found means to enter the country without the King's knowledge, they closed round the waggons with every demonstration of hostility, accosting us with insolence, and peremptorily commanding the drivers to halt; several at the same time placing themselves in front to obstruct the passage. The Hottentots looked aghast, and Cœur de Lion, in a state of extreme agitation, fainted when he saw a number of wounded warriors borne past on the shields of their comrades, whilst others groaned under the weight of accoutrements that had been stripped from the bodies of the slain.

Our situation was now critical—Andries whether from terror, or the disgust excited by his supercession at Kapain, showed no disposition to extricate us by an explanation of the true state of affairs. No one else understood a word of the language. The crowd was fast encroaching upon us, and their pacific intentions becoming momentarily more questionable. Some even clambered into the waggons, overhauling their contents, whilst others cast a longing eye at the oxen and sheep. The unhappy Andries was at length seized by a brawny savage, an event which proved highly favorable to us, for in his agony of distress at the supposed approach of death, he found his tongue, and stuttered out a brief intimation of our having been the honored guests of

the King.   The name of Moselekatse acted like
magic on his followers.   The barbarians were instantly appeased, and in a few seconds, were peti-
tioning in an abject tone for ʼnuff, beads, and tobacco—allowing us to proceed on our way rejoicing.

The warriors were all clad in their full costume,
which was more complete than that I have already described.   It consisted of a thick fur kilt called *Um-*
cooloobooloo, composed of treble rows of cats or
monkeys tails descending nearly to the knee.   A
tippet formed of white cows' tails encircled the shoulders, and covered the upper part of the body, the
knees, wrists, elbows, and ancles, being ornamented
with a single ox tail fastened above the joint.   Several of their shields bore marks of the recent conflict,
being drilled with musquet balls, and they carried
with them the arms of those who had perished, to
place them at the foot of the King—having left the
bodies of their comrades, as usual, a prey to vultures
and hyænas—for no funeral obsequies ever honor
the deeds, or crown the devotion and bravery of a
Matibili warrior.

Nothing could be more savage, wild and martial,
than the appearance presented by the barbarian army returning to their despotic Sovereign, wreathed
with laurels and laden with spoils.   We continued
to meet large straggling parties during the whole
of the day, and could not have passed fewer than
five or six thousand head of captured cattle.

MATABILI WARRIOR.

Contrary to the practice of the Kafirs, the Matabili prefer attacking in open ground, rushing in at
once upon their foes, striking their shields by way
of intimidation, and stabbing with their short spears,
of which a bundle of five or six is taken when going
to war. So terrible is this mode of combat to the
unwarlike Bechuana, that one Matabili champion
is a match for fifty of them.   In the late affair, however, they received a severe lesson in the superiority
of fire arms, of which, since the signal defeat of
Barends' Griquas in 1831, Moselekatse had entertained a great contempt.   Kalipi had found the emigrant Farmers several days march to the Southward
of the position they occupied when Erasmus' effects
were captured.   Being apprized of the approach of
the barbarian horde, they had drawn up their waggons in a close circle, fortifying the enclosure with
thorn branches, and defending themselves so stoutly,
that they beat off the assailants with terrible slaughter, wounding Kalipi, and obliging him to retire
from the conflict.   Plunder is the principal object
of all savage warfare, and although, fortunately for
the cause of humanity, he failed in carrying into
effect the orders of his incensed and blood-thirsty
master, to massacre the males without quarter, spar-
ing only the women and young girls that were calculated to grace the imperial seraglio—Kalipi had
yet succeeded in the more lucrative object of his

22

expedition—he retired from the field of carnage, sweeping before him the whole of the flocks and herds of the emigrants, that were grazing in thousands upon the verdant plains of the Likwa,—leaving the late flourishing camp, an immoveable and shattered wreck in the wilderness.

We soon descended into a fine valley in which were situated nine of Moselekatse's principal kraals, around which countless cattle were grazing. From one of these villages, the last Matabili station in this direction, we were rejoined by Mohanycom, who brought with him 'Lingap, the captain of our escort, and a whole host of ladies, who were desirous of ascertaining the quality of our "Irish blackguard." They all saluted us with *Dakha bono, Qui!* " I see you! give me some snuff!"   Winding up a little acclivity we presently entered a grand and extensive forest, with occasional open spots, which abounded to an incredible degree with Hartebeests, Sassabys, Gnoos, and Quaggas. Here too we saw the first traces of the Elephant—Mimosa trees torn up by the roots, and sturdy branches, which rent from the parent stock, overhung the path.   Hundreds of deep holes impressed by the feet of these gigantic quadrupeds during some recent heavy rain, with heaps of fresh excrement, were every where to be seen.   Andries, who thought every animal less than an Elephant beneath his notice, now became frantic. Stopping the waggon which he was leading, he waved his cap aloft, threw a mass of dung into the air, and huzzaed till he was hoarse.

Arriving at the end of the forest we again descended, and found ourselves under one of the secondary ranges of the Cashan mountains, on the bank of the Bagobone river, where we halted in a meadow, having travelled twelve miles. Here again the scenery was wild and romantic. The mountains rose on either hand in bold majestic forms, clothed in parts with luxuriant verdure—their steep rocky sides besprinkled in others with occasional light bushes, which enlivened the rich and varied tints of the broken crags. Rugged cliffs margined the bubbling river and shut in the lower prospect, whilst the great range of the Cashan mountains towered above them in the distance, their spiry blue summits appearing to us, who had for months seen nothing larger than an ant hill, almost to rival the Alps in grandeur.

Whilst the Hottentots were engaged in making a fence for the cattle, I entered one of the nearest groves, for the purpose of obtaining food for the people, and presently brought down a Water Buck,* a rare and splendid Antelope, which is not

---

* *Aigocerus Ellipsiprymnus.* Delineated in the African Views.

to be met with until after crossing the Mariqua. The report of my rifle disturbed a Lion and Lioness from a bush close by, and they instantly slunk into the jungle. Having covered up the carcase with bushes, I returned to the waggons and found that Piet had already arrived with an abundant supply of Gnoo's flesh. He too had narrowly escaped stumbling over a Lion in long grass. These troublesome beasts appeared to be so numerous, that we made a more substantial fence than usual for the oxen, and had no reason to regret having taken the precaution; as numbers were roaring and prowling round the camp towards morning, endeavoring to effect an entrance.

Over the evening fire Lingap favored us with the particulars that he had been able to collect regarding the attack on the emigrant Farmers, extolling Kalipi's bravery to the skies. Himself a warrior of tried courage, he had formed one of the Commando that captured Erasmus' waggons. His eyes glistened as he spoke of the pleasure he had derived from feeling his spear enter white flesh. It slipped in, he said, grasping his assegai and suiting the action to the word, so much more satisfactorily than into the tough hide of a black savage, that he preferred sticking a Dutchman to eating the King's beef. When sufficiently sated with roast meat, and primed with snuff, he treated us to a love ditty, in the course of which he looked most killing. Both he and

Mohanycom were much elated at Kalipi's success, and as the evening advanced, being joined by a large party of friends, they all struck up a war chorus in praise of the King, which they continued until a late hour, howling and dancing until they were exhausted. We could never arrive at any interpretation of their songs, and of this in particular, beyond what I have already given. Strange though it must appear, it is a fact that, whether from fear or superstition, the devotion of these savages to their tyrannic Chieftain amounts to positive adoration. Present or absent he absorbs all their praises, and is the only idol they worship. The following were the words repeated with occasional transposition, ten thousand times.

O Lĭlli bŭkālū, Būnkā Bāee
O nwăng-ă-nū sŭbŏokană-shee.
Ai bŭnkă bàee—Hibo, hi bo, hi bo bo-shee.

Dancing served in the place of music, and was nothing more than an accompaniment to the song, of which the pathos and feeling were indicated by the contortions of the body, and by the various figures described with the hands in which they flourished a club of Rhinoceros' horn. The feet regulated the time, and imparted the locomotive effect in which they rejoice. At first they were slowly lifted, to descend again with a single or double stamp; and the sticks being gently clashed at the same moment, the correspondence was both diverting and striking. But as the performers warmed upon the exercise, their gesticulations became more and more diversified, vehement and energetic—leaping, striding, vaulting, and running, they perpetually crossed each others' orbits, stabbing, parrying, thrusting, advancing, and retreating, with so light a foot, and so rigid a muscle, that the eye could with difficulty follow the velocity of their motions; now darting to the right, and then as abruptly recoiling to the left, they brandished their sticks aloft, increasing in vehemence by each detour; then vaulting several feet into the air, leaping, galloping, and charging, in pantomimic conflict, they made the ground resound under their feet, and raised a cloud of dust by the eagerness and rapidity of the exercise—until, foaming and frenzied by their tortuous movements, they fairly sank beneath the tempest which they had stirred. To the bystander this scene conveyed all the reality of the wildest conflict of savage life; the darkness of the night, with the peculiar light shed over the features of the frantic group by the blazing fire, contributing greatly to heighten the impression it produced. In consequence of the absence of the warriors, we had not an opportunity of witnessing any of the great national dances in which the King himself acts a prominent part, but the effect of these public *spectacles* may be estimated by what I have described.

CHAPTER XIX.

RHINOCEROS AND WILD BUFFALO HUNTING ALONG
THE CASHAN MOUNTAINS.

LEAVING the waggons to proceed to the ground
where our operations against the Elephants were to
commence, I went with 'Lingap to the carcase of
the Antelope I concealed yesterday, near which I
killed two females of the same species. I believe I
may with safety assert that I am the only European
that ever shot a Water Buck. It is about the size of
an ass, and of somewhat browner colour. The hair
is coarse, like that of the Indian Rusa Stag, and in
texture resembles split whalebone. The appearance
of the male animal is stately; the eyes are large and
brilliant; the horns ponderous, three feet in length,
white, ringed, and placed almost perpendicularly on
the head, the points being curved to the front. A
mane encircles the neck, and an elliptical white band,
the tail, which is tufted at the extremity. The female is similar, but hornless and rather smaller.
The flesh of both is coarse, and so highly ill savoured
that even savages are unable to eat it. On cutting
off the head, the effluvia literally drove me from
the spot. Mr. Stedman had the merit a few years

ago of bringing this Antelope under the observation
of the scientific world, and Dr. Smith brought down
other two specimens with the late expedition.

On the bank of the river I observed the perfect
skeleton of an Elephant. Near to it 'Lingap suddenly stopped, and pointing with his assegai to a
bush a few yards off, whispered " *Tao,*" and I immediately perceived three Lionesses asleep. Ensconc-
ing himself behind his shield, he made signs to me
to fire, which I did into the middle of the party, at
the same moment springing behind a tree which completely screened me. Thus unceremoniously awakened, the three ladies broke covert, roaring in concert,
and dashed into the thick bushes, while we walked
as fast as possible in the opposite direction. In the
course of a few minutes we heard several discharges
of musquetry, and an infuriated Rhinoceros, streaming with blood, rushed over the brow of the eminence
that we were ascending, and was within pistol shot
before we were aware of his approach. No bush
presenting itself behind which to hide, I threw my
cap at him, and 'Lingap striking his shield and shouting with stentorian lungs, the enraged beast turned
off. I saluted him from both barrels, and he was
immediately afterward overturned by a running fire
from the Hottentots, every one of whom I now saw
had left the waggons at the mercy of the oxen,
conduct for which we reprimanded them severely,

threatening to withhold further supplies of ammunition.

Three hours travelling between two ranges of the Cashan mountains, brought us to the Ooli river, a pretty little stream, upon the further bank of which we halted. A party of savages joined us, having feasted heartily upon the Gnoo killed yesterday, and as we did not require their services we sent them to eat up the Rhinoceros, with injunctions to return in the evening. The banks of the Ooli are precipitous, and clothed with extensive mimosa groves, abounding with wild Buffaloes, Pallahs, and Guinea Fowl.* We made a large bag of the latter, and obtained a supply of Ostrich eggs. In order to drive the Elephants into the plain, preparatory to hunting them the next day, we set fire to the grass, and moved the camp to a more secure position, where the savages who had returned, assisted in fortifying our stockade against the Lions.

At day break the following morning, we crossed an extensive valley which skirts the mountain range, passing the ruins of several stone kraals, which in former times served to confine the cattle of numerous Bechuana tribes then living in peaceful possession of the country. These crumbling memorials now afford evidence of the extent to which this lovely spot was populated before the devastating wars of

* *Numida Meliagris.*

23

Moselekatse laid it waste, and indicate also a refine-
ment in the art of building that I had not met with
before. Our guides eagerly plucked several plants
of tobacco that grew wild about the enclosures, dry-
ing them for the manufacture of snuff. Soon afterwards we entered a gorge of the mountains, and began to ascend. The ravages of Elephants were here
still more conspicuous, and foot prints of the preceding day were numerous. We paused on the mountains to admire the stupendous depth and formidable
character of the ravines and chasms, which have been
scooped out by the mighty torrents of water that
roll down during the rainy season, with fury irresis-
tible, uprooting ancient trees, and hurling into the
plain below huge masses of rock, which, once put
in motion bound from ledge to ledge until they
reach the bottom of the valley. Nearly all the rivers
in this part of Africa, take their source in the
Cashan range. It divides the waters that flow to
the Eastward into the Mozambique sea, from those
that run to the Westward into the Atlantic Ocean;
and the country on both sides being abundantly irri-
gated, is far better calculated both for grazing and
cultivation than any part of the district that we
found the Matabili occupying. The fear of Din-
gan, however, has led them to neglect it, and to establish themselves in a more secure position. A gigantic savage of a subordinate tribe of the Baquaina, a

conquered nation to the Northward, here accidentally joined us.   He was a perfect ogre in dimensions, six feet four inches high, and stout in proportion.   From him we learned that there was a large herd of Elephants on the opposite side of the mountains, out of which he had speared a young one the day before.   We proceeded under his guidance, and threading a pass in the mountains formed by the dry channel of a ravine, through which a waggon might be brought with little difficulty, sat down to breakfast by a refreshing mountain rill.   A large colony of Pig-faced Baboons,* shortly made their appearance above us, some slowly advancing with an inquisitive look, others deliberately seating themselves on the rocks, as though debating on the propriety of our unceremonious trespass on their domains.   Their inhospitable treatment at length obliging us to make an example, we fired two shots among them.   Numbers assembled round the spot where the first had struck, scraping the lead with their nails, and scrutinizing it with ludicrous gestures and grimace.   The second, however, knocked over one of their elders, an enormous fellow, who was strutting about erect, laying down the law—and who, juding from his venerable appearance, must have been at least a great-grand-sire.   This national calamity caused incredible consternation, and many affecting

* *Cynocephalus Porcarius.*

domestic scenes.   The party dispersed in all directions, mothers snatching up their infants, and bearing
them in their arms out of the reach of danger with
an impulse and action perfectly human.

Conducted by an Elephant path, we descended
through the forest to a secluded dell on the northern
side of the range.   Beyond, the whole plain was
studded with detached pyramidical stony hills, amongst
which we could perceive the extensive remains of
cattle enclosures and ruins, similar to those we had
passed in the morning, testifying of "cities long gone
by."   The tracts of the Elephants leading back
again to the mountains, we reascended by a steep
path considerably to the Westward of the defile
through which we had come, and, on arriving at the
summit, perceived our waggons like small white
specks in the distant valley.   Bare and sterile rocks
occupy the highest elevation of these mountains,
commanding an extensive view, and forming a strong
contrast with the middle and lower regions, so thickly covered with verdure and forests, the latter chiefly
occupying the ravines.   Having reconnoitered the
whole country through a telescope, without being
able to discern the animals of which we were in quest,
we descended by a steep foot-path, the face of the
mountain being strewed with round white pebbles.
Near the summit grew a venerable mimosa, which
completely overshadowed the path, and a little on

one side of it we observed a large heap which had been formed by each passenger contributing one of these pebbles as he passed. Our savages added their mite, simply picking up the nearest, and casting it irreverently towards the hill. This being the only approach to external worship or religious ceremony that we had seen, we naturally became very inquisitive on the subject, but could elicit no satisfactory information. Mohanycom said it was "the King," from which very sapient reply we were left at liberty to conclude, either that the hill was a monument of respect to royalty, or that they had been engaged in an idolatrous rite. The former is the most probable, for, amongst the Matabili, the reigning monarch, whilst he absorbs all their praises, is the only deity. He it is, in the opinion of this benighted race, that "maketh the rain to fall and the grass to grow, that seeth the evil and the good, and in whose hands are the issues of life and death." They have no idea of a Creator, so far as we could learn, or knowledge of a future state; nor could we ascertain that by the term King, they ever referred to any being beyond the despot who presides over their mortal destinies.

On reaching the foot of the mountains, we found a portion of the skull of the Elephant's calf that our colossal savage friend had destroyed the day before. It was all that the Hyænas had left, of the little that he had considered too hard for his own digestion.

The tracks of the drove had gone Eastward over the country where we had already hunted, and as it waxed late we made the best of our way to the camp. I shot two Quaggas for our savage allies, who returned during the night laden with flesh, and bringing with them a Wild Hog,* that they had buried in the morning in a Porcupine's earth, to which it had been driven by their dogs.

The grass on the opposite side of the mountains having been burnt, we resolved by the advice of the natives, to skirt them on the South side for a day or two.   As soon as it was light, I set out with Mohanycom, and killed a spotted Hyæna,† that had been attracted with many others by the smell of the pork to our camp. I was glad to have my revenge, for they had annoyed our cattle all night long, moaning funereally in concert with the dismal yelling of Jackals,‡ and roaring of Lions, with whose melody our only surviving dog never failed to chime in. The sole of my shoe coming off, I had the felicity of running barefooted over sharp flints to overtake the waggons, which had crossed four inconsiderable mountain streams, and were entering a field of tall reed-grass, that waved above the heads of the oxen. An immense white Rhinoceros suddenly started from his slumbers, and rushed furiously at the leading

---

* *Sus Larvatus.*   † *Hyæna Crocuta.*
          ‡ *Canis Mesomelas.*

waggon, crushing the dry reeds before him, and alarming the cattle by his loud snorting, and hostile demonstrations. A volley, however, cooled his courage, and he retired to a suitable bush where we despatched him. Three more Rhinoceroses were added to the list on our way to the Massellan river, which flowing through the mountains, joins the Lingkling, a tributary to the Limpopo.

Although said to be very expert in following the tracks of wild animals, the Hottentots are far less skilful than the Asiatics, and I not unfrequently eclipsed them myself. Piet was the most accomplished in wood craft, and besides being possessed of considerably more nerve, was the only one of our followers upon whom I could depend for any assistance in the field. The rest were ready enough to go out that they might obtain a supply of ammunition, and gain a pretext for evading their other duties—but their natural indolence extending itself even to their recreations, they never hesitated to abandon me at their convenience, in order to divert themselves with the more common species of game, which could be circumvented with little exertion. The savages never accompanied us beyond the carcase of the first large animal slain, upon which having gorged to repletion, they fell fast asleep over the fire.

On the 5th November, we followed the traces of Elephants along the side of the mountains for miles,

through stupendous forests, all the Hottentots excepting Piet dropping in the rear in succession, either
to solace themselves with a pipe, or to expend their
ammunition upon ignoble game. Time not permitting
us to continue the search, we descended into a valley,
bent upon the destruction of a Roan Antelope,* a
large herd of which rare animals were quietly grazing. A pair of white Rhinoceroses opposed our
descent, and being unwilling to fire at them, we had
some trouble in freeing ourselves from their company. A large herd of wild Swine † or as Indians
term it, a *sounder* of Hog, carrying their long whip
like tails erect, then passed in order of review, and
immediately afterwards two bull Buffaloes were observed within pistol shot. It was a perfect panorama of game; I had with great difficulty restrained
Piet from firing, and was almost within reach of the
Bucks, when a Hottentot suddenly discharging his
gun put every thing to flight. The Buffaloes passed
me quite close on their way to the hills. I fractured
the hind leg of the largest, and mounting my horse,
closed with him immediately, and after two gallant
charges performed upon three legs, he fell, never to
rise again. This was a noble specimen of the African Buffalo, standing sixteen hands and a half at the
shoulder. His ponderous horns measured four feet

---

* *Aigocerus Equina.* Delineated in the Africa Views.
† *Phascochærus Africanus.*

from tip to tip, and like a mass of rock, overshadow-
ing his small sinister grey eyes, imparted to his countenance the most cunning, gloomy, and vindictive
expression.   The savages instantly set to work upon
the carcase with their teeth and assegais—Piet providing himself with portions of the hide for shoe soles,
and of the flesh, which though coarse, is a tolerable
imitation of beef.

From the summit of a hill which commanded an
extensive prospect over a straggling forest, I shortly
afterwards perceived a large herd of Buffaloes, quietly chewing the cud beneath an umbrageous tree.
Creeping close upon them, I killed a Bull with a single
ball, but the confused echo, reverberating among the
mountains alarming the survivors, about fifty in number, they dashed panic stricken from their conceal-
ment, ignorant whence the sound proceeded, and every
thing yielding to their giant strength, I narrowly
escaped being trampled underfoot in their progress.
We moved five miles to the Eastward in the afternoon, stopping to take up the head of the Buffalo,
which Andries could with difficulty lift upon the waggon.   Myriads of vultures, and the clouds of smoke,
which arose from the fires of the giant and his associates, directed us to the spot.   In commemoration, I
presume, of the exploit of Guy Fawkes, they had kindled a bon fire, which bid fair to destroy all the grass
in the country, the flames fanned by the wind already

beginning to ascend the hills.   Nothing can be conceived more horribly disgusting than the appearance
presented by the savages, who, gorged to the throat,
and besmeared with blood, grease, and filth from the
entrails, sat nodding torpidly round the remains of
the carcase, sucking marrow from the bones, whilst
their lean famished curs were regaling themselves
upon the garbage.   Every bush was garnished with
flaps of meat, and every man had turned beef butcher,
whilst swollen vultures * were perched upon the adjacent trees, and others yet ungorged were inhaling the
odours that arose.

   The sun set upon us with every demonstration of
rain.   The night was dark and gusty.   Thunder
pealing amongst the mountains, and vivid flashes of
forked lightning presaged a coming storm; fortunately, however, it expended it's fury in the hills, and
only visited us with a few drops.   Before going to
bed, I had been gazing for hours upon the singular
and sublime effect produced by the extensive and
rapidly spreading combustion of the grass.   A strong
South Easterly wind setting towards the hills, was
driving the devouring element with a loud crackling
noise, up the steep grassy sides, in long red lines,
which, extending for miles, swept along the heights
with devastating fury, brilliantly illuminating the land-

----

  * *Vultus Fulvus, and Vultus'Auricularis:* White and Black
Aas-vogel of the Cape Colonist.

scape, and threatening to denude the whole country of its vegetation.　Suddenly the storm burst above the scene.　The wind immediately hushed; a death-like stillness succeeded to the crackling of the flames. Every spark of the conflagration was extinguished in an instant by the deluge that descended, and the Egyptian-like darkness of the night was unbroken even by a solitary star.

CHAPTER XX.

ELEPHANT HUNTING IN THE CASHAN MOUNTAINS.

BEFORE daybreak the following morning, it was discovered that the oxen having been alarmed by Lions,
had made their escape from the pound. A party was
despatched in pursuit of them, and we proceeded
into the hills to look for Buffaloes. The thunder-
storm having purified the atmosphere, had rendered
the weather delightfully cool, and a deep wooded defile which had not been approached by the conflagration of the day before, was filled with game that had
fled before the flames. A Rhinoceros was killed almost immediately, and before we had reloaded, a
noble herd of near one hundred and fifty Buffaloes
was perceived on a slope overhanging a sedgy stream.
Having crept within five and twenty yards, we despatched two Bulls before the alarm was spread.
Crashing through the forest, they overturned decay-
ed trees in their route, and swept along the brow of
the opposite hill in fearful confusion, squeezed together in a compact phalanx, and raising an incredible
cloud of dust to mark their course. We mounted
our horses, and after sticking some time in the treach-

erous mud of the rivulet, gained the opposite bank
and brought two more to bay, which were despatched after several charges. Our savage friends,
still torpid from their yesterday's feast, had not made
their appearance; we therefore despatched Claas,
after breakfast was over, to bring in some marrow
bones, in the act of collecting which delicacies, he
was put to flight by a Lion that jumped out of a
bush close to him, and did not leave him time to think
of his gun. After some hours, however, he mustered
courage to proceed with a large party to recover it.

Early in the afternoon the Hottentots returned
with the oxen, and we proceeded without loss of time
to the Eastward, following the course of the mountains through very high grass, and passing between
two conical hills of singular appearance which stood
like sentinels on either hand; after crossing six inconsiderable streams, we with some difficulty gained the
vicinity of a remarkably abrupt opening in the range,
which through a telescope appeared to afford a practicable road to the Northward. Both our waggons
stuck fast in the Sant river, and were with difficulty
extricated by the united efforts of the teams. The
heat was intense, not a breath stirred, and heavy
black clouds fast collecting bade us prepare for a deluge. We therefore formed the camp in a sheltered
and elevated position, under the lee of a high stone
enclosure, which only required the entrance to be

closed with bushes to make a secure pound for the cattle. Scarcely were these arrangements completed, when a stream of liquid fire ran along the ground, and a deafening thunder clap, exploding close above us, was instantly followed by a torrent of rain, which "came dancing to the earth," not in drops, but in continuous streams, and with indescribable violence, during the greater part of the night; the thunder now receding and rumbling less and less distinctly, but more incessantly among the distant mountains—now pealing in echoes over the nearer hills, and now returning to burst with redoubled violence above our heads.

> ————————————————"Far along
> From peak to peak, the rattling crags among,
> Leapt the wild thunder, not from one lone cloud,
> But every mountain soon had found a tongue."

The horses and oxen were presently standing knee deep in water; our followers remained sitting all night in the baggage waggon which leaked considerably, but our own, being better covered, fortunately resisted the pitiless storm. Sleep was however out of the question, the earth actually threatening to give way under us, and the lightning being so painfully vivid that we were glad to hide our heads under the pillow.

Those only who have witnessed the setting in of the South West monsoon in India, are capable of fully understanding the awful tempest I have attempted to describe. About an hour before dawn its fury began to abate, and at sunrise it was perfectly fine, but the rivers were quite impassable. I proceeded with some of the Hottentots to reconnoitre the pass, but found that it was impassable for waggons, being nothing more than a narrow channel flanked by perpendicular crags, between which the Sant river rushes on its way to join the Lingkling, making a number of very abrupt windings through a most impracticable country, intersected by a succession of rocky acclivities. From the highest peak we saw several herds of Buffaloes, and whilst descending, came upon the tracks of a huge Elephant that had passed about an hour before. This being the largest foot print we had seen, I had the curiosity to measure it, in order to ascertain the animal's height—twice the circumference of an Elephant's foot being, it is notorious, the exact height at the shoulder. It yielded a product of about twelve feet, which notwithstanding the traditions that have been handed down, I believe to be the maximum height attained by the African Elephant.* We followed the trail across the Sant river, which had now considerably subsided—and finding that it proceeded Eastward along the mountain chain, returned to our encampment for horses and ammunition.

* *Elephas Africanus.* Delineated in the African Views.

Leaving the waggons to proceed to a spot agreed upon, we again took the field about ten o'clock, and pursued the track indefatigably for eight miles, over a country presenting every variety of feature. At one time we crossed bare stony ridges, at another threaded the intricacies of shady but dilapidated forests; now struggled through high fields of waving grass, and again emerged into open downs. At length we arrived amongst extensive groups of grassy hillocks, covered with loose stones, interspersed with streams, and occasional patches of forest in which the recent ravages of Elephants were surprising. Here to our inexpressible gratification we descried a large herd of those long sought animals, lazily browsing at the head of a distant valley, our attention having been first directed to it, by the strong and not to be mistaken effluvia with which the wind was impregnated. Never having before seen the noble Elephant in his native jungles, we gazed on the sight before us with intense, and indescribable interest. Our feelings on the occasion even extended to our followers. As for Andries he became so agitated that he could scarcely articulate. With open eyes and quivering lips he at length stuttered forth " *Dar stand de Oliphant.*" Mohanycom and 'Lingap were immediately despatched to drive the herd back into the valley, up which we rode slowly and without noise, against the wind; and arriving within one hundred

and fifty yards unperceived, we made our horses fast,
and took up a commanding position in an old stone
kraal. The shouting of the savages, who now appeared on the height rattling their shields, caused the
huge animals to move unsuspiciously towards us,
and even within ten yards of our ambush. The group
consisted of nine, all females with large tusks. We
selected the finest, and with perfect deliberation fired
a volley of five balls into her. She stumbled, but
recovering herself, uttered a shrill note of lamenta-
tion, when the whole party threw their trunks above
their heads, and instantly clambered up the adjacent
hill with incredible celerity, their huge fan-like ears,
flapping in the ratio of their speed. We instantly
mounted our horses, and the sharp loose stones not
suiting the feet of the wounded lady, soon closed
with her. Streaming with blood, and infuriated with
rage, she turned upon us with uplifted trunk, and it
was not until after repeated discharges, that a ball
took effect in her brain, and threw her lifeless on
the earth, which resounded with the fall.

Turning our attention from the exciting scene I
have described, we found that a second valley had
opened upon us, surrounded by bare stony hills, and
traversed by a thinly wooded ravine. Here a grand
and magnificent panorama was before us, which beggars all description. The whole face of the landscape
was actually covered with wild Elephants. There

25

could not have been fewer than three hundred within the scope of our vision. Every height and green knoll was dotted over with groups of them, whilst the bottom of the glen exhibited a dense and sable living mass—their colossal forms being at one moment partially concealed by the trees which they were disfiguring with giant strength; and at others seen majestically emerging into the open glades, bearing in their trunks the branches of trees with which they indolently protected themselves from the flies. The back ground was filled by a limited peep of the blue mountainous range, which here assumed a remarkably precipitous character, and completed a picture at once soul-stirring and sublime!

Our approach being still against the wind was unobserved, and created little alarm, until the herd that we had left behind, suddenly showed itself, recklessly thundering down the side of the hill to join the main body, and passing so close to us, that we could not refrain from firing a broad side into one of them, which however bravely withstood it. We secured our horses on the summit of a stony ridge, and then stationing ourselves at an opportune place on a ledge overlooking the wooded defile, sent Andries to manœuvre so that as many of the Elephants as possible should pass before us in order of reveiw, that we might accertain by a close inspection, whether there was not a male amongst them. Filing sluggishly along, they occasionally halted beneath an umbrageous tree within fifteen yards of us, lazily fanning themselves with their ample ears, blowing away the flies with their trunks, and uttering the feeble and peculiar cry so familiar to Indians.　They all proved to be ladies, and most of them mothers, followed by their little old fashioned calves each trudging close to the heels of her dam and mimicking all her actions.　Thus situated we might have killed any number we pleased, their heads being frequently turned towards us, in such a position, and so close, that a single ball in the brain would have sufficed for each; but whilst we were yet hesitating, a bullet suddenly whizzed past Richardson's ear and put the whole herd to immediate flight.　We had barely time to recede behind a tree, before a party of about twenty with several little ones in their wake were upon us, striding at their utmost speed, and trumpeting loudly with uplifted heads.　I rested my rifle against the tree, and firing behind the shoulder of the leader, she dropped instantly.　Another large detachment appearing close behind us at the same moment we were compelled to retreat, dodging from tree to tree, stumbling amongst sharp stones, and ever coming upon fresh parties of the enemy.　This scence of ludicrous confusion did not long continue—and soon approaching the prostrate lady, we put an end to her struggles by a shot in the forehead.　Andries now came up in high good humour at his achievements, and in the most bravado manner discharged his piece into the dead carcase, under the pretence that the animal was shamming. His object evidently was to confound the shots—for thrusting his middle finger into the orifice made by my two ounce ball, he with the most modest assurance declared himself the author of the deed, being pleased altogether to overlook the fact of the mortal shot having entered the Elephant on the side opposite to that on which he was stationed, and that his own ball, whether designedly or not, had all but expended my worthy and esteemed fellow traveller.

On our way to the camp, of the exact position of which we were uncertain in consequence of the late inundation, we passed three other large herds of Elephants. One of these standing directly in the route, we attacked it and pursued the fugitives about a mile over loose stones. Much has been said of the attachment of Elephants to their young, but neither on this, nor on any subsequent occasion, did we perceive them evince the smallest concern for their safety. On the contrary they left them to shift for themselves, and Mohanycom and'Lingap, who were behind us, assegaied one, the tail of which they brought in. We slew another old female as we ascended the brow of an eminence, and at the same moment perceived our waggons within a few hundred yards of the spot. The whole herd dashed through the camp causing

indescribable consternation amongst cattle and followers, but fortunately no accident occurred, and after the
fatiguing day's work we had undergone, we were not
sorry to find ourselves at home.

Watery clouds hung about the sun as he set heavily
behind the mountains. Loud peals of crashing thunder rent the air, and ere it was dark, we had a repetition of yesterday's storm, the river roaring past us
with frightful fury. Troops of Elepants flying from
the scene of slaughter, passed close to our waggons
during the darkness, their wild voices echoing a-
mongst the mountains, and sounding like trumpets
above the tempest. It was impossible to keep the
fires burning; and the oxen and sheep were alarmed
to such a degree, that they broke from the kraal,
and sought safety in the wilderness. Tired as I
was, the excitement I had undergone banished sleep
from my eyes. I ruminated on the spirit-stirring
events of the day, and burned with impatience to
renew them. Heedless of the withering blast that
howled without, I felt that my most sanguine expectations had been realized, and that we had already
been amply repaid for the difficulties, privations and
dangers, that we had encountered in our toilsome
journey towards this fairy land of sport.

CHAPTER XXI.

ELEPHANT HUNTING CONTINUED; AND LION SHOOT-
ING FROM THE WAGGONS.

IT was still raining heavily when the day gloomily
dawned. The mountain torrents having overflown
their banks, the valley in which we were encamped
had become a continuous pool of water; and those
of our followers, who had not slung their hammocks
beneath the waggons, were partially submerged.
High roads had been ploughed through the mire by
the passage of the Elephants, and whole acres of
grass, by which we were surrounded the preceding
evening, had been completely trampled down. Soon
after sunrise it cleared up, and the cattle having
been recovered, we armed a party with hatchets, and
proceeded on foot to cut out the teeth of the slain Elephants; but walking was exceedingly toilsome, and
our feet sinking to the ancles in black mud, were extricated with inconceivable difficulty. Taking advantage of our situation, an irritated Rhinoceros sallied from behind an old stone wall; and the damp
causing three of the guns to miss fire, he was actually amongst us when my ball fortunately pierced his
eye, and he fell dead at our feet.

Not an Elephant was to be seen on the ground that was yesterday teeming with them; but on reaching the glen which had been the scene of our exploits during the early part of the action, a calf about three and a half feet high, walked forth from a bush, and saluted us with mournful piping notes. We had observed the unhappy little wretch hovering about its mother after she fell, and having probably been unable to overtake the herd, it had passed a dreary night in the wood. Entwining its little proboscis about our legs, the sagacious creature, after demonstrating its delight at our arrival by a thousand ungainly antics, accompanied the party to the body of its dam; which swollen to an enormous size, was surrounded by an inquest of vultures. Seated in gaunt array, with their shoulders shrugged, these loathsome fowls were awaiting its decomposition with forced resignation: the tough hide having defied all the efforts of their beaks, with which the eyes and softer parts had been vigorously assailed. The conduct of the quaint little calf now became quite affecting, and elicited the sympathy of every one. It ran round its mother's corse with touching demonstrations of grief, piping sorrowfully, and vainly attempting to raise her with its tiny trunk. I confess that I had felt compunctions in committing the murder the day before, and now half resolved never to assist in another; for in addition to the moving behaviour of the young Elephant, I had been unable to divest myself of the idea that I was firing at my old favorite *Mowla-Bukhsh*, from whose gallant back I had vanquished so many of my feline foes in Guzerat—an impression, which however ridiculous it must appear, detracted considerably from the satisfaction I experienced.

The operation of hewing out three pair of tusks, occupied several hours, their roots, imbedded in massy sockets, spreading over the greater portion of the face. My Indian friends will marvel when they hear of tusks being extracted from the jaws of a female Elephant—but, with very few exceptions, all that we saw had these accessories, measuring from three to four feet in length. I have already stated my belief that the maximum height of the African male is twelve feet; that of the female averages eight and a half—the enormous magnitude of the ears, which not only cover the whole of the shoulder, but overlap each other on the neck, to the complete exclusion of the *Mahout* or Driver, constituting another striking feature of difference between the two species. The forehead is remarkably large and prominent, and consists of two walls or tables; between which, a wide cellular space intervening, a ball, hardened with tin or quicksilver, readily penetrates to the brain and proves instantaneously fatal.

The barbarous tribes that people Southern Africa have never dreamt of the possibility of rendering this lordly quadruped serviceable in a domestic capacity; and even amongst the Colonists, there exists an unaccountable superstition that his subjugation is not to be accomplished.　His capture however, might readily be achieved; and, as he appears to possess all the aptitude of his Asiatic relative, the only difficulty that presents itself, is the general absence, within our territories, of sufficient food for his support.　Were he once domesticated, and arrayed against the beasts of the forest, Africa would realize the very *beau ideal* of magnificent sport.　It is also worthy of remark that no attempt has ever been made on the part of the Colonists to naturalize another most useful animal, the Camel although soil, climate, and productions appear alike to favor its introduction.

We succeeded, after considerable labor, in extracting the ball which Andries pretended to have fired yesterday; and the grooves of my rifle being conspicuous upon it, that worthy, but unabashed, squire was constrained not only to relinquish his claim to the merit of having slain the Elephant—but also to forego his fancied right to the ivory.　The miniature Elephant, finding that its mother heeded not its caresses, voluntarily followed our party to the waggons, where it was received with shouts of welcome from the people, and a band of all sorts of melody from the cattle.　It died, however, in spite of every care, in the course of a few days; as did two others, much older, that we subsequently captured.

The day again closed with a thunder-storm, which twice passed off, and twice revisited us in the course of the night. The rivers, which had subsided during the day, became once more agitated, and instead of the trumpet accompaniment from Elephants, we were serenaded by a legion of jackals. An opening shriek from one of these crafty animals, resounding during the conflict of the elements, amid craggy rocks and solitary glens, was the signal for a general chorus; and, re-answered by a long protracted scream from an hundred throats, did not fail in its effect upon our harrassed cattle, causing the sheep to break out of the enclosure, notwithstanding our efforts to control them.

Although the ground was very heavy, we resolved upon shifting the camp a few miles to the Eastward, in order to be within reach of the Elephants. All the mountain rills were full, but they were not of sufficient magnitude to obstruct the waggons. As we proceeded, several Elephants were observed clambering with the agility of Chamois, to the very summit of the chain. Shortly after we had halted, I went out alone, and ascending by a narrow path trodden by wild animals, entered a strip of forest occupying an extensive ravine. On the outside of this, stood a mighty bull Elephant, his trunk entwined around his tusk, and, but for the flapping of his huge ears, motionless as a statue. Securing my mare to a tree

I crept silently behind a block of stone, and levelled
my rifle at his ample forehead.　The earth trembled
under the weight of the enormous brute as he dropped heavily, uttering one deep groan, and expiring
without a struggle.　His height at the shoulder was
eleven feet and a half, and his tusks measured more
than seven in length.　The echo of the shot, reverberating through hill and dale, caused the mare to
break her tether and abscond, and brought large
tribes of pig-faced baboons from their sylvan haunts,
to afford me any thing but sympathy.　Their ridiculous grimaces, however, could not fail to elicit my
mirth, whatever might have been my humour.　It
was long before I recovered my horse, and I did not
regain the waggons until after night-fall.　The new
moon brought, if possible, a more abundant supply
of rain than usual; nor did the Lions fail to take
advantage of the nocturnal tempest, having twice
endeavored to effect an entrance into the cattle fold.
It continued, until nine o'clock the next morning,
to pour with such violence, that we were unable to
open the canvas curtains of the waggon.　Peeping
out, however, to ascertain if there was any prospect
of its clearing up, we perceived three Lions squatted
within an hundred yards, in the open plain, atten-
tively watching the oxen.　Our rifles were hastily
seized, but the dampness of the atmosphere prevented
their exploding.　One after another, too, the Hotten-

tots sprang out of the pack waggon, and snapped
their guns at the unwelcome intruders, as they trot-
ted sulkily away, and took up their position on a
stony eminence at no great distance. Fresh caps
and priming were applied, and a broad side was followed by the instantaneous demise of the largest,
whose cranium was perforated by two bullets at the
same instant. Swinging their tails over their backs,
the survivors took warning by the fate of their companion, and dashed into the thicket with a roar. In
another half hour, the voice of *Leo* was again heard
at the foot of the mountains, about a quarter of a
mile from the camp; and from the waggon-top we
could perceive a savage monster rampant, with his
tail hoisted and whirling in a circle—charging furiously along the base of the range—and in desperate
wrath, making towards John April, who was tending
the sheep. Every one instinctively grasped his weapon, and rushed to the rescue, calling loudly to warn
the expected victim of his danger. Without taking
the smallest notice of him, however, the infuriated
monster dashed past, roaring and lashing his sides
until concealed in the mist. Those who have seen
the monarch of the forest in crippling captivity only,
immured in a cage barely double his own length,
with his sinews relaxed by confinement, have seen
but the shadow of that animal, which "clears the
desert with his rolling eye."

The South African Lion, differs little from that
found in Guzerat, in Western India,* measuring
between ten and eleven feet in extreme length—but
generally possesses a finer mane, a peculiarity which
is attributable to the less jungly character of the
country that he infests, and to the more advanced
age which he is suffered to attain. Amongst the
Cape Colonists it is a fashionable belief, that there
are two distinct species of the African Lion—the
yellow, and the black—and that the one is infinitely less ferocious than the other. But I need scarcely inform the well instructed reader, that both the
the color and the size depend chiefly upon the animal's age; the developement of the physical powers,
and of the mane also, being principally influenced
by a like contingency. That which has been de-
signated the "maneless Lion of Guzerat," is nothing more than a young Lion whose mane has not
shot forth; and I give this opinion with less hesitation, having slain the "King of beasts" in every
stage from whelphood to imbecility.

---

* The reader is aware that the Tiger is not a denizen of
Africa. Both the Leopard, and the Hunting Leopard occur,
but differ in no respect from those found in India.

CHAPTER XXII.

SHOOTING THE HIPPOPOTAMUS, AND HUNTING IN
THE VALLEY OF THE LIMPOPO.

It was unfortunately requisite, during the greater part of our journey, to furnish the Hottentots with ammunition for their protection whilst tending the cattle; and their incessant firing, which no remonstrance could control, soon disturbing the whole of the game in our neighbourhood, we found it useless to remain more than one day at any place. Compared with the quantity of powder expended by these men, the number of animals they killed was exceedingly limited—the supply of meat for the camp generally depending upon my success; but the beasts of the forest, having been unmolested all their lives, and unaccustomed to the report of the gun, fled before their attacks in consternation; so that within a few hours after the formation of the camp in a spot abounding with game, not a living quadruped was to be seen.

The country through which we travelled being chiefly characterized by open plains or straggling forests, it will readily be conceived that *woodcraft* availed little in the destruction of game. Many of the species that occur are naturally slow and heavy; and the gregarious habits of the fleeter, rendering them easy of approach on horseback, almost every animal, from the mighty Elephant to the most diminutive Antelope, must be pursued in the saddle. Not only, however, does the success of a hunting party mainly depend upon the number and condition of the horses—which are almost daily required also for the recovery of straying cattle—but its safety in event of an attack from the savage tribes, is equally involved. We could therefore have found ample employment for forty, instead of sixteen, half starved, shoeless Rozinantes, with nothing but grass to eat, and not so much even as a cloth to protect them from the cold and wet during a succession of inclement nights. But whilst none of our many trading advisers, who had doubtless experienced the difficulty of destroying on foot sufficient game for the subsistence of their followers, had suggested our going better provided; they had unfortunately succeeded in dissuading us from carrying a supply of shoes or grain, the absence of both of which essentials we never ceased to deplore. The anxiety may be estimated with which we watched the now daily improving condition of our meagre steeds, and assiduously endeavoured to free them from the clusters of bursting ticks, which having been contracted amongst the bushes, threatened to relieve them of the little blood they possessed. A sturdy stall fed Arab, would have now been worth his weight in gold ; but ragged as the Cape horses undoubtedly are, it is but justice to their manifold merits to declare, that they only require feeding to render them most useful allies during an African campaign. Hardy, docile, and enduring, any number may be driven on the line of march, by a single Hottentot ; and they are soon habituated to graze unattended within sight of the waggons, where-ever grass is abundant. In the chase, the most formidable animal does not inspire them with the slightest alarm ; and the bridle being thrown over their heads, they may generally be left standing in the wilderness for hours together, without attempting to stir from the spot.

Our next movement brought us to the source of the Oori or Limpopo—the Gareep of Moselekatse's dominions. Fed by many fine streams from the Cashan range, this enchanting river springs into existence as if by magic ; and rolling its deep and tranquil waters between tiers of weeping willows, through a passage in the mountain barrier, takes its course to the Northward. Here we enjoyed the novel diversion of Hippopotamus * shooting—that animal abounding in the Limpopo, and dividing the empire with its amphibious neighbour the Crocodile. Throughout

* *Hippopotamus Amphibius.* Delineated in the African Views.

the night, the unwieldy monsters might be heard
snorting and blowing during their aquatic gambols,
and we not unfrequently detected them in the act of
sallying from their reed-grown coverts, to graze by
the serene light of the moon; never, however, venturing to any distance from the river, the strong hold to
which they betake themselves on the smallest alarm.
Occasionally during the day, they were to be seen
basking on the shore amid ooze and mud; but shots
were more constantly to be had at their uncouth heads,
when protruded from the water to draw breath, and
if killed, the body rose to the surface. Vulnerable
only behind the ear, however, or in the eye, which is
placed in a prominence, so as to resemble the garret
window of a Dutch house, they require the perfection
of rifle practice, and after a few shots become exceedingly shy, exhibiting the snout only, and as
instantly, withdrawing it. The flesh is delicious, resembling pork in flavour, and abounding in fat, which
in the colony, is deservedly esteemed the greatest of delicacies. The hide is upwards of an inch
and a half in thickness, and being scarcely flexible,
may be dragged from the ribs in strips like the planks
from a ship's side. Of these are manufactured a superior description of *sjambok,* the elastic whip already
noticed as being an indispensable piece of furniture
to every Boor proceeding on a journey. Our followers encumbered the waggons with a large invest-

ment of them, and of the canine teeth, the ivory of which is extremely profitable.

Of all the Mammalia, whose portraits, drawn from ill stuffed specimens have been foisted upon the world, *Behemoth* has perhaps been the most ludicrously misrepresented. I sought in vain for that colossal head—for those cavern-like jaws, garnished with elephantine tusk—or those ponderous feet with which " the formidable and ferocious quadruped" is wont " to trample down whole fields of corn during a single night!" Defenceless and inoffensive, his shapeless carcase is but feebly supported upon short and disproportioned legs, and his belly almost trailing upon the ground, he may not inaptly be likened to an overgrown pig. The color is pinkish brown, clouded and freckled with a darker tint. Of many that we shot, the largest measured less than five feet at the shoulder; and the reality falling so lamentably short of the monstrous conception I had formed, the " River Horse," or "Sea Cow,"* was the first, and indeed, the only South African quadruped in which I felt disappointed.

The country now literally presented the appearance of a menagerie; the host of Rhinoceroses in

---

* The Hippopotamus is termed by the Colonists *Zekoe* or Sea-Cow the least applicable designation perhaps, not excepting that of the *River Horse*, that could have been conferred.

particular, that daily exhibited themselves, almost exceeding belief. Whilst the camp was being formed, an ugly head might be seen protruded from every bush, and the possession of the ground was often stoutly disputed. In the field, these animals lost no opportunity of rendering themselves obnoxious— frequently charging at my elbow, when in the act of drawing the trigger at some other object—and pursuing our horses with indefatigable and ludicrous industry, carrying their noses close to the ground, and uttering a sound between a grunt, and a smothered whistle. In removing the horn with an axe, the brain was discovered, seated in a cavity below it, at the very extremity of the snout—a phenomenon in the idiosyncrasy of this animal, which may in some measure account for its want of intelligence and piggish obstinacy; as well as for the extraordinary acuteness of smell with which it is endowed. Irascible beyond all other quadrupeds, the African Rhinoceros appears subject even to unprovoked paroxysms of reckless fury; but the sphere of vision is so exceedingly limited, that its attacks although sudden and impetuous, are easily eluded, and a shot behind the shoulder, discharged from the distance of twenty or thirty yards, generally proves fatal.

On our way from the waggons to a hill not half a mile distant, we counted no less than twenty-two of the white species of Rhinoceros, and were compelled in self defence to slaughter four. On another occasion, I was besieged in a bush by three at once, and had no little difficulty in beating off the assailants. Wild Buffaloes too might often be seen from the waggons. Riding up a narrow defile, flanked by steep banks, I one morning found myself suddenly confronted with the van of a vast troop of these formidable animals, which were ascending from the opposite side—their malevolent grey eyes scowling beneath a threatening brow. Unable to turn, they must have charged over me, had my horse not contrived to scramble up the bank; from the top of which I fired both barrels into the leader, a ponderous bull, whose appearance stamped him father of the herd. Falling on his knees, the patriarch was instantly trampled underfoot by his followers as they charged, bellowing in close squadron, down the declivity with the fury of a passing whirlwind, and making the woods re·echo to the clatter of their hoofs.

In the vegetable world, a great variety of novel and interesting forms, grace the banks of the Limpopo, but the airy acacia is still pre-eminently beautiful. Green and shady belts, bedizened with golden blossoms and purple pods, or fringed with the cradle nests of the pensile grosbeak, extend on either side— their mazes being intersected by paths worn by Hippopotami during their nocturnal rambles. The recesses of these fairy groves are the favorite haunts

of many forest-loving Antelopes. The graceful Pallah, with knotted, and eccentrically inflected horns of
extraordinary proportions, is found in large families.
Shy and capricious in its habits, the elegance of its
form, and the delicate finish of its limbs, are unri-
valled. The usual succentorial hoofs are wanting,
but the hinder legs are furnished with remarkable
cushions of wiry hair, which occur in no other
species, and remind us of the heels of a Mercury.
This favored spot too, is a chosen resort of the majestic Water Buck, which I now found might be ridden down with facility; a discovery that enabled me
to obtain many splendid specimens. This rare and
remarkable animal which has been already described,
is never found at a distance from the banks of tropi-
cal rivers, in the waters of which he delights to
plunge.

Another rare species—the Roan Antelope, or Bastard Gemsbok—is an inhabitant of the elevated downs
and ridges about the source of this river, and being
utterly destitute of speed, may be ridden to a stand-
still without difficulty. This most imposing animal,
which charges viciously when unable to continue
its flight, is the size of a large horse; and ex
cepting the head and tail, which are jet black, is uniformly of a delicate roan color. It is heavily built,
and has an upright mane, long asinine ears, and robust scimitar-shaped recurved horns. Here too, I

first met with, and slew the Koodoo.* Majestic in its carriage, and brilliant in its color, this species may with propriety be styled the king of the tribe. Other Antelopes are stately, elegant, or curious—but the solitude-seeking Koodoo is absolutely regal! The ground color is a lively French grey approaching to blue, with several transverse white bands passing over the back and loins; a copious mane, and deeply fringed, tricolored dewlap, setting off a pair of ponderous, yet symmetrical horns, spirally twisted, and exceeding three feet in length. These are thrown along the back, as the stately wearer dashes through the mazes of the forest, or clambers the mountain side. The old bulls are invariably found apart from the females, which herd together in small troops, and are destitute of horns.

Every open glade abounds with the more common species of game, such as the Brindled Gnoo, Hartebeest, Sassayby, and Quagga, together with the Ostrich and Wild Hog; the tusks of this latter most hideous animal attaining in some instances to an enormous size, although its stature is insignificant. Among the sedge grown rivulets, the Riet Buck is common; and the mountain range and its grassy environs, are the resort of six smaller species of Antelope, hitherto unnoticed in these pages; viz. the Klipspringer,

---

* *Strepsiceros Koodoo.* Delineated in the African views.

Rheebuck, Rooe Rheebuck or Nagor, Ourebi, Steenbuck, and Duiker,* of each of which I obtained
several specimens. Although described in the Appendix, the remarkable character of the two first
demand further notice; the Klipspringer, which is
closely allied to the Chamois of Europe, and coney-
like, has its house on the mountain-top, being furnished with singularly coarse hair, imparting the appearance of an Hedge Hog; whilst the fur of the Rheebuck again, is of a curly woolly nature, resembling
that of the Wild Rabbit.

Excepting the Guinea Fowl, which usually abounded in the vicinity of wood and water, feathered game
was comparatively scarce throughout our journey.
Occasionally however, and here in particular, we
found two species of the bustard, or *Paow* of the
Colonists—two of the Florican or *Koraan*—with four
distinct kinds of Partridge.   To these however, I had
little leisure to attend, my time being fully occupied
from dawn until dark, in the pursuit of far more
attractive objects.

In the extensive and romantic valley of the Limpopo which strongly contrasts with its own solitude,
and with the arid lands which must be traversed to
arrive within its limits, Dame Nature has doubtless

---

* *Oreotragus Saltatrix, Redunca Capreolus, R. Lalandii,
R. Scoparia, Tragulus Rupestris,* and *Cephalopus Mergens.*

been unusually lavish of her gifts. A bold mountain landscape is chequered by innumerable rivulets abounding in fish, and watering a soil rich in luxuriant vegetation. Forests, producing timber of the finest growth, are tenanted by a multitude of birds, which, if not generally musical, are all gorgeously attired; and the meadows throughout are decked with blossoming geraniums, and with an endless profusion of the gayest flowers, fancifully distributed in almost artificial parterres. Let the fore-ground of this picture, which is by no means extravagantly drawn, be filled in by the animal creation roaming in a state of undisturbed freedom, such as I have attempted to describe and this hunter's paradise, will surely not require to be colored by the feelings of an enthusiastic sportsman, to stand out in striking relief from amongst the loveliest spots in the universe.

CHAPTER XXIII.

EXCURSION TO THE EASTWARD OF THE LIMPOPO,
AND JOURNEY ACROSS THE CASHAN MOUNTAINS
TO THE NORTHWARD.

The perils of waggon-travelling were now so materially increased by the rugged character of the
country, that in order to follow a retreating herd of
Elephants it was found necessary to leave the camp
standing—a measure to which we were further driv-
en by a positive refusal on the part of the guides
to accompany us to the Eastward of the Limpopo;
alleging their apprehension of hostilities from Dingaan as a reason for their non-compliance in this instance with the King's orders to escort us wherever
we pleased. Crossing the river, therefore, we skirted
the mountain range on horseback, arriving at the
close of the second day's hunting, below its highest
point; the sources of the Bekane and Umpeban
here marking the site of the last great battle fought
between the armies of Moselekatse and Dingaan, in
which that of the former was completely routed.
These rivers speedily become confluent; and after
describing a nearly semicircular course, join the Limpopo, a considerable distance to the Northward of the

28

range, where the country assumes a more rugged
character than ever, being intersected by detached
stony hills and mountain chains of barren and forbidding aspect. To the Southward it becomes very
open and level, with occasional clumps of forest; but
although the black soil continued, the vegetation was
becoming visibly less and less abundant.

Although unquestionably the highest part of Southern Africa, if measured from the level of the sea, yet
the actual altitude of the Cashan mountains, jutting up as they do, from an elevated base, is not so
great as might be expected. From one point which
we ascended, the extraordinary refraction of the atmosphere enabled us to obtain a glimpse in the direction of Delagoa, of a very distant range stretching
North and South, and said to form the boundary of
Moselekatse's conquests in that direction, during his
progress from the Zooloo country to that he at present
occupies. It is in this tract of country, to the Eastward of the beautiful but unhealthy slopes in which
the Vaal river takes its origin, that Louis Triechard,
the leader of the first party of Colonial Emigrants has
long been located, on the banks of what appears to
be a very large river, reported by the natives to be
tributary to the Limpopo; but of which the source
and course remain unexplored. The first accounts
of its existence were brought to the Colony by
Robert Scoon, the trader to whose name I have before

alluded. Coming accidentally upon it whilst hunting Elephants, he followed the banks for several days
without being able to discover a ford, and such is
the sluggish character of the stream, that it was some
time before he could even determine the course;
pieces of wood which were thrown in remaining almost stationary on the surface. An exploring party
of the Emigrants under a Boor named Bronkhorst,
subsequently visited this water from Triechard's
camp, and described its breadth to be more than a
mile, from which circumstance, combined with its
proximity to the head of the Vaal river, it is probable that it is a lagoon.

I shall not tax the patience of those of my readers, who may not be votaries of the chase, by a
repetition of hunting scenes. We returned to our
camp on the fourteenth, laden with spoils, having also
fully establishhed the possibility of dispensing, even
to cooking apparatus, with every article of baggage.
Carrying nothing but the raiment on our backs, the
saddle served for a pillow, and the horse-rug for a
blanket. Our tent was the starry canopy of heaven;
we drank of the waters of the chrystal stream, and
our viands were the produce of our trusty rifles.
It is said that the epicures of Rome esteemed the
the trunk of an elephant an extraordinary luxury;
and descending to more modern times we find our
brother traveller, Vaillant, feasting upon the foot
with extraordinary relish. To the attention of the

city alderman, however, I must be allowed to recommend the slice round the eye, which appears
to have been hitherto overlooked by *bon vivans.*
Upon this dainty morsel, roasted upon a stick before
a blazing fire, or singed among the embers, so as to
come under the Hottentot denomination of *Carbo-
naadtje*, on devilled-grill, we frequently feasted;
and I can aver, without the smallest fear of contra-
diction, that the dish rather resembled the fragment
of a shoe, picked up after a conflagration, than meat
which could boast of having been subjected to a culinary process.

Nothing momentous had transpired during our
absence, Cœur de Lion our Deputy having proved
himself a bold and vigilant Commander. The merciless inroads of the Lions, and the trouble that their
attacks involved, had at length taught our followers
the necessity of keeping up constant watch-fires;
and whenever the night was fine—which " by the
King's orders," was sometimes the case—the guides
howled forth his praises, glutted themselves, and
took snuff by turns. The wild wood rang with their
shrill herdsman's whistle, and reiterated chorus of
" *Hi-bo-bo*;" and when the night was spent, they
leisurely fetched a large stone, upon which downy
pillow having first refreshed the edges of their weapons, they placed their woolly heads by the fire-side.

In these regions, where the heavenly bodies are

seen through the clearest of mediums, a star-lit firmament is remarkably brilliant and beautiful. We frequently sat for some hours, over unadulterated "tea-water," witnessing Mohanycom's ludicrous imitations of the dancing of our country-women at the Cape, or listening to tales of the success of the King's arms. One favorite theme was the defeat of Sobiqua, King of the Wangkets, in accomplishing whose downfall 'Lingap, had aided and abetted. Like many other African potentates, he had been found guilty of possessing too many cattle, and was presently compelled to fly to the Kalahari desert, with the wreck of his tribe. Conjecture, too, was alive, as to the fate of a Commando, that had four years before been despatched for the subjugation of the *Damaras*, but of which no tidings had ever been received; and the proceedings of a Dutch trader were not unfrequently brought on the *tapis*. It appeared that this wretch had undertaken in return for a quantity of ivory, to add a white female to the beauties of the King's seraglio; and had actually succeeded in enticing a Farmer, with his fair *vrouw*, to the very borders of the country, within which a Commando was in readiness to seize the lady. The diabolical scheme being suspected however, his designs were frustrated; and a fear of Moselekatse's implacable revenge has obliged him to relinquish all trade with the savages, whilst the Colonists on the other hand, have placed the delinquent beyond the pale of society.

Our horses having now greatly improved in condition, we resolved to proceed immediately to the
country of the Bakone or Baquaina, where Cameleopards were reported by the savages to be very abundant; and accordingly on the 15th November, having
previously cleared away several of the trees, we
crossed over to the North side of the Cashan mountains, by a perilous and barely practicable path.
The waggons were several times only prevented from
being dashed to pieces by means of guy-ropes,
which fortunately preserved their equilibrium, and we
were enabled to encamp on the Western banks of the
Limpopo, some distance below the point where it
winds through the bowels of the mountains, which
rise on either hand in abrupt precipices, as though
torn asunder by some mighty convulsion of nature.
Here the country again assumes a more level character, but is broken to the Eastward by detached
hills and low ridges, imperceptibly increasing in importance, until they grow into a great range of
mountains, known to the natives as the Mural.
These may be said to take their origin about one
degree North of the parallel of Delagoa, assuming
a nearly northerly direction, and dividing the tracts
occupied by the Baquaina and Babariri.   During
the rainy season especially, they are infested by a
large species of gad-fly, nearly the size of a honey-
bee, the bite of which, like that of a similar pest

in Abyssinia, proves fatal to cattle. A desire to
escape the officious visits of these destructive insects, whose persecutions relieved us of two of our
oxen, soon obliged us to abandon the willow-fringed
river, which threads the mountains for a considerable distance; and, after crossing the Lingkling, the
embouchure of which is not many miles above
that of the Umpeban, our difficulties were not a little
increased by the broken and stony character of the
country.

On the 17th, whilst crossing a nameless and insignificant stream, the treacherous appearance of which
had induced us to follow a path ploughed by Hippopotami, the pack-waggon became suddenly ingulfed
in a quagmire. The *trektouw*, or leathern trace,
having been nibbled by Alligators, twice snapped in
the attempt to extricate it by double purchase; and
all other resources failing, we were at length actually compelled to dig it out! This subsequently
unfortunate vehicle was shortly afterwards upset for
the first time during our journey, by the carelessness
of Frederick, who had been appointed to the post of
leader of the team, *vice* April, removed. With one
hind wheel on the slope of a steep bank, and the
other in a deep hollow, it vibrated for some seconds,
as though the turn of a hair were to decide whether
it should stand or fall. " It's over"—"now it's safe"
—" No, gone by heavens" burst from half a dozen

mouths at once; and just sufficient time having elapsed to admit of the inmates effecting their escape,
down it went with an appalling crash, the wheels
appearing uppermost, and the motley contents displaying themselves in admirable disorder. Peltry,
merchandise, and hunting trophies—camp furniture,
tinman's wares, and oilman's stores, were speedily
strewed upon the plain; whilst ten thousand leaden
bullets, having been liberated by the sudden shock,
from the sacks in which they were put up, might be
seen emulating each other in a race to arrive at the
lower ground. To a spectator unacquainted with
the construction of a Cape waggon, no one compo-
nent part of which is attached to another, this would
have appeared an irrecoverable and total wreck. In
the course of two hours, however, every thing was
in its proper place again, and the vehicle in motion,
a trifling distortion of the awning being the only
trace left to remind us of the catastrophe. It served as a lesson nevertheless, to trim the waggons with
greater care; and as we had now eaten some way
into the stores, the hunting trophies were removed
from the awning, to which they had hitherto been
lashed, and stowed away in the hold as pig ballast.
Yet even this precaution did not exempt us from
further misfortune—the same ill-fated van was again
overthrown in a few days with most alarming detri-
ment to its contents—the portable sextant, amongst

other things being flattened in one of the side pockets.

The third day after crossing the mountains, we encamped on the Machachochan river, near the scene of the signal defeat of Barend Barend's Griquas in 1831, an event to which I have before had occasion to allude. A conical mountain, seen from a considerable distance in every direction, points to the spot; and it's base is a perfect Golgotha, thickly strewed with the whitened bones of men and, horses broken guns, and tattered furniture. Taking advantage of the absence of Moselekatse's army, on an expedition against a tribe to the Northward, a thousand mounted Bastaards dashed across the River Vaal, and obtained possession of vast herds of cattle without opposition. Elated by success, they were encamped, on their return, in straggling detachments; and whilst slumbering in that ill timed security for which the tribe is remarkable, were surprised about an hour before day light—the approved opportunity in savage warfare—by a band of unpractised soldiers, who had been hastily called together to meet the emergency. Such was the panic created, that many fell by the guns of their comrades, and few indeed escaped to tell the fate of the less fortunate. Dowd, the Chief whom we met at Daniel's kuil, and Hendrik Hendrik, a Griqua Captain residing at Phillipolis, state themselves to be the only survivors of that dis-

29

astrous day. Ensconced in a thick bush, they kept up an incessant fire while their ammunition lasted; jumping on the first horses they could catch, and riding for their lives, the instant the dawn appeared. The scene of carnage was visited by Moselekatse, and as he viewed the carcases of his foes " strewing the earth like broken glass," his exultation knew no bounds; the contempt he had entertained for fire arms being fully confirmed by this signal defeat. Barend Barend, who was infirm in years, had not accompanied the invading army beyond the Vaal river, but died shortly after the destruction of his clan.

CHAPTER XXIV.

HUNTING THE CAMELEOPARD, OR GIRAFFE.

To the sportsman, the most thrilling passage in my adventures, is now to be recounted. In my own breast, it awakens a renewal of past impressions, more lively than any written description can render intelligible; and far abler pens than mine, dipped in more glowing tints, would still fall short of the reality, and leave much to be supplied by the imagination. Three hundred gigantic Elephants, browsing in majestic tranquillity amidst the wild magnificence of an African landscape, and a wide stretching plain, darkened far as the eye can reach, with a moving phalanx of Gnoos and Quaggas, whose numbers literally baffle computation, are sights but rarely to be witnessed; but who amongst our brother Nimrods shall hear of riding familiarly by the side of a troop of colossal Giraffes, and not feel his spirit stirred within him? He that would behold so marvellous a sight must leave the haunts of man, and dive, as we did, into pathless wilds, traversed only by the brute creation—into wide wastes, where the grim Lion prowls, monarch of all he surveys, and where the gaunt Hyæna and Wild Dog fearlessly pursue their prey.

Many days had now elapsed since we had even seen the Cameleopard—and then only in small numbers, and under the most unfavorable circumstances. The blood coursed through my veins like quicksilver, therefore, as on the morning of the 19th, from the back of *Breslar,* my most trusty steed, with a firm wooded plain before me, I counted thirty two of these animals, industriously stretching their pea-cock necks to crop the tiny leaves which fluttered above their heads, in a mimosa grove that beauti-fied the scenery. They were within a hundred yards of me, but having previously determined to try the *boarding* system, I reserved my fire. Although I had taken the field expressly to look for Giraffes, and had put four of the Hottentots on horseback, all ex-cepting Piet had as usual slipped off unperceived in pursuit of a troop of Koodoos. Our stealthy approach was soon opposed by an ill tempered Rhinoceros, which with her ugly calf, stood directly in the path; and the twinkling of her bright little eyes, accompani-ed by a restless rolling of the body, giving earnest of her intention to charge, I directed Piet to salute her with a broadside, at the same moment putting spurs to my horse. At the report of the gun, and the sudden clattering of hoofs, away bounded the Gi-raffes in grostesque confusion—clearing the ground

Dean & Munday Lithog. 7.s.w. Threadneedle St. London.

by a succession of frog-like hops, and soon leaving
me far in the rear. Twice were their towering
forms concealed from view by a park of trees, which
we entered almost at the same instant; and twice on
emerging from the labyrinth, did I perceive them tilt-
ing over an eminence immeasurably in advance. A
white turban, that I wore round my hunting cap,
being dragged off by a projecting bough, was instantly charged by three Rhinoceroses; and looking over
my shoulder, I could see them long afterwards, fag-
ging themselves to overtake me. In the course
of five minutes, the fugitives arrived at a small river,
the treacherous sands of which receiving their long
legs, their flight was greatly retarded; and after
floundering to the opposite side, and scrambling to the
top of the bank, I perceived that their race was run.
Patting the steaming neck of my good steed, I urged
him again to his utmost, and instantly found myself
by the side of the herd. The stately bull, being
readily distinguishable from the rest by his dark
chesnut robe, and superior stature, I applied the
muzzle of my rifle behind his dappled shoulder, with
the right hand, and drew both triggers; but he still
continued to shuffle along, and being afraid of losing him, should I dismount, among the extensive mimosa groves, with which the landscape was now obscured, I sat in my saddle, loading and firing behind
the elbow, and then placing myself across his path,

until, the tears trickling from his full brilliant eye,
his lofty frame began to totter, and at the seventeenth
discharge from the deadly grooved bore, bowing his
graceful head from the skies his proud form was
prostrate in the dust.   Never shall I forget the tin-
gling excitement of that moment!   Alone, in the wild
wood, I hurried with bursting exultation, and un-
saddling my steed, sank exhausted beside the noble
prize I had won.

When I leisurely contemplated the massive frame
before me, seeming as though it had been cast in a
mould of brass, and protected by a hide of an inch
and a half in thickness, it was no longer matter of
astonishment that a bullet discharged from a distance of eighty or ninety yards should have been attended with little effect upon such amazing strength.
The extreme height from the crown of the elegantly
moulded head to the hoof of this magnificent animal,
was eighteen feet; the whole being equally divided
into neck, body, and leg.   Two hours were passed
in completing a drawing; and Piet still not making
his appearance, I cut off the tail, which exceeded
five feet in length, and was measurelessly the most es-
timable trophy I had gained ; but proceeding to saddle my horse, which I had left quietly grazing by the
side of a running brook, my chagrin may be conceived, when I discovered that he had taken advantage
of my occupation to free himself from his halter, and

abscond. Being ten miles from the waggons, and in
a perfectly strange country, I felt convinced that the
only chance of recovering my pet, was by following
the trail, whilst doing which with infinite difficulty,
the ground scarcely deigning to receive a foot-print,
I had the satisfaction of meeting Piet and Mohanycom, who had fortunatly seen and recaptured the
truant. Returning to the Giraffe, we all feasted
heartily upon the flesh, which although highly scented
at this season, with the rank Mokaala blossoms, was
far from despicable; and after losing our way in consequence of the twin-like resemblance of two scarp-
ed hills, we regained the waggons after sunset.

The spell was now broken, and the secret of
Cameleopard hunting discovered. The next day
Richardson and myself killed three; one, a female,
slipping upon muddy ground, and falling with great
violence, before she had been wounded, a shot in the
head despatching her as she lay. From this time we
could reckon confidently upon two out of each troop
that we were fortunate enough to find, always approaching as near as possible, in order to ensure a
good start, galloping into the middle of them, *boarding* the largest, and riding with him until he fell. The
rapidity with which these awkwardly formed animals
can move, is beyond all things surprising, our best
horses being unable to close with them under two
miles. Their gallop is a succession of jumping

strides, the fore and hind leg on the same side moving together instead of diagonally, as in most other
quadrupeds, the former being kept close together,
and the latter so wide apart, that in riding by the
animals side, the hoof may be seen striking on the
'outside of the horse, momentarily threatening to
overthrow him. Its motion altogether, reminded
me rather of the pitching of a ship, or rolling of a
rocking horse, than of any thing living; and the
remarkable gait is rendered still more automaton-
like, by the switching, at regular intervals, of the
long black tail, which is invariably curled above
the back, and by the corresponding action of the
neck, swinging as it does like a pendulum, and literally imparting to the animal the appearance of a
piece of machinery in motion. Naturally gentle,
timid, and peaceable, the unfortunate Giraffe has no
means of protecting itself but with its heels; but
even when hemmed into a corner, it seldom resorted
to this mode of defence. I have before noticed the
courage evinced by our horses, in the pursuit of game.
Even when brought into actual contact with these
almost unearthly quadrupeds, they evinced no symptom of alarm, a circumstance which may possible be
traced to their meagre diet.

The colossal height, and apparent disproportions
of this extraordinary animal, long classed it with
the Unicorn, and the Sphinx of the ancients, and

induced a belief that it belonged rather to the group of Chimeras with which the regions of imagination are tenanted, than existed amongst the actual works of nature. Of its form and habits, no very precise notions were obtained, until within the last forty years; and even now, the extant delineations are far from the truth, having been taken from crippled prisoners instead of from specimens free in their native deserts. The Giraffe is by no means a common animal, even at its head quarters. We seldom found them without having followed the trail, and never saw more than five and thirty in a day.* The senses of sight, hearing, and smell, are acute and delicate; the eyes, which are soft and gentle, eclipsing those of the oft sung gazelle of the East, and being so constructed that without turning the head, the animal can see both before and behind it at the same time. On the forehead, there is a remarkable prominence; and the tongue has the power of mobility increased to an extraordinary degree, accompanied with the

* A traveller whom I met in the Cape Colony, assured me before I visited the interior, that he had himself counted eight hundred Giraffes in a single day; and during his travels, had ridden down *hundreds*. On my return, however after a little cross examination, the number destroyed dwindled gradually down into *one;* which solitary individual appeared, upon further investigation, to have been taken in a pit-fall!

faculty of extension, which enables it, in miniature, to perform the office of the Elephant's proboscis.   The lofty maned neck, possessing only seven joints, appears to move on a pivot, instead of being flexible like that of the Swan or Peacock, to which, from its length, it has been likened.

The Giraffe utters no cry whatever.   Both sexes have horns, covered with hair, and are similarly marked with an angular and somewhat symmetrical pattern.   The male increases in depth of color, according to the age, and in some specimens is nearly black; but the female is smaller in stature, and of a lighter color, approaching to yellow.   Although very extensive, the range of its *habitat* is exclusively confined to those regions in which the species of mimosa termed mokaala, or *Kameel-doorn* is abundant, the leaves, shoots, and blossoms, of that tree being its ordinary food.

On the 22d, being encamped on the banks of a small stream, a Cameleopard was killed by a Lion, whilst in the act of drinking at no great distance from the waggons.   It was a noisy affair, but an inspection of the scene on which it occurred, proved that the giant strength of the victim had been paralysed in an instant.   Authors have asserted that the king of beasts is sometimes carried fifteen or twenty miles, "riding proudly" on the back of the Gi_ raffe; but notwithstanding the amazing power of this superb animal, I am disposed to question his ability to maintain a race under such merciless jockeyship!

CHAPTER XXV.

RETURN TO THE SOUTHWARD FROM THE TROPIC OF
CAPRICORN.

ALTHOUGH hunting the Cameleopard, we continued
to advance to the Northward, by marches of ten and
fifteen miles a day, over extensive rugged tracts, strewed with numerous stone walls, once thronged by thou-
but now presenting no vestige of inhabitants. Wherever we turned, the hand of the Destroyer was apparent:

——————" The locusts wasting swarm,
Which mightiest nations dread,"

is not more destructive to vegetation, than he has
been to the population of this section of Southern
Africa. We frequently travelled for days without
meeting a solitary human being—occasionally only
falling in with the small and starving remnant of
some pastoral tribe of Bechuana, that had been plundered by Moselekatse's warriors. These famished
wretches, some of whom had been herding the King's
cattle during the absence of Kalipi's Commando, hovered around us, disputing with Vultures and Hyænas
the carcases we left, which they devoured with such

brutish avidity as scarcely to leave a bone to attest the slaughter.

The moon was full on the night of the 23rd, and a spotted, or "laughing" Hyæna, superior in size to the largest mastiff, was shot through the head, by the clear light it afforded, as he was in the act of skulking under the sheep-pen. The great muscular power of this animal, which is called by the Colonists, "the Wolf," renders it exceedingly formidable; the difficulty of determining the sex, being the most remarkable feature it possesses. On the 27th we again encamped on the banks of the Limpopo, in which a Buffalo was shot as it was swimming across. Few other sporting incidents occurred of an extraordinary character, except the death of a very large black Rhinoceros, which being pent up in an old stone enclosure, received no less than twenty-seven shots before it fell. A troop of Brindled Gnoos, being pursued by another of these animals, dashed into a narrow defile in the hills, at the outlet of which, having stationed myself, I disposed of two with each barrel.

As we approached the junction of the Mariqua with the Limpopo, in about latitude 24° 10′, bushes usurped the place of trees; the country daily became less inviting, and the game in consequence less and less abundant, although a supply was still always to be obtained. The few inhabitants that we now met with, refused to hold any communication with our escort—seating themselves at a distance, and declining the proferred snuff-box. These men were the wreck of the Bakone or Baquaina, once the most powerful and prosperous of the Bechuana nations. Conquered by Moselekatse, however, and Caama * their King having been slain, they fled to this part of the country, and are now reduced to an extremity of misery and want, little short of actual starvation—the emaciated forms of many too plainly testifying to their precarious means of subsistence.

The obtaining of information relative to the country and inhabitants had uniformly been attended with much difficulty; but our guides, who had evidently received instructions from the King, to entice us as far as possible from the scene of contention with the Emigrant Boors, in the hope of eventually inducing us to return by Kapain, instead of by the Likwa, being now apprised of our intention of discontinuing our journey Northward, brought seven savages who volunteered information regarding the *great inland lake,* and even proposed for a suitable remuneration in beads, to accompany us thither as guides. They stated that this vast fresh water sea, towards the discovery of which geographical attention has long been directed, and the existence of which was first

* King Hartebeest !

fully established by Dr Smith's expedition, might easily be reached from our present position in *two moons*, through the country of the Bukaws; a small intervening desert tract being passable at this season, and the recent heavy rains having filled the pools upon which the supply of water depends. Nothing could be more tantalizing than this proposal made at a time when our oxen were in superb condition, our supplies abundant, and our followers in better heart than usual; but knowing from experience how little reliance can be placed upon a savage's estimate of distance, we were not without reasonable apprehensions of being detained beyond the Bukaws until after next rains, and thus exceeding our leave. All circumstances but this, conspiring to favour both the successful continuance of our journey, and the discovery of the " great water,"—it was with feelings of no ordinary regret and disappointment, that we felt ourselves thus compelled to return, at the very moment when a prize of such value appeared actually within our grasp.

Although not more than fifty miles to the South of the tropic of Capricorn, we did not find the heat by any means oppressive; a circumstance which was of course in a great measure to be attributed to the season. After the thunderstorm which usually ushered in the night, the mornings had been always remarkably cool; and even during the middle of the day the range of the thermometer in the waggons had rarely exceeded 85°.   Before turning to the South-ward, we crossed the Limpopo, and made an excursion of forty miles to the North-eastward, on horseback, with a design of determining the course assumed by this interesting feature in the geography of Southern Africa.   So far as it was possible to comprehend the descriptions given by savages, which are not the clearest in the world, this river, after being joined by another, called the Clabatz, or Balapatse, which rises in the Mural mountains, turns suddenly through that chain, and flows into the unexplored country of the Babariri, towards Delagoa, distant probably about three hundred and fifty miles.   This account is in a great measure confirmed by information given me by David Hume, an exceedingly clear headed, observing traveller.   By whomsoever it may eventu-ally be traced, therefore, the Limpopo will in all pro-bability be found identical with the *Manice*, the ri-ver which was surveyed by Captain Owen, from its embouchure in Delagoa bay, as far as latitude 25° 21 South, and longitude 33° 52′ East.

For the satisfaction of those of my readers, who take an interest in the geography of the African quarter of the globe, it may be proper here to state, that with a view of ascertaining our position on the map, I adopted the very simple, but excellent method pursued by Burchell, during his travels.   The exact

distance passed over each day was calculated by a
table, computed from the circumference of the larger
waggon wheel, multiplied by the number of revolu-
tions performed per minute ; the time that the vehicle
was actually in motion being carefully noted by an
inside passenger, as well as the course by compass.
This plan, with occasional correction from the now
broken pocket sextant, used on a sheet of pasteboard
by way of false horizon, had determined our position in so level a country with 'sufficient accuracy.
Rude as it may appear, few inland portions of this
vast continent, have been surveyed by a more scientific process; and during the early part of our journey, especially while travelling between known
points, I had frequent opportunities of satisfying
myself of its practical correctness.

Judging therefore, from a minute daily register
kept throughout our journey, we must now have
been about the tropic, our distance to the North of
the known latitude of Mosega being upwards of
one hundred and fifty miles. We retraced our steps
on the 1st December, the previous night having been
passed at a kraal of starving Baquaina, for whom
we had killed a Rhinoceros. Fearful indeed was
the uproar that attended the division of the carcase
—a large party of ladies, possessing remarkably
slender wardrobes, rushing forth like witches, and
leaving nothing in the course of a few hours but a
pool of blood.

Thus far we had been treated by the guides with
tolerable civility. No sooner, however, had we turned to the Southward than they began to evince the
greatest impatience at their detention, complaining
loudly of their limited rations of snuff and bread,
and insolently urging our return to the Cashan
mountains with all expedition, upon the plea that the
King would be displeased at our making so long a
stay; His Majesty having, they said, instructed them
that we were only to hunt during one moon. Knowing this to be false, we continued hunting Giraffes,
and paid little attention to their remonstrances; but
on arriving opposite the scene of the Griqua defeat,
we were joined on the 6th by four Matabili warriors
from Kapain, who stated that they had been following our waggon tracks, by command of the King,
for ten days past, in order peremptorily to direct our
return to the Cashan mountains, where we should be
met by our friend Um'Nombate, who had a further
message to communicate. This mysterious intimation
had the effect of conjuring back the dormant apprehensions of the Hottentots; Andries, as usual, gloomily persisting that the King had never intended to
let us go through by the Vaal river, and was now
about to recal the permission we had extorted. Although we stoutly combatted these dismal forebodings, there really appeared to be some grounds for
entertaining them—it being impossible to imagine

why else the minister should have been sent. The
result of our deliberations however, was, that nothing short of main force should induce us to relinquish
the permission we had purchased ; and that having
successfully struggled thus far with difficulties and
annoyances, we would now

> ————————" Not bate a jot
> Of heart or hope, but still bear up and steer
> Right onwards."

With this determination we hurried our advance towards a large Matabili kraal, which, situated to the
North of the Cashan range among a group of pyramidical hills, had been selected as the point of ren-
dezvous with the ambassador. On arriving there
however, crowds of both sexes issuing forth, we
were informed that he was still a day's journey
in advance; and were thus provokingly hurried from
place to place, until late on the evening of the
8th, when we reached a small collection of deserted
wigwams, on the Sant river, immediately under the
mountains. But even here we were destined to
experience further disappointment and suspense—
the Catiff guides declaring that the object of our
search, who was still not forthcoming, must have
been *asleep* in one of the kraals that we had passed
in the morning! Suspecting the story of his advent
to be a hoax, invented merely to annoy us, we
now distinctly intimated to the messengers, that if

the minister did not make his appearance in the
course of the following forenoon, we should not wait
for him; and with this understanding, they left the
waggons, accompanied by the guides, faithfully promising to return with the great man in the morning.

CHAPTER XXVI.

INTERVIEW WITH UM'NOMBATE, AND JOURNEY
THROUGH THE CASHAN MOUNTAINS TO
THE SOUTH-EASTWARD.

Contrary to our expectations, Um'Nombate was
actually descried at an early hour the next morning,
approaching our waggons with a large retinue and
three wretched oxen. The important preliminary of
snuff-taking having been duly concluded, the crafty old courtier, without making the slightest allusion
to the object of his visit, delivered abundant compliments on the part of His Majesty, regarding whose
august health we made befitting enquiries. The table having in the mean time been spread with dainty
viands, amongst the most inviting of which I may be
permitted to notice a pile of Rhinoceros' steaks, we
proceeded to breakfast, and were not a little diverted
by the grand vizier's uncouth attempts at the use of
the knife and fork. Copying the polished example
set by Mrs. John Smith of Somerset, he presently
cut the corner of his mouth, repeatedly placing his
sight in imminent jeopardy, by bringing his hand to
the bleeding orifice, instead of the point of the fork,
which, loaded with meat, appeared above his head.

His son, a fine young savage to whom we were for-
mally introduced, sat upon a tar barrel at the head
of the table, but wisely preferred making use of his
nails and assagai; whilst the retinue, squatting themselves behind the old man's chair, quarrelled like
dogs for the scraps which he was pleased from time
to time to throw to them. In the course of a few minutes, the board was swept of its smoking load, and
tea having been baled out of a large kettle to
the whole party, the repast was concluded by the
greedy consumption of half a pound of snuff.

After a long and mysterious conference with the
guides, which was conducted at a distance, in an under tone of voice and with great earnestness, Um'-
Nombate proceeded to open the business of his em-
bassy by presenting to each of us first, and then to
Andries, a Leopard's skin, a bag of kafir corn, and
a scrubby ox. The animal sent expressly for Andries besides being hornless, was wall-eyed on the
dexter side—a peculiarity which elicited many personal jokes at the expense of our trusty follower,
whom His Majesty, when in merry mood, was in
the habit of addressing by the familiar soubriquet of
Mutlee or cock-eye. The pleasantry of the conceit
being fully appreciated, that designation was immediately bestowed upon the Ox; and we learned shortly afterwards that Andries had engaged to return
from the Colony, and enter the despot's service, upon

condition of being rewarded by the hand of Truëy the Griqua captive.

After a few unimportant remarks relative to the country we had visited, the game, and the liberal supply of rain, which it had been the King's gracious pleasure to send us, the ambassador proceeded without further preamble, to disclose his important errand, by acquainting us with His Majesty's sudden determination to become the proprietor of a fowling piece upon the detonating principle; at the same time declaring his own readiness immediately to receive charge of the weapon, together with any other trifling presents that we might be desirous of sending. We evaded compliance with the first part of this very modest demand, by promising, when the Elephant hunting should be concluded, to send a gun by our escort, party on its return *from the Vaal river;* at the same time meeting the spirit of the request, by producing another coil of the identical brass wire which had proved so attractive at Kapain—several articles of crockery ware—a gross of gilt regimental buttons, —and a brown jug, with raised representations of Toby Philpot in five different stages of intoxication —from which most appropriate vessel we begged that His Majesty would be pleased to quaff his beer in future.

The mention of the Vaal river passing off without any remark, our anxiety on that score was relieved;

and the jug having been duly admired, we proceeded
to complain of the mutinous behaviour of the guides,
who we requested might be exchanged for others.
Mohanycom being the channel through which this
communication must pass had an opportunity of
distorting it as he pleased, and delivered a smooth
honied speech in reply, the substance of which was
that no further difficulties would be made. A warrior answering to the name of *Maphook*, was then
directed by the ambassador to reinforce our escort;
and having duly enlisted himself under our banner,
they all received injunctions to accompany us, by any
route we fancied, to the Vaal river but on no account to return thence without the percussion gun.

Having requested Um'Nombate to express to his
Royal Master the gratification that we had derived
from our visit to his extensive preserves, I proceeded
to the exhibition of the drawings I had made of the
different game animals which was attended with the
usual theatric effect. The production of " the noble
Elephant," caused an involuntary elevation of the eye-
lids, although no remark was made. On seeing the
Giraffe, every one exclaimed *'Intootla! 'Intootla!!
'Intootla !!!* at the same time standing on tip-toe,
and stretching his neck to the utmost extent. *Tao*, or
the Lion, caused a general flourish of weapons and
beating of shields; and *'Imfooboo*, the Hippopotamus, whilst it nearly threw the old man into fits,

elicited the observation that I "undoubtedly took *very strong medicine!* After some other equally sapient remarks, the peer arose, and reminding us of his Sovereign's caution to return by Kuruman if we visited him again, which he trusted we would, took leave of us in the usual manner, and set out on his return carrying the brown jug in his own hand.

We forthwith continued our journey to the South-eastward with renewed spirits, passing through the mountains by the opening described in a former chapter, and arriving with some hair breadth escapes, at one of our former stations on the South side of the range. The next day, our route lying across a belt of hillocks with many steep acclivities, our progress was repeatedly delayed by the breaking of one of the tow ropes, the half starved dogs of the savages, which not unfrequently devoured the *veldt-scoen*, or untanned leather shoes of our followers, having at our last station gnawed through some of the straps. A large herd of wild Buffaloes being observed at a little distance, my companion and myself mounted our horses, and soon despatched a splendid bull. Whilst several of the followers were employed in flaying the animal, we returned to the waggons, and sent Andries with a pack-horse for the hide, of which a new *trek touw* was to be manufactured. He presently returned at speed, to acquaint us that Piet had been badly wounded in the

32

leg by the accidental discharge of a gun; and 'Lingap who accompanied him, after pointing with breathless dismay to a hole perforated by the same bullet through his own shield, proceeded to a minute practical illustration of the affair, by placing Andries' clumsy piece against a tree in such a way, that it also fell down, and was discharged, but fortunately without doing further mischief. The unhappy Piet was brought in shortly afterwards, when our nervous anxiety respecting him were not a little relieved by an inspection of the limb, which although dreadfully burnt and lacerated was providentially unbroken. Our skill in surgery being exercised with good effect, the wound healed rapidly; and I, feeling obliged to the patient for the little assistance he had occasionally afforded me in the field, again resigned my cot to him during the day; a piece of kindness, which, like the rest of his unthankful tribe, he mistook for weakness, repaying me in the end by the grossest ingratitude.

Every feature of this part of the country was beautiful beyond description. Grassy meads, spangled with brilliant flowers, extended between rich masses of grove and forest. Stately trees were festooned with clambering vines, or scented creepers. Here the gorgeous aloe reared its coral tufts above the olive brake—and there the meadows were flushed with the crimson or lilac hues of the poppy, and

amaryllis. Amongst a variety of animals, a herd of
Elephants was visible from the waggons; and the
·next day, from the top of a commanding eminence,
we again saw the face of the highly picturesqne landscape covered with these stately beasts browsing in
indolent security, and bathing in the pellucid stream.
Upon being attacked, one hundred at least,

> " Trampling their path through wood and brake,
> And canes which crackling fell before their way,"

rushed franticly down a ravine, with upraised ears,
and tossing trunks, screaming wildly, and levelling
every thing before them. A shot fired from the
bank, while it sealed the fate of the leader, turned
the rest back again, and this persecution was repeated until they became fairly stupified. On one
occasion they attempted to retrieve the day by a
headlong charge from several quarters at the same
moment, and we were often so surrounded by small
detachments, that it appeared doubtful which party
would be obliged to quit the field. The sound of
our voices however uniformly turned the scale, and
declared man the victor. Among several hundred
females and calves, we could find but one bull; and
as we were tracking him on horseback through a
heavy forest by his life blood welling from fifty
wounds, a savage Rhinoceros dashed out of a bush
into the very middle of our party, overthrowing several, but injuring none. Andries, though he was

ever thrusting upon us his code of sage laws regarding Elephant hunting, was always the first to infringe
it; and wantonly firing at a peaceably disposed
Rhinoceros, while we were upon the hot trail of Elephants in the early part of the day, his horse got
away, and he was knocked over; the damage sustained by the hinder part of his leathern trowsers,
which were rent by the animal's horn, proving how
nearly we had been bereft for ever of his valuable
services.

Both our vehicles were now so crammed with *spolia* that being unable to find room for any more
ivory, we were reluctantly compelled to leave the
ground strewed with that valuable commodity. Great
difficulty was experienced in getting our heavily laden waggons clear of the formidable belt of wooded
hillocks which, intersected by deep ravines, form the
suburbs of the Cashan range. In some places,
the paths worn by the huge tenants of this almost
trackless region being too narrow, it was found
necessary to send a party of pioneers to widen them
—thus literally cutting our way through the country,
and making the hitherto silent forest ring to the un-
wonted sound of the axe.

Scarcely a day passed without our seeing two
or three Lions, but like the rest of the animal creation, they uniformly retreated when disturbed by
the approach of man. However troublesome we

found the instrusions of the feline race during the night, they seldom at any other time, showed the least disposition to molest us, unless we commenced hostilities; and this, owing to the badness of the horses, we rarely felt disposed to do. Returning one afternoon with Maphook to a Koodoo that I had shot, in order to take up the head, which I had concealed in a bush, I was surprised to find an enormous Lion * feasting upon the carcase; an odious assemblage of eager vultures, as usual, garrisoning the trees, and awaiting their turn when the gorged monarch should make way for them. Immediately upon my appearance, he walked heavily off, expressing by a stifled growl his displeasure at being thus unceremoniously disturbed at dinner. It was not destined, however, that our acquaintance should cease here; for passing the scene of this introductory interview the following morning, Richardson and myself were suddenly made aware of the monster's presence by perceiving a pair of gooseberry eyes glaring upon us from beneath a shady bush; and instantly upon reining up our horses, the grim savage bolted out with a roar, like thunder, and bounded across the plain with the agility of a grey hound. The luxuriant beauty of his shaggy black mane, which almost swept the ground, tempted us contrary to

* *Felis Leo.* Delineated in the African Views.

established rule, to give him battle with the design of obtaining possession of his spoils; and he no sooner found himself hotly pursued than be faced about, and stood at bay in a mimosa grove, measuring the strength of his assailants with a port the most noble and imposing. Disliking our appearance however, and not relishing the smell of gunpowder, he soon abandoned the grove, and took up his position on the summit of an adjacent stony hill, the base of which being thickly clothed with thorn trees, we could only obtain a view of him from the distance of three hundred yards. Crouched on this fortified pinnacle, like the sculptured figure at the entrance of a nobleman's park, the enemy disdainfully surveyed us for several minutes, daring us to approach with an air of conscious power and pride, which well beseemed his grizzled form. As the rifle balls struck the ground nearer and nearer at each discharge, his wrath, as indicated by his glistening eyes, increased roar, and impatient switching of the tail, was clearly getting the mastery over his prudence. Presently a shot broke his leg. Down he came upon the other three, with reckless impetuosity, his tail straight out and whirling on its axis, his mane bristling on end, and his eye balls flashing rage and vengeance. Unable however to overtake our horses, he shortly retreated under a heavy fire, limping and discomfited to his strong hold. Again we bombarded him, and

again exasperated, he rushed into the plain with
headlong fury—the blood now streaming from his
open jaws, and dying his mane with crimson. It
was a gallant charge, but it was to be his last. A
well directed shot arresting him in full career, he
pitched with violence upon his skull, and throwing
a complete somerset, subsided amid a cloud of dust.

CHAPTER XXVII.

THE list of large animals killed during the Campaign, now exceeded four hundred head of various sorts and sizes. Of these the minimum height at the shoulder had been three feet, and not a few had measured ten and twelve. Within the last few days, I had obtained several superb specimens, especially of the Koodoo and Bastard Gemsbok; and excepting some of the smaller antelopes, which only occur in parts of the country that we were subsequently to visit, my collection of horns and *exuviæ* had by this time extended itself to every known species of game quadruped in Southern Africa. But a still prouder trophy than all, was yet in abeyance, and before leaving this hunters' Elysium, my researches were to be crowned by a truly splendid addition to the catalogue of Mammalia.

My double barrelled rifle having again suffered in a fall with my horse, I took the field on the 13th December with a heavy weapon constructed upon the primitive principle of flint and steel, which, as a *pis aller*, I had obtained from Mr. Moffat.　Our party were in full pursuit of a wounded Elephant, when a herd of unusually dark looking Antelopes attracted observation in an adjacent valley.　Reconnoitring them through a pocket telescope from the acclivity on which we stood, I at once exclaimed that they were perfectly new to science; and having announced my determination of pursuing them, if requisite, to the world's end, I dashed down the slope, followed by the derision of the Hottentots, for my unsportsmanlike attention to an "ugly buck," *one* specimen of which, however, I assured them, I would rather have possessed than all the Elephants in Africa!　In an instant I was in the middle of the herd, which was then crossing the valley—nine chesnut colored does leading, and two magnificent coal black bucks—all with scimitar shaped horns—bringing up the rear.　Hastily dismounting, I was delighted to observe them stand for a few seconds within fifty yards, and stare at me with amazement.　In vain was it however, that I pulled the trigger of my rifle; three several times the heavy machinery of the lock descended with alarming vehemence, but no report followed the concussion; and the herd having in the mean time ascended a steep hill, I fairly rode my horse to a stand in the attempt to overtake them.　Cursing my hard fortune, as I dashed the hateful weapon to the ground, I hastened to the camp, to repair my broken rifle;

33

armed with which, and mounted on a fresh steed I returned with my companion to the spot; where, having taken up the foot marks, we followed them, with unwearied perseverance among the hills, during the whole of that and the following day, without attaining even a glimpse of the objects of our quest.   At noon of the third day, however, peeping cautiously over a bank, our laudable assiduity was rewarded by the gratifying sight of the two bucks grazing by them-selves, unconscious of our approach, in a stony valley.   Having disposed our forces, after a moment's consultation, so as to intercept the game from a tangled labyrinth of ravines, the attack was made.   The hind leg of the handsomer of the two was dangling in an instant, and in another he was sprawling on the earth.   Quickly recovering himself however, he led me more than a mile over the sharp stones ere he was brought to bay, when twice charging gallantly, he was at length overthrown, and slain.

It were vain to attempt a description of the sensations I experienced, when thus, after three days of toilsome tracking, and feverish anxiety unalleviated by any incident that could inspire the smallest hope of ultimate success, I at length found myself in actual possession of so brilliant an addition to the riches of Natural History.   My prize evidently belonged to the Antilopine subgenus *Aigocerus*, and was equal in stature to a large galloway.   The horns,

which were flat, and upwards of three feet in length
swept gracefully over the back in the form of a crescent.   A bushy black mane extended from the lively
chesnut colored ears, to the middle of the back; the
tail was long and tufted; and the glossy jet black
hue of the greater portion of the body, contrasted
beautifully with a snow-white face and belly.*   I
thought I could never have looked at, or admired it
sufficiently.   A drawing and description having been
completed on the spot, the skin was carefully

* The following were the dimensions of this singular and
beautiful Antelope, which is faithfully depicted in the African
Views.

	Inches.		Inches.
Height at the wither	54	Croup to hock	36
Length of body	44	Hock to foot	18½
Ditto neck	17	Breadth of fore arm	6
Do. head	19	Ditto thigh	6
Do. tail	25	Do. fore leg	2½
Do. hind quarter	19	Do. hind leg	3
Depth of chest	30	Do. neck	16
Length of fore arm	16	Length of horns	37
Fore knee to foot	15	Asunder at base	1
Height of mane	6½	Ditto tips	9½
		Length of ears	10

During the first day, I had opportunities of distinctly remarking that the females were all furnished with crescent
shaped horns; and although of smaller stature than the
males, were similarly marked—a deep chesnut brown taking
the place of jet black.   The species was evidently not recognized by the natives, although to conceal their ignorance,
they pronounced it to be *Kookaam*, which signifies the Oryx,
an animal of such extremely rare occurrence in Moselekatse's country, that they had in all probability never seen it.

removed and conveyed upon a pack horse in triumph to the camp ; and it may possibly interest those of my readers, who shall have followed me during the last three days, to learn, that I succeeded, with infinite difficulty, in bringing this unique and interesting specimen of African Zoology, in a state of high preservation to Cape Town; where in October last, it was elegantly set up by Monsieur Verreaux, the French Naturalist, and obligingly taken to England, by my well known friend Captain Alexander, 42d Royal Highlanders.

Notwithstanding the arrangements made by Um-'Nombate, our escort was daily becoming more unruly and impatient; and upon our attempting to move some miles further to the Eastward, in order if possible to obtain a female specimen of the new species, they positively refused to accompany us in any direction but that of the Vaal river. The most tempting bribes failed to shake their resolution; and upon our threatening to send an express to the King, for which duty Andries eagerly volunteered, they sat sullenly grinding tobacco with the most provoking indifference. Just at this time, the murrain attacked our oxen; and the horses moreover, being so galled and reduced in condition that many were unfit for further work, it was resolved that since the objects of our expedition had been thus far fully accomplished, we should at once set out upon our return to the Colony by the unexplored route.

Right joyfully was this announcement received by our followers. Ever discontented with their present lot, the Hottentots had long impatiently sighed for the drunken brawls of the canteen, and the bewitching smiles of their absent sweethearts. Cœur de Lion could instantly perceive in dim perspective the auspicious termination of *his* perils by sea and land; nor was the worshipper of the cow, in his turn, less pleased at the increased prospect of escape from a land so little suited to the prejudices of his *caste*. The bovine appearance of most of the African animals, having precluded this faithful follower from partaking of their flesh, he had suffered greater privations than any one, and had not unfrequently been compelled to observe a fast. Without a moment's loss of time, Kobus repaired his dilapidated violin, which in a fit of passion he had broken over a comrade's head: and a wild-peppermint-tea party, with dancing to its discordant notes round our gipsy fire, celebrated the approaching termination of the campaign.

At noon on the 16th of December then, bidding a final adieu to the enchanting forests of Cashan, we turned our faces to the Southward, and having crossed a small range of hills, which were all that divided us from the vast plains of the Vaal river, entered at once upon a new region, totally different in character from all that we had hitherto traversed. Such

had been the recent abundance of water, that our
people had for some time past allowed the wholesome
practise of filling the water flagons, to fall into desue-
tude; and we had in consequence the felicity of
passing the night without any of that necessary, although we travelled until dark in the hope of finding
it. A ponderous bull Eland, with only one horn,
being observed in the neighbourhood, Richardson and
myself drove him up to the caravan, where his blood
was eagerly quaffed both by the savages and Hottentots.

In the total absence of material for the construction of a pound, the cattle became so restless during
the night, that we were glad to resume our journey
two hours before dawn. Numerous Hartebeests and
Quaggas were disturbed by our advance; and the
white tailed Gnoo, which now occurred for the first
time since passing Kuruman, startled at the approach
of our waggons, was again bellowing, stamping, and
tossing its eccentric head. As the day broke, boundless meads kept extending to the eye, covered with
luxuriant herbage and enamelled with rich parterres
of brilliant flowers. These were animated by droves
of portly Elands, moving in long procession across the
silent and treeless landscape. The rank odour of
these animals, resembling the exhalation from a cattle close, could be winded from a great distance; and
it is a singular fact that their bodies are infested by

the ticks and parasitic flies commonly found in such places.

Pursuing a herd of many hundred Elands, which literally resembled a vast drove of stall fed oxen, we were joined in the chase by the prettily striped foal of a Quagga, which neighed and frisked by the side of our horses for a considerable time, before it discovered its mistake. The lighter bodied cows skipped nimbly over each others' heads, while the unweildy bulls laboured in the rear, their sleek sides shaking with fat, and frothing with perspiration. Two minutes were sufficient to reduce them all to a walk, and although some turned in desperation upon their pursuers, these enormous creatures are so easily disposed of that the whole herd might have been slaughtered. Their flesh being so greatly superior to that of any other animal, was always eagerly sought after; and on this occasion, we killed a sufficient number to afford a stock of tongues and briskets for salting, in case the country in advance, of which every one was equally ignorant, should not afford a supply of game. Leaving the carcases a banquet for the Vultures, we placed these delicacies on our meagre steeds, and rejoined the *cafila* in the afternoon. Weary and exhausted for want of water, we were not a little rejoiced on our arrival to find it drawn up on the banks of the beautiful Chonapas, a deep gurgling stream tenanted by Hippopotami, and meandering amid clusters of sighing reeds. Some of our people were busily engaged in the manufacture of a Buffalo hide drag rope for the approaching journey, and others had gone in search of fire-wood. Not a dry twig was to be obtained however, in the whole country, and it was found necessary to break up one of our boxes in order to boil the water and dress some fish that had been taken. The savages had always evinced the strongest antipathy to the finny tribe, flying in dismay if one were suddenly exhibited; and Andries here attempting some ill-timed practical joke of the kind upon Maphook, the savage sprang tiger-like upon his back, and throwing him to the ground, handled him so roughly, that our crest-fallen hero was fain to sue for quarter.

From our present position, the Vaal river was stated by the guides to be only two days journey to the Southward, the range of mountains in which it rises being indistinctly visible to the Southeast. Having conducted us thus far on our journey, they now declared their intention of returning immediately to the King, for whom they had the impudence to demand the gun, as well as the promised wages of their own services; adding, in reply to our remonstrances, that as we were now standing on the ground where the Emigrants had been routed, they found it impossible to proceed further, or to overcome the dread they entertained of their enemies the Dutchmen. An intimate acquaintance with the lying propensities of the savages, combined with other circumstances, satisfied us that the unusual appearance of sheep-droppings, to which they referred in support of their assertions, had been occasioned during Kalipi's return with the booty. Feeling confident therefore that they had no cause for alarm, and having every reason to be apprehensive for our own safety, should they desert us under existing circumstances, we steadily refused to comply with their demand. Upon this they assumed a tone of ultra insolence, and in the end menaced us with an attack from a neighbouring Matibili outpost, if we longer withheld the presents.

Without any just grounds for doubting the good faith of the King, we had been a little suspicious of the real object of Um'Nombate's visit, and after this threat, felt doubtful to what extent the guides might be acting under the royal instructions, with a design of deterring us from proceeding. Personal considerations would have justified, if they did not demand, our putting the caitiffs to death upon the spot ; but after some deliberation, it was resolved, after adopting precautionary measures against a night surprize, that we should see whether the morrow's dawn might not find them in a more accommodating humour. Ammunition was accordingly served out, and a place allotted to every one in case of an attack—the horses being secured to the front of our own waggons, lest the weak nerves of the Hottentots should induce them to jump upon their backs on the first appearance of danger. As a last arrangement before going to bed, Ethaldur—whose nights if passed at a distance from the "Licensed retailer of wine and brandy," were usually restless—was selected to perform the important part of *Cerberus,* in which duty he was voluntarily assisted by Cœur de Lion, who declared his utter inability to close his eyes. "Did I not tell you," croaked the former of these bold spirits to his companion, as, pipe in mouth, he proceeded to mount guard—"Did I not tell you that we should all have our throats cut, so sure as we came out by the Vaal Rivière!"

CHAPTER XXVIII.

DESERTION OF OUR ESCORT, AND ARRIVAL AT THE
RIVER VAAL.

AWAKING as the bright morning star shot above
the Eastern horizon, I perceived four Elands standing
within a few yards of the camp, undetected by the
vigilance of the sentinels, whose eyes nevertheless
were wide open. Directions for yoking the oxen
were no sooner given, than the guides commenced
packing their goods and chattels, and otherwise preparing for their return to the King. Seeing the impossibility of inducing them to accompany us farther
on our journey, and apprehensive of their resentment
if the rewards with held, we made a merit of necse-
sity, and attempted to restore them to good humour, by presenting each in his turn with a red woollen night cap, and a complete suit of European cloth-
ing, together with some beads which had been expressly reserved for their use. The only remaining
coil of brass wire was likewise handed over with a
box of lucifers, and a few mould candles, as a farewell offering to His Majesty, to whom we desired a
complimentary message expressive of our regret at
having been deprived of the means of sending him

the gun from the Vaal river. Hereupon, spurning the proferred treasures from them, the savages indignantly demanded if such rubbish could be considered a suitable recompense for their long and meritorious services, feigning at the same times as if about to retire. After some consultation however, they carefully scraped together the scattered beads, hanging each a hoop of wire about his neck; and placing their shields and bundles on their heads, departed angrily, Mohanycom declaring with a mysterious air as he opened his shark-like jaws in our presence for the last time, that "when the mightiest of Monarchs should behold such trash, his royal heart would be *very sore!*"

Without either guide, escort, or interpreter—in the midst of an unkown wilderness, bordering on the recent scene of bloody strife, and still scoured by the contending parties—our little band was now left in a highly unenviable position. After providing us, as he supposed, with a guard to the verge of his dominions, His Majesty had not in all probability, deemed it necessary to acquaint the different frontier outposts of our approaching exit; and deprived as we now were of the means of holding communication with his warriors, should we fall in with them, the least evil that could be anticipated in the present excited state of their feelings, would be a journey back to Kapain. Adding to the above prospect, the pro-

bability of annoyance or misrepresentation on the
part of the recreant escort, we plainly perceived that
the sooner we were out of Moselekatse's country, the
better it was likely to fare with ourselves.

The Matabili were fast receding in single file towards the Northern horizon, when we commenced
our retreat to the Southward; and crossing the river
by a natural causeway which formed a small cas-
cade, shaped our course along the bank. A verdant
meadow on which numerous Elands were grazing in
herds like tame cattle, stretched away before us, and
was traversed throughout its length, by the silver
stream of the tortuous Chonapas, winding between
fringes of waving bulrushes. The direction it assumed, convincing us that it must be a tributary of the
river to which we were journeying, we determined by
hugging the bank, to avoid the chance of passing the
night without water; and to guard as far as possible
against other misfortunes, a new order of march was
ordained—the oxen, horses, and sheep, being driven
close to the waggons *en masse*, and not suffered to
straggle as of yore.

We had proceeded some ten miles in this fashion,
when two human figures were descried at a distance,
accompanied by several dogs. Immediately on perceiving us, they concealed themselves beneath a bush,
and on our approach, fled in the greatest consternation, sitting gloomily down as " men without hope,"

when our horses were actually at their heels. Ex-
pecting nothing at our hands but instant death, these
miserable savages were not a little surprised at receiving a liberal supply of tobacco, and an invitation to
the waggons, where they feasted so heartly, that although anxious to accompany our party, they were
utterly, unable to keep pace. Before losing sight of
them we discovered that they were members of the
Barapootsa tribe, acknowledging an independent
King named *Bapootsa,* and occupying the hills at
the head of the Likwa; which river, they assured
us, we could not possibly reach before the next night.
In accordance with African caprice, which assigns a
parasol to the male instead of to the female sex,
these gentlemen were each provided with a long staff
decorated with the black body feathers of the Ostrich.
Besides affording protection from the sun's rays, these
implements not unfrequently prove serviceable in the
chase; and being stuck into the ground at the proper
moment, divert the attention of a charging Lion
from the object of his vengeance, and thus enable
the rest of the party, to rush in, and dispatch him
with their assagais.

By sunset, having abandoned two of the sick ox-
en, and accomplished twenty-five miles, our further
advance was prevented by the pack waggon sticking
fast in a morass. It was at length extricated at the
expense of a *trek-touw,* to repair which a tax was

levied on the hides of two Elands that were grazing in the neighbourhood, and we then drew up in a strong position, before an old stone enclosure, which served as a cattle pound, the rear being fortified by an isolated tumulus. Andries having confidently predicted some unpleasant occurrence, Cœur de Lion perched himself upon the summit of this eminence, and maintained another weary vigil throughout the night, the early half of which was illumined by a brilliant moon.

We commenced another forced march before day light on the 19th, still taking the course of the Chonapas for our guide. Several long strings of wild Buffaloes passed a-head of us on their way up from the river, and a Lion, with tail erect, was observed in full career after a troop of scouring Gnoos. The capricious distribution of animal forms, is no where more remarkable than in Africa, and to solve the mysterious causes by which it is influenced has long been reckoned among the most puzzling problems in the great scheme of the creation. As if by magic the Brindled Gnoo had suddenly given place during the last three days, to the common, or white tailed species, and not another specimen occurred during the remainder of our journey. Whilst hunting the *Wilde Beest,* as the latter species is termed by the

* *Anglice.* Wild Ox.

Cape Colonists, the abstraction already recorded of my
shoes by His Amazooloo Majesty, had nearly been the
cause of a serious disaster. In order to avoid the disagreeable alternative of walking barefooted, I had been
compelled to adopt a pair rudely manufactured of untanned hide; and the sole becoming entangled in the
stirrup, while, with both hands encumbered, I was in
the act of jumping off to administer the *coup de
grace,* I fell on my back; and the wounded animal
bellowing and struggling at the same instant, my
horse started off, and before I could extricate myself,
had kicked me severely on the knee and ancle, besides dragging me a sufficient distance over the loose
stones, to remove the whole of my clothes, and a
large portion of the skin from by back.

Merciless and repeated applications of the whip-
cord and double thong, enabled us with the loss of
another ox, to achieve twenty-five miles more by
four o'clock in the afternoon. The blue mountain
range, now on our left, had gradually assumed a
deeper and deeper tint, and as we advanced over the
trackless plain like a ship through the ocean, was
fast developing its rugged character. At length,
lifting up our eyes, we beheld before us afar off, a
long dark streak of bushes, stretching parallel to the
horizon, and marking the course of the stream of
which we were in search. Shouts of exultation burst
from the mouths of the Hottentots, as they sprang

from the waggon boxes from which they had been gazing, and cracked their long whips with encreased energy. The patient oxen broke into a trot—the object upon which all eyes were rivetted became better and better defined, our friendly pilot stream rapidly encreased in breath, and as the sun disappeared below the horizon, we were standing on the banks of the river Vaal.

This remote arm of the Gareep, or Great Orange river, forms the Southern limit of the territory to which Moselekatse lays claim. Rising nearly opposite to Delagoa bay, about three degrees to the Westward of that port, and joining the parent stream some two hundred and fifty geographical miles below the confluence of the Chonapas, it traverses the South African continent from East to West like a great artery, and discharges its waters into the Atlantic ocean. At the spot where we reached it, the breadth did not exceed one hundred and fifty yards, but the fresh deposition of rubbish on the bank, showed that the water had very lately risen at least ten feet above its present level—and from the strength and muddiness of the current, we were not a little apprehensive that it might be again flooded during the night, and obstruct our progress for many days. The absence nevertheless of any thing approaching to a practicable ford, obliged us to take cur chance.

The river was literally teeming with Hippopotami,

35

about forty of those amphibious monsters protruding their laughable countenances at the same time, and grampus-like, blowing a spout of muddy water as if in honor of our arrival. Although two Lions had been seen the moment before, the Hottentots, to a man, without unycking the oxen, left the waggons standing on the brink of the high bank, and rushed like school boys to the water's edge. A gigantic Hippopotamus was making directly for the shore by a succession of plunges, his broad snout appearing nearer and nearer, every time he rose, puffing to the surface. I was in the act of firing in at his garret window, when I perceived the tail of a couchant Lioness knocking angrily within a few yards of my foot. So completely was her attention engrossed by the waggons, that although close behind her, she did not perceive either Piet or myself, and was retiring, when one of the followers foolishly firing at her, she galloped back through the middle of our party, and being joined by a Lion disappeared among the bushes.

The savage loneliness of this wild spot, might well have constituted it the metropolis of *Feræ;* but in spite of all the warnings we had received, it was with the greatest difficulty, and not before we had set the example in person, that the perverse Hottentots could be induced to suspend hostilities against the *Zeekoes*, and construct a thorn fence for the security of the cattle. Scarcely was it completed before there set in a drenching and dismal night, which has left behind it, on my mind, an indelible impression. If the panorama that presented itself on our first arrival, had agreeably recalled to recollection the inconsistent medleys of a dream, the gloomy terrors of the night that now succeeded, might fitly be likened to an incubus. "Darkness that could be felt," and torrents of rain, accompanied by vivid flashes of lightning, and peals of deafening thunder, were rendered trebly terrible by the howling of the wind, the incessant snorting of Hippopotami in the river, and the prowling of Lions around our slender fortification. About midnight the affrighted oxen contrived to effect their escape, and after fruitless attempts to recover them, we were left in no very enviable plight, to muse, while we counted the tedious hours until morning, upon the improbability of our ever finding them again.

CHAPTER XXIX.

EXIT FROM MOSELEKATSE'S DOMINIONS, AND PAS-
SAGE ACROSS THE NAMA-HARI.

The twentieth of December, though it placed us
beyond the Matabili territories, was a day of exces-
sive toil, and but little progress. As soon as it was
light enough to see, Andries started on horseback
in quest of a ford; and all but one of the oxen having by the most unlooked-for good fortune, been recovered, we shortly afterwards moved down the river,
the waters of which had risen upwards of a foot during the night. After crossing many perilous ravines,
we at length became alarmed at the protracted non-
appearance of our scout, and had just resolved to
send back in search of him when he rejoined us, triumphantly bearing the teeth of a sea-cow—whilst
extracting which for his own private advantage, he
had unfortunately suffered his masters to overshoot,
by several miles, what he termed an admirable ford.
Retracing our steps to this spot, we found the current waist deep, the bank acclivitous, and the bed
strewed with large blocks of granite; but having
first taken the precaution of sending a horseman re-

peatedly across, we determined to attempt the passage   After much violent bumping, the leading
waggon reached the opposite side without any difficulty, but not so its consort. Owing to some mismanagement on the part of the driver, the luckless
"omnibus," when about half way over, became
firmly wedged between two masses of rock; and although every one stripped to the skin, and "applied
his shoulders to the wheel," three provoking hours
were passed in abortive attempts to extricate it.
Whips, shin-bones, and *trek-touws*, were alike fruit-
lessly broken, and fresh oxen repeatedly applied
without the smallest advantage; and the river rising
rapidly, we had almost despaired of saving our property, when cracks and yells, followed by the simul-
taneous struggling of twenty-four of our sturdiest
beasts, were answered by the grating of a wheel.
An interval of intense anxiety succeeded. One after another, the fore and hind nave on the same side,
rose slowly above the surface of the water, and the
fall of the slanting vehicle appeared inevitable. To
our joy, a sudden jerk restored it, tottering, to the
perpendicular—pair after pair of the long string of
oxen obtained their footing on the bank—once again
the whips resounded in the hollow, and the dripping
van emerged in safety from the flood.

Another hour had passed away before our little
flock of sheep could be reclaimed. These stubborn

animals, having in the first instance been forced into
the stream by dint of much pelting and persecution,
had been carried down a considerable distance; and,
as a matter of of course, whilst all hands were engaged in extricating the waggon, had strayed into the
thicket. At length every thing was ready. Little
dreaming of the distance that still divided them from
their beloved gin-shop, the Hottentots cheered and
fired a salute, as they turned their backs upon the
"yellow river," and upon the execrated dominions
of His beer-drinking Majesty.

We had not advanced more than three miles, before our progress was opposed by a furious storm of
hail and thunder. Many of the stones were half an
inch in diameter, and the oxen being unable to
face them, turned their backs to the pitiless shower
and stood in the yokes. With some difficulty we at
last gained the shelter of a neighbouring hill, in an
amphitheatre enclosed by which, we passed the night.
To Andries in particular, this friendly spot wore an
aspect of charmed interest, it having been described
by 'Lingap, with what truth I know not, as the scene
Truëy's enslavement. To me it is remarkable from
of the circumstance of my having there, for the last
time, seen and destroyed the Rhinoceros.

Thus far on our pilgrimage we had been directed
in some measure by the course of rivers and mountains, but during the remainder of our journey we

were to be guided by the compass alone. A perfectly unexplored country intervened betwixt us and the Colony, and the distance that we had travelled south of the known latitude of Moscga, convinced me that we were still much further from it than the maps would indicate. It was believed by the Hottentots, that a southerly course would have led us to Lishuani, the residence of Peter David, conjectured to be about one hundred and fifty miles from the present position. In order to reach the Missionary station of Phillipolis therefore, which was supposed to be rather less than double that distance, it was determined to adopt South-westerly route. Day after day as I pricked off on the chart the progress that we had made, was I strengthened in the opinion I had formed, and the sequel fully confirmed its correctness.

The first day we travelled over an uninterrupted plain strewed with small land tortoises, and covered with a profusion of gay flowers, amongst which the Marigold predominated. A sultry and tedious march of nine hours, brought us at length to a bog, with a scanty pool of excessively fetid mineral water, which nothing but the direst necessity could have induced us to taste. The number of animals collected in the vicinity first drew our attention to this treasure, which was surrounded by a clump of bulrushes, with a strong calcareous incrustation at their roots. So

exhausted were the oxen, after their three hours cold
bath the preceding day, that they would hardly have
reached this oasis, had the fresh scent of a Lion not
recruited their vigour.   However tired the poor
beasts might be, a sniff of one of their feline enemies
never failed to put them in the highest spirits.   Several Gnoos rushed with them to the water's edge, as
if to dispute their share, and I shot one from the
waggon; but in the total absence of fuel, we were
driven to the necessity of burning one of the spare
waggon poles, in order to cook a portion of the flesh.

A heavy dew fell during the night, and was followed by a dense fog, in spite of which we were fain to
decamp from this inhospitable bivouac, at an early
hour.   The face of the country here, so beautifully
clothed with herbage and flowers, would appear to
be kept fresh and verdant by these nightly dews and
humid mists, rather than by the partial showers
which, few and far between are wont to visit it.   The
being able to sleep in the open air with perfect im-
punity, is a convincing proof that in Africa, these
vapours are little prejudicial to health.   As the fog
dispersed, long files of Quaggas were observed moving across the distant profile of the plain, like a rival
caravan on its march; a range of mountains could
shortly afterwards be distinguished to the westward,
and about noon, the hawk-eyed Hottentots, who
possessed an extraordinary facility of detecting objects

at a distance, descried a troop of savages. Of the two parties, it is difficult to say which was thrown into the greatest consternation by the mutual discovery—but I can only aver, that while every preparation was making on our side for a gallant defence, the enemy were observed in ignominious retreat.

After we had advanced twenty-five miles, a long line of Karree trees darkening the horizon, proclaimed our approach to a river; and late in the afternoon to our surprise we struck upon a sudden bend of the Vaal river, which here winds abruptly between willowed banks round, a narrow peninsula, the neck of which is not more than six hundred yards across. The cavalcade was in the act of drawing up near some deserted Bushman wigwams, when three Lionesses leaped out of a bush immediately on our flank; and Piet, who declared that he could discern the head of a fourth, having cracked his long whip forth there stalked also a venerable Lion, evidently subdued and enfeebled by years. A bullet discharged at him from the waggon box, having penetrated the patriarch's shoulder, he thrust his hoary head into a bush, and was gathered unto his fathers. It was not, however, until Richardson, with a party on horseback, had tested his demise by repeated vollies, that his remains were dragged out for inspection.

My knee was still so painful from the effect of the kick I had received, that I was unable to mount a

36

horse. The task of providing food for the followers, had therefore devolved principally upon my fellow *voyageur*. Elands were still abundant, and as a *dernier resort* we had upwards of twenty sheep left, notwithstanding the ravages committed on our herd by wild beasts. The hardiness evinced by our little flock became daily more the theme of admiration, an instance of foot soreness rarely occurring during the longest march. When it did, the cripple either rode in the omnibus, or was placed at the disposal of the fire-worshipper, at whose hands it had little mercy to expect. The prevailing scarcity of fuel in this part of the country, induced us to take in a good supply before again leaving the river; and in order to make room for it, and relieve the oxen as much as possible; nearly all their necks having been rendered raw by drawing in wet yokes, we threw out every article that could possibly be dispensed with, amongst the most bulky of which was a large supply of *Zekoe fat,* commissioned by our friends in the Colony.

On the 23d, having skirted the river about five miles, we unexpectedly found ourselves at the embouchure of one of its principal tributaries, the Nama Hari or Donkin, a river which takes its source one hundred and fifty miles to the Eastward, midway between Port Natal and Delagoa bay, in the great mountain range that divides Caffraria from the Bechuana country. The point of confluence of these streams is situated at the very apex of the bend already described; and the meeting of their troubled waters, rolling towards each other from opposite points of the compass, was an imposing and unusual spectacle. As we were witnessing it from the brink of the precipitous and well rounded scarp, which forms the salient angle, *Behemoth* at intervals thrust out his broad snout for a moment to gaze at us, or suddenly emerging with a snort and splash, from beneath the belt of Chaldean willows* which graced the opposite shore, plunged his shapeless bulk into the flood. About sunset, having advanced ten miles up the right bank of the Nama Hari without discovering a ford, we halted at a spot where the banks might with some labor have been pared down sufficiently to admit of our waggons crossing; but our scouts discovering a practicable road two miles higher up, we were fortunately spared the trouble.

Two hours toil the following morning placed us safely on the Southern bank of the Nama Hari; and after filling up our water casks, and endeavouring to persuade the cattle to drink their fill, which at so early an hour they refused to do, we resumed a South-westerly course, and again made sail over the interminable plain. Our attention was presently

* Salix Babylonica.

arrested by the fresh *spoor* of several horsemen in
pursuit of Elands; and some of the Hottentots, feeling convinced that the hunters would prove to be a
band of Bastards from Lishuani, determined to follow
them, and enquire the news. A few hours afterwards, however, they returned in dismay, with the intelligence that they had unexpectedly come upon a
spot near the river, where the ground was spread
with human skeletons as with a table-cloth, under
which circumstances they had thought it prudent to
return.

The day was distressingly sultry, and by the
time we had advanced twenty-five miles, three more
of our invalid oxen had been left to perish. Tanta-
lized by the dancing mirage, we had scoured the
country in every direction, without being able to discover a drop of water, although the thirsty earth
was seamed with dry tanks and gullies. Late in the
afternoon, still plodding our weary way over the
cheerless expanse, we were vainly listening for the
melodious croaking of some friendly frog, which
alone was likely to be the index to the element we
required, when our eyes were unexpectedly greeted
by a waggon road. The appearance of the deeply
ploughed ruts, the first that we had seen since
leaving Tolaan, showed that upwards of twenty
laden vehicles had passed about twelve months before,
during a fall of rain. Trusting that they might lead

us to water, we followed them as long as day light
lasted.   Then the sky became overcast, and flashes
of lightning, at short intervals, showing us something on the verge of the horizon which loomed
like a thick bush, we persevered towards it.   Alas!
like the delusive lakes in the morning, it was meta-
morphosed on our approach, into a few dwarf shrubs
barely a foot in height.   Unable to proceed further,
we halted in the middle of the bleak and exposed
heath without either fuel or water beyond the scanty
supply in the waggons.   The sheep were placed in
a circle formed by haltering the horses together;
and to prevent the oxen from straying, we were
compelled to secure them to the waggon wheels,
although the unfortunate beasts had passed twelve
hours in the yoke, without tasting a morsel of food.

CHAPTER XXX

THREE DAYS' SOLITARY WANDERING IN THE WILDERNESS.

CHRISTMAS day was pregnant with an event, which for some time cast a dismal gloom over the party, and had nearly caused my separation from it during the remainder of the journey. Three hours before that festive morn had dawned upon us, our search for water was renewed—the moon enabling us to trace the waggon road, although at every step it was becoming less and less distinct. Arriving as the day broke, at the summit of a gentle ascent, which here disturbing the monotony of the otherwise uniformly level flat, had obstructed our view to the Southward, another vast landscape presented itself to our gaze. Endless meads, clad in a vernal and variegated robe of gay but scentless flowers, in whose presence the desert seemed to smile, spreading away before us, exhibited the motley confusion of a Turkey carpet. One isolated tumulus stood like a pine-apple in the centre, and in the distance, three rectangular table topped mountains, of singularly uniform appearance, reminded the spectator of terraced barrack-rooms—shooting boxes perhaps,

erected by the giants of olden times.   Hair brained
Gnoos, careering over the plain, hailed our advance
—now stopping inquisitively to scrutinize the waggons—then lashing their dark sides with their snowy
tails, as they hastily retreated.   Large troops of
Blesbucks,* or White faced Antelopes, a pied species that we had rarely met with before, likewise
chequered the scene; and with herds of Springbucks,
Quaggas, and Ostriches, announced the proximity of
water.   Presently, to our delight, we descried a
"reed encircled fountain" at which after twenty-
eight hours of total abstinence, the dying oxen were
enabled to slake their terrible thirst.   A strong calcareous deposit adhering to the vegetation, rendered
the water extremely bitter to the taste, and it was
by the exercise of the long whips alone that the
cattle were prevented from plunging into the pool,
before our casks had been filled.

The accidental, but important discovery of portions of a broken yoke key, here enabled the Hottentots to decide the knotty and long argued question, whether the outward bound tracks upon which
we were proceeding, were those of Dutch, or of
Griqua waggons.   Opinion being now unanimous in
favor of the former, it was determined to follow them
as long as they should preserve a South-westerly

* *Gazella Albifrons.*   Delineated in the African Views.

direction. The total absence of fuel obliged us after
an hour's halt, to continue our march over numerous
salt-pans, upon which herds of Blesbucks were busily licking the chrystalized efflorescence. Alarmed
at our approach, vast troops of them were continually sweeping past against the wind, carrying their
broad white noses close to the ground like a pack of
harriers in full cry. Never having killed any of
these Antelopes, and our stock of provisions requiring to be recruited, I mounted *Breslar*, my favorite
Rozinante, and never heeding whither I sped, dashed
into the thick of them. The pine-apple hill bore
east about five miles, and I fancied was a never failing land mark to direct my return to the road, which
although faint, could readily be distinguished by a
practised eye. Dealing death around, I continued to
scour the plain, the herd before me increasing from
hundreds to thousands, and reinforcements still pouring in from all directions, when crying "Hold,
enough," I stayed my hand from slaughter. Having divested some of the slain from their brilliant
party colored robes, and packed the *spolia* on my
horse, I set out to rejoin the waggons, but ah! how
vainly did I seek for them. Again and again I strain-
ed my eyes for the road, and cantered to and fro between the string of frosted salt-pans, and the little hill,
which, floating in the sea of mirage that environed
me, seemed as if poised in the sky. The monotony

of the landscape baffled all my attempts at recognition, and my search was utterly fruitless. Every
feature of the cone was precisely the same—the table mountains were completely obscured by the
vapour—and in the constant recurrence of similar
forms, I lost the points of the compass, and at last
became totally bewildered.

To retrace my steps over plains so trampled by
innumerable herds was clearly impossible. At one
moment as if in mockery, a solitary Quagga, magni-
fied ten thousand times by the treacherous mirage,
loomed like the white tilt of a waggon; but my joy
at the supposed discovery was invariably followed by
the bitterest disappointment. Again a group of
pigmy Bushwomen, walking unnoticed among a herd
of Blesbucks, and seen through the same deceptive
medium, personated our followers with the cattle.
Alas! these too fled at my approach, and jabbered
like baboons when I had overtaken them. Several
hours had thus passed in idle search. Spent by fatigue and anxiety, my parched tongue rattling like a
board against the palate of my mouth, I wandered on
over flowery wastes, still lengthening as I advanced.
Dry tanks surrounded by a garden of pinks and
marigolds, served only to increase my sufferings,
but neither fount, nor pool, nor running stream,
greeted my straining gaze. At length the refraction
dissipating with the declining day, the three table-

topped mountains became again visible in the horizon.   With the consoling reflection that at all events
I was now advancing in the same direction as the
caravan, I hastened forward, and before dusk, found
myself not a little revived by a draught of the clearest water from a serpentine river flowing to the Westward; the banks of which were trimmed with reeds
and dwarf willows, while portions of its sandy bed
were imprinted with the heavy foot-steps of a troop
of Lions.

The mind becomes even more readily habituated
to hardship and suffering than the body.   Every
thing around me was vague and conjectural, and
wore an aspect calculated to inspire despondency;
yet I no sooner became convinced that I was actually
lost in the heart of a howling wilderness, inhabited
if at all, by barbarous and hostile tribes; than I felt
fully prepared to meet the emergency.   The setting
sun having given me the bearing of the table mountains, considerably to the Westward of South, it was
evident, that without being aware of it, I had crossed
the road, and ridden too far to the Eastward.   In the
hope of yet retrieving my error, I hurried down the
river as fast as possible, but night closing in, I was fain
to prepare for a bivouack among the bushes.   The
stars were completely concealed behind a clouded sky,
and repeated flashes of lightning were accompanied by

distant thunder. Having completed all my preparations, I was listening with breathless attention for the
cracking of a whip, or the signal guns which I knew
would be fired from the waggons, when to my inexpressible delight, a joyous beacon fire shone suddenly
forth on the river. Upon consideration, I felt puz-
zled to account for its appearance in a spot which I
had so recently passed, but concluding that the
waggons had subsequently arrived there, I laid the
flattering unction to my soul, and groped my way
towards it. My disappointment and disgust may
better be imagined than described when by the light
of the fire, I discovered a gang of Bushmen with
their imp-like squaws, carousing over a carcase. I
slunk silently back to my den, fully impressed with
the necessity of remaining perfectly quiet, but scarcely hoping that my horse would be so fortunate as to
escape the observation of these lynx-eyed vagabonds.

The uneasy snorting of my unfotunate steed, and
his constant efforts to get loose, soon apprised me
of the presence of Lions at no great distance to
windward, but the fear of attracting my two legged
enemies to the spot prevented my kindling a fire for
his protection, or even for dressing a *Koorhaan** with
which I had taken care to provide myself. Dying of

* Florican.

hunger, and my "girdle of famine"* tightened to the last hole, I felt strangely tempted to devour my Christmas repast uncooked. About midnight however, having prepared a deep oven, I ventured to light a fire, and the fowl being duly baked and disposed of, I presently betook myself to sleep.

The following morning set in with tremendous rain. Drenched, cold, and cramped, I arose from my aquatic bed, and at once perceived that all hope of finding the trail of our waggons was at an end. The soil consisting chiefly of a red loamy earth from which the faintly marked tracks were easily obliterated, I resolved to follow the course of the river several miles further, to the Westward; and then, should I fail in finding the waggons, to cross the country in a direct line to the conical hill, which was still a conspicuous land mark—thus certainly intersecting the road, if indeed any traces of it remained, of which I began to be doubtful. To this programme I rigorously adhered, walking the greater part of the way to save my harrassed steed, upon whose back I now comtemplated the probability of having to seek my way to the Colony—a probability which was mightily increased about sunset, when I found myself preparing to perfect my acquaintance with the cone, by roosting on its summit,

"In a deep cave dug by no mortal hand."

---

* The leathern strap worn round the waist is called by the savages a *Lambele* strap, or hunger girdle.

During this second day's weary pilgrimage, scorched by the ardent and reflected rays of a summer sun, I arrived at an extensive pond covered with water lilies, and bordered by a broad belt of flags and rushes. Hastily approaching the margin, I became suddenly ingulfed in a pit fall, six feet in depth, filled with mire and water, from which I extricated myself with inconceivable difficulty. On recovering my shoes out of the stiff blue clay at the bottom, I perceived that the whole tank was closely invested by a chain of these traps, which had been carefully covered over by my friends the Bushmen. Having shot a Springbuck, I here scorched enough of the flesh to satisfy the cravings of hunger, and slinging a fine fat leg on either side of the saddle took up my night's lodging as already described, without having been able to discover the smallest traces of the road.

The night was serene and starlight. From the top of my strong hold I looked out upon the tranquil expanse beneath me, and listened for hours to catch some friendly melody that might direct my bewildered footsteps. Where, alas! was the "busy hum of men?" The shrill neighing of the Wild Ass, the bleat of the timid Springbuck, or the bellow of the Gnoo, with the deep-drawn distant sighing of a prowling Lion, occasionally borne along upon the breeze, alone disturbed the grave-like stillness of the wilderness! Seriously did I now debate with myself upon the propriety of making for the Colony, instead of prolonging my search. It is true that every thing betwixt me and it was wrapped in uncertainty, and that to arrive there I should have to pass alone through an unknown and inhospitable region, but on the other hand, I had already done all that human ingenuity could devise without the smallest success. I estimated my distance from the New Hantam, to be about two hundred miles; and being well provided with ammunition, there was a fair prospect of my being able to reach that district in six or seven days, unless the scarcity of game should oblige me to sacrifice my steed. Taking into consideration however, the long and dismal state of uncertainty that the measure would entail upon my companion, I finally determined to make one more huntsman-like cast, before giving up the search in despair.

Another day dawned, and again I saddled my trusty beast, and struck into the pathless waste, intending to make a wide sweep to the Northward and Westward, where it was possible that rain might not have fallen. About noon, lifting up my eyes from the ground, on which they had vainly sought for any indication of the party having passed, to my inexpressible joy and delight, I recognised the sedge-grown fountain at which we had breakfasted on Christmas morning! Vaulting into the saddle, I eagerly dashed towards the spot, and in-

stantly hit upon the trail of our waggons, steadily
following up which, I shortly fell in with a party of
Bechuana of both sexes, who proved to be members
of the remnant of a tribe called Lihoya, and were
engaged in eating up a Blesbuck that had been
caught in one of their pit-falls. Having, through the
agency of a broken cigar, negociated a treaty of
alliance with these terrified savages, who as usual
had fled on perceiving me, I pointed to the wheel-
tracks, and gave them by signs to understand that I
was in search of my waggons. They instantly understood my meaning, and holding up both hands,
pointed to the Western horizon. The ladies, although very nervous at first, had in the mean time
conceived a violent attachment for the brass buttons
of my jacket—pointing to them, and repeatedly exclaiming with dry mouths, " *Tullana, Tullana!* " *
Upon my presenting these, together with a knife with
which their amputation had been performed, they
became perfectly insane, and declared their intention
of accompanying me in person for the purpose of
receiving further presents. Placing myself under
the willing guidance of this savage party, I struck
across the plain, and in the course of another hour
was within sight of the waggons. Jaded and way-
worn, it was with profound gratitude to a protecting

---

* *Anglice,* Buttons, buttons!

Providence, that I thus found myself restored to the cafila, after three days of anxious wandering over an unexplored and inhospitable wilderness.

Great was the anxiety, and many were the dismal forebodings to which my mysterious absence had given birth. A general gloom had pervaded the camp, and it was conjectured that I had reached "that bourne, whence no traveller returns." There being no fuel with which to kindle a beacon fire, whips had been cracked, and musquets discharged at inter-vals, both during the day and night; and my horse's *spoor* having been completely effaced by the rain, three separate parties had gone out in search of me, in different directions. Those only who have ex-perienced the warm cordiality which grows up be-tween partners in so wild and adventurous an ex-pedition as that in which my companion and myself had embarked, are capable of fully understanding the nature of the welcome I received—the sensations created by my safe and unhoped-for return even ex-tending themselves to the disaffected of our followers. On comparing notes with my fellow traveller, I was concerned to find that in some respects he had scarcely fared better than myself—the knuckle bone of a tainted ham, and a cup full of dirty water, having constituted his Christmas dinner.

CHAPTER XXXI.

JOURNEY RESUMED, TO THE 'GY KOUP, OR VET
RIVIERE OF THE EMIGRANTS.

Misfortunes, according to the old adage, never
come singly; and I have assuredly no grounds for
recording a special exception to the rule in our favor.
Shortly after my restoration on the 27th, the sudden
brewing of a whirlwind, or more properly speaking,
of a *simoom* in miniature, whilst it caused the partial destruction of one of the waggon awnings, led
also to the temporary loss of our live stock; the natural consequence of the latter calamity being, that
one of the best oxen fell into a pit, and two of the
sheep into the maw of the Hyæna. This extra-
nary squall of dust and gravel, which raged as if all
inanimate nature had been stirred into commotion,
was the forerunner of a thunder storm, that lasted
the greater part of the night, and ultimately gave
place to a drenching and steady rain during the
whole of the following day. Towards evening, our
allies, the Lihoya, honestly brought in the remaining
sheep, and our position being very exposed, we made
an attempt to reach the river; but after travelling
five miles were compelled to halt at a puddle of rain

water, where we passed the dreary wet night of the
28th as we had spent its predecessor, without either
fuel or shelter.

The next morning brought us to the scene of my
bivouack on Christmas night, and according to my
prediction, we experienced no little difficulty in
discovering a spot where the capriciously winding
river might be crossed. The interval was turned to
account by Cœur de Lion in cooking provisions,
a man having been sent in advance to collect fuel,
which however proved to be abundant. At length
the exploring parties returned—one of them having
discovered a practicable ford two miles higher up
the stream, whilst the other had fallen in, to the
Westward, with the skeletons of several horses, together with some fresh human remains, which, from the
dimension of the *crania* they declared to be those of
Dutch Boors. A favorite wheel-ox, that had fallen
sick the preceding day, being now unable to proceed
further, Claas, at his own request, was permitted to
put the unfortunate beast out of its misery—a task
which he accomplished in five clumsy shots.

The perpendicular character of the bank, rendered
a *skid*, or as it it termed by the Colonists, a *remscoen*,
necessary upon each hind wheel, in addition to the
drag-chain; but even after this precaution, the weight
of the vehicles caused them to descend with frightful
velocity. Safely arrived at the bottom, the long

waggon presently settled down to the axle in a
quicksand, the team also sinking to their bellies;
and it was not until our remaining supply of flour and
sugar had been spoiled in the water, during an attempt
which was made to drag the van out backwards, that
the latter was at length unloaded, and towed on
shore by the application of a twenty-four ox power.
In commemoration of this disaster, the treacherous
stream was christened by the Hottentots, *Sant
Riviere*, or sand river, by which homely designation
it will be recognised in the map, as a tributary of the
Likwa.

We had not advanced above ten miles, before a
violent storm of hail and rain obliged us again to
halt in the open heath. Piet, who had gone in advance to reconnoitre, lost his way, and did not rejoin
the party until midnight, having at length been attracted by the signals made, and by Coeur de Lion's kitch-
en fire, which on account of the weather, had with
considerable difficulty been kindled in an ant hill.
The country over which we passed, was usually covered with dome-shaped mounds of clay, thrown up
by the pismire, and invariably scooped out either by
the long nails of the ant eater, or by Bushmen, so as
resemble a baker's oven. In wet weather especially,
or during a dearth of fuel, these mounds were our
stoutest allies; but on the other hand, the Hottentots not unfrequently put the strength of our waggons to the test by driving carelessly over them.

Two distinct animals are found in this part of the country, that alike burrow in the ground, and appear to subsist entirely upon ants and termites, leaving upon every habitation thrown up by those minute insects, unequivocal marks of their desolating visits. Of these the Ant-bear, or *Aard vark** of the Colonists, is the more common; it is from six to seven feet in extreme length, covered with coarse brown hair, and furnished with a slimy, flexible tongue, capable of being protruded to the extent of eighteen or twenty inches, beyond the attenuated snout. It possesses the singular peculiarity of walking, or rather hobbling, upon the sides instead of upon the soles, of its fore-feet. The latter are provided with four robust nails, which form a complete rake, and with which the animal digs into the bowels of the mound, its taper tongue being always in readiness to seize the swarming inmates as fast as they issue from their beleaguered abode.

Although differing greatly in external appearance, the equipments as well as the habits, of the second species, are essentially the same. Seen from a distance the *Pangolin*, or Manis, † might easily be mistaken for a small Alligator. The upper parts of the body are clad in a complete suit of flexible armour, consisting of numerous stout horny scales, overlapping each other like the tiles of a house, and

---

* *Orycteropus Capensis.*   † *Manis Temminckii.*

presenting an appearance precisely similar to the bark of the brab tree. Possessing also, the power of of rolling itself into a ball like a hedgehog, this otherwise defenceless animal is at once rendered perfectly invulnerable to the attacks of its foes.

The soil in this neighbourhood was black; and owing to the great quantity of rain that had fallen during the night, we found ourselves fairly water-logged in the morning. This was considered a rare opportunity for breaking in some of the oxen that had never yet bowed their stiff necks to the yoke, and their rebellious spirits once subdued by the un-sparing administration of the whip, they presently dragged us out of our difficulties. Ascending gradu-ally to the base of the three table mountains, which like natural buttresses protruded their bold outlines into the monotonous landscape, an extensive and stir-ring prospect burst upon our astonished gaze. Gone were the level plains, over which the lingering eye had wandered for days without once finding an object upon which it could repose. Hill and dale, moun-tain and valley, stretched away at our feet in fair variety, terminated in the remote horizon by the craggy summits of the well known *Wittebergen*— those

> " Sterile mountains, rough and steep,
> That bound abrupt the valley deep,
> Heaving to the clear, blue, sky
> Their ribs of granite, bare and dry."

Half crazy with delight, and never dreaming of the distance that still intervened, or the troubles that were yet in store, every one instantly affected to recognise some landmark with which he was familiar; and whilst many actually talked themselves into a belief that they could distinguish the smoke from the missionary's chimney at Phillipolis, still one hundred and fifty miles distant, Andries positively asserted that a line of bushes which skirted the remaining portion of level land, was the *Modder Riviere.*

As we gradually descended towards this stream of promise, which ultimately proved to the 'Gy Koup, or Vet riviere of the Emigrants—rising near the missionary station of Umpukani, and also a tributary to the Likwa—we passed over a low tract about eight or ten miles in extent, strongly impregnated with salt, and abounding in lakes and pools. The number of wild animals congregated on this swampy flat, almost realised fable; the roads made by their incessant tramp, resembling so many well travelled highways. At every step incredible herds of Bontebucks,* Blesbucks, and Springbucks, with troops of Gnoos, and squadrons of the common, or stripeless, Quagga, were performing their complicated evolutions; and not unfrequently, a knot of Ostriches decked in their white plumes played the part of ge-

---

* *Gazella Pygarga.* Delineated in the African Views.

neral officer and staff with such strict propriety, as
still further to remind the spectator of a cavalry
review. Late in the afternoon, we struck into a
waggon track, and crossed the river by a made road,
to a deserted camp of the Emigrant farmers, whose
temporary reed huts formed so inviting a shelter, that
it was resolved to halt for a day—as well for the purpose of recruiting the oxen, three more of which
were unable to proceed from the effects of distemper, as to manufacture a new *trek-touw*, wash our
linen, eject the host of ticks which had taken possession of the waggons, and give the Hottentots an
opportunity of dancing in the new year.

Together with the old year, we had fairly bidden
adieu to the great plains of the Vaal river, which to
the traveller appear to be completely taken possession of by wild animals, and may with strict propriety be termed the domain of savage nature. A
region to the perception as vast and trackless as the
ocean, and like it presenting an undisturbed horizon,
is spread out, from the Cashan mountains, into one
level and treeless expanse of serene and sunny plain.
In vain we seek for the bewitching variety of hill or
dale, forest or glade, which constitutes the charm of
landscape—the eye wanders on without the smallest
check over endless flats, which are utterly wearisome
from their extent and monotony. Yet nature has endeavored in some measure to supply the deficiency,

by decking them out in her gayest flowers, and in some of the most eccentric and attractive forms that exist in the vegetable world. The chandelier plant, and purple amaryllis, with many other splendid bulbs, grow wild in profusion; and being interspersed with geraniums, a several species of the cactus, and an endless variety of the succulent green-house plant, called the Hottentot fig, literally impart to the waste the appearance of a flower garden.

The monotony of this extraordinary wilderness, is at length broken in upon by the Wittebergen, or Quathlamba mountains, a broad basaltic belt that skirts the Eastern coast at a distance varying from sixty to ninety miles for the shore, and divides Caffraria from Bechuana land. This wild chaos of rocks and cliffs—of barren ridges and towering peaks, worn by time into castellated fortresses, and other fantastic shapes, resembles the ruins of a world; and being intersected by yawning chasms, offers an impassable barrier. Both the Caledon, and the Nu-Gareep, take their source in this vast chain, and its wild fastnesses not only afford shelter to the *Manta-tees* under King Sikonyela, and to many other broken tribes who have been driven from their native homes by " war's alarms"—but they have lately been discovered by adventurous French Missionaries, to be the haunts of two Cannibal tribes, called the *Barimo* and *Ba-Mahakana*.

December and January constituting the hottest season, we crossed the plains of the Vaal river at the proper time for suffering all the inconvenience of rain, without enjoying any of its advantages. In common with other countries remote from the sea coast, this portion of the continent receives its rain in thunder showers during the summer months; and there being none during the rest of the year, the climate, notwithstanding frequent nocturnal dews, is characterised by extreme aridity. The sun shines with matchless splendor through a sky of delicious blue, which is rarely visited by a cloud; and during his meridian blaze over a level expanse, in many parts strongly impregnated with salt, the delusion of mirage is nowhere more perfect. Optical lakes impart to the wanderer fevered with thirst, the torments of Tantalus; yet even on these naked plains he will experience none of the debilitating fervor of an Indian sun.

Although thinly populated by skulking broods of Bushmen, and by the starving remnants of nomadic pastoral tribes, which have been broken up by war and violence, this is a land in which no man permanently dwells—neither is the soil any man's property, being abandoned as water or fuel fails. Nearly all the rivers by which it is traversed are periodical, and the few pools that exist, being dried up at certain seasons, the miserable wretches, whose existence depends upon the wild animals,

39

migrate with them to distant parts, keeping within the verge of expiring verdure. Amongst the savage nations of South Africa, as elsewhere, a principle of extinction has for ages past been in active operation. Regions now silent and deserted, once contained their busy throng, whose numbers and strength have been gradually brought down by war and want. Whole tribes have been rooted out from their hereditary homes, and have either disappeared from the face of the earth, or, pursued by the " gaunt and bony arm" of famine, still wander with fluctuating fortunes over these measureless tracts. For hundreds of miles therefore, the eye is not greeted by the smallest trace of human industry, or by any vestige of human habitation—the wild and interminable expanse ever presenting the same appearance—that of one vast, uninhabited solitude.

CHAPTER XXXII.

PLUNDERED BY BUSHMAN HORDES, AND LEFT A
WRECK IN THE DESERT.

Resuming our pilgrimage on the morning of the
1st January 1837, our road wound among singular
groups of detached hills, which wore the appearance
of having accidentally fallen there after the formation of the plain; blue peaks and mountain ridges
stretching along the horizon, and deepening their
tints as we advanced. Again, the valleys were spread,
as with flocks of sheep, with countless herds of
graceful Springbucks, displaying the snowwhite folds
on their haunches while they vaulted over each others
heads; and for the first time since quitting the Colony, several Secretary birds were now observed strutting about the plain, in search of snakes, upon which
reptiles they principally subsist. In many places the
ground was strewed with the blanched skeletons of
Gnoos and other wild animals, which had evidently
been slaughtered by Bushmen, and the traces of
these *Troglodytes* waxed hourly more apparent, as
the country became more inhabitable; the base of
one hill in particular, in which some of their caves
were discovered, presenting the appearance of a

Golgotha—several hundred Gnoos and Bontibucks' skulls being collected in a single heap.

The Bontibuck is the twentieth and last known species of the Antelope tribe* that is to be met with in Southern Africa, remote from the sea-coast. It was formerly common in the Cape Colony, and a few are even still preserved in the district of Swellendam, a fine of five hundred Rix Dollars being attached to their destruction, unless by special licence from Government. In point of shape and size, the Bontibuck bears a close resemblance to the Blesbuck, being equally robust, humpbacked and broad nosed; but it is more remarkably piebald, the legs being perfectly white, and the horns black, instead of being light colored. The two animals have in common, a broad blaze down the face, a *glazed* blue back, and fiery red eyes. The horns are placed vertically on the summit of the head, and both species alike invariably scour against the wind, with their noses close to the ground. Numbers of these Antelopes had fallen to our rifles during the last few days, and several of the common Quagga also. That quadruped had now entirely supplanted Burchell's

---

* I have retained the term *Antelope* as applied to the Eland, Gnoo, Koodoo, and others, with the view of avoiding confusion. The.modern classification of these animals will be found in the Appendix.

Zebra, and its flesh although infinitely more yellow, rank, and oily than that of a horse, was greatly esteemed by the Hottentots.

During this part of our journey, I again met with the Oryx, or Gemsbok, which splendid Antelope has been described in an early chapter of my narrative, as the animal that in ·all probability gave birth to the figure of the fabulous Unicorn. When seen *en profile*, the long straight horns so exactly cover each other, that the existence of two might almost be doubted; and whilst rude delineations in this posture, have been discovered in many of the Bushman caves, the Algazel, a corresponding species in North Africa, is to be found similarly represented on the sculptured monuments of ancient Egypt and Nubia. The Oryx is a powerful and dangerous antagonist, charging viciously, and defending itself when hard pressed, with wonderful intrepidity and address. Its skeleton has not unfrequently been found locked in that of a Lion—the latter having been transfixed by its formidable horns, in a conflict which has proved fatal to both the combatants.

With the Ostrich,* which was usually common during our journey, I conclude my notice of objects that especially interest the sportsman. Miserably mounted as we were, any attempt to overtake this

---

* *Struthio Camelus.* Delineated in the African Views.

gigantic bird would have been vain, but a shot could always be obtained at arm's length by galloping to a point in the course it had selected, and from which it rarely swerved. The male bird often measures nine feet at the crown of the head, and exceeds three hundred pounds in weight—the thigh being equal in size to the largest leg of mutton. Excepting the costly white plumes, so prized by the fair sex, and which are chiefly obtained from the wing, instead of from the tail, as generally imagined, the color of the body is the deepest black in the male bird, and in the female a dingy brown. While running, the wings are raised above the back, and the clatter of the feet, which are only provided with two toes, resembles that made by a horse in trotting. The Bechuana, with what truth I know not, are said occasionally to domesticate this bird for equestrian purposes; and the puny Bushman avails himself of the disguise afforded by its skin, to mix with a troop of wild animals, and select his victim. At the twang of his tiny bow, away scours the herd in dire consternation, and more alarmed than all, off scuds the impostor with them, again propelling a shaft as soon as the panic has subsided. The destruction committed in this manner is incredible—a slender reed, only slightly tipped with bone or iron, but imbued with a subtle poison, and launched with unerring dexterity, being sufficient to destroy the most powerful animal.

Late in the afternoon, as we were journeying,
several imp-like figures of human form, were observed
through a telescope, making with all despatch for
a neighbouring hill, the summit of which was crowded with them. Anxious to obtain information regarding our position, we halted the caravan, and
made friendly signs to induce the wild beings to approach. After warily reconnoitring us from their
fastnesses, nine of them at length ventured down, and
having replied to our questions in fear and trembl-
ing, received some tobacco, and retreated. Their
intercourse being conducted with such circumspec-
tion, the sum total of intelligence gained was, that
Piet Whitefoot, the Coranna Captain, resided about
three days' journey to the Westward. At sunset, having advanced twenty miles, we crossed a small stream,
and drew up on the bank, making the whole of
the cattle fast to the waggons, lest they should fall
into the hands of the Lilliputians, several of whose
watch fires were visible on the surrounding hills.

The following morning we unyoked for half an
hour at a small river, near a nest which contained
upwards of thirty women. These gypsies as usual,
approached the waggons with great familiarity, pointing to the flatness of their stomachs, and suing for
tobacco, which luxury was doled out to them by the
inch. Twenty miles more brought us to another
deserted camp of the Emigrant farmers, in which

amongst other interesting marks of human labor, stood a lofty scaffolding, used in the manufacture of *riems* or leathern halters. Hence, a made road led us across a stream of considerable size, pronounced by the followers, with their usual sagacity, to be the *Reit* river, although subsequently it was discovered to be the *Modder*, rising near the Missionary station of Thaba Uncha, and joining the Likwa a little above the *embouchure* of the Nu Gareep. The sheep having been placed in a deep pit to prevent them from straying, were visited during the night by a party of Hyænas, which slaughtered three, and drove the residue to the summit of a high hill, where they were found the following morning.

Having travelled until dark on the 3d without being able to discover any water, we halted in a wide plain under an isolated hill, which, it will be seen, was destined to be the scene of sad disaster and anxiety. A party of Bushwomen who had their den among the rocks at its base, presently arrived, bringing fuel and eatable wild roots for barter. One of them, whose foot measured barely four inches in length, was a most bewitching creature, and completely turned the heads of the Hottentots. Besides being far more elaborately embellished with red clay and ornaments of fat—and perhaps even more redolent of villainous smells than any lady we had hitherto seen, this Venus carried a jackal's tail by way of a pocket

handkerchief, and spoke the mellifluous Dutch language with surprising fluency.   It appeared that she
had effected her escape from a Boor residing in the
Sneuwebergen, whose slave she had been from in-
fancy; but we could elicit little information of value,
beyond the existence of a dirty pool about two miles
distant, whither the cattle were immediately driven.

Since leaving the Cashan mountains, one or two
of our oxen had been almost daily abandoned; but
including *Mutlee,* the old cow, and a dwarf bull—
neither of which royal gifts could be worked in the
teams—we were still the proprietors of thirty-eight
of sorts.   They had fasted the preceding night, and
the plain being very open, we left them to graze in
a verdant hollow from which it did not appear probable that they would stray.   About midnight however,
the roar of a lion being followed by a general rush
towards the waggons, Andries was appointed to keep
watch; but spent with fatigue he did not preserve his
vigil long, and the consequence was that at day-break
not an ox was to be seen.   This being an event of
every day occurrence created so little uneasiness at
first, that Andries whose business it also was to look
for them, instead of atoning for his carelessness by
a suitable display of activity, took his leisure to indulge in a little more gossip with the pretty Bush girl,
who very knowingly persuaded him that she had seen
the cattle not a quarter of a mile off, only a minute

40

before. In the course of an hour however, the Hottentots who had gone out to look for them, returned for horses—the appearance of the trail leading them to believe that the oxen had been chased by Lions. Owing to some intestine feuds and jealousies, difficult to be explained, Piet alone obtained a steed, but Andries and Cobus were also mounted the moment we discovered the real state of affairs, and although much valuable time had been unnecessarily thrown away, still no doubt was entertained that the oxen would eventually be re covered. All that day however, and part of the next were passed it a state of anxiety and suspense. During the night it rained a deluge, and about 2 P. M. on the 5th, Piet returned, empty handed for ammunition, or rather for no reason at all, having left the other two men upon the tracks, which still indicating a chase—led in the direction of some distant hills. Owing to the hardness of the ground, he had been unable to discover the cause of the panic.

In this posture of affairs, I determined to proceed in person without another moment's delay, and whilst mounting my horse, faithfully promised my comrade not to show my face again until I had recovered our cattle. Alas! it was destined that I should not redeem my pledge. I had cantered about eight miles, less than half way to the hills, when Andries and Cobus were descried approaching at speed, with

the dismal intelligence that the oxen were in the hands
of a troop of Bushmen, occupying the summit of the
nearest hill, whence one of the pigmies, in broken
Dutch, had challenged the gallant equestrians to do
them battle. Cobus, who the morning before, when
he dreamt not of the real state of the case, had ridden
forth gasconading of his prowess in arms, now repeated several times emphatically that the contemptible spokesman had actually defied him in terms
derogating from his valour. " Here" said he, " Here
stand your oxen; come up if you're a man! Take
them ye poltroons if ye dare !" Yet although
mounted, and abundantly supplied with munition,
these hulking white-livered villains did not blush to
acknowledge that their personal fears had induced
them to decline the invitation. Neither was it possible now to persuade them to turn back with me;
the enemy, they declared, being so exceedingly numerous, and ensconced in so strong a position, that
nothing could be attempted with so small a force.

Here then, like sailors who have foundered upon a
rock when within sight of their destined haven, were
we—after weathering many a storm, and accomplishing the most hazardous portion of our journey—left at
last, a wreck in the desert. The spirit of Ethaldur
groaned within him, when he thus saw his prediction
on the eve of being verified, and the lower jaw of
Cœur de Lion dropped until his beard was dangling

at his girdle. To add to *his* misfortunes, the scanty
pool upon which our supply of water depended, be-
·ing drained to the dregs, it had become necessary to
perform a journey of *six miles* over an enemy's
country, in order to replenish the tea kettle.

The vindictive and improvident character of the
Bushman hordes, rendered it extremely probable that
the whole of our unfortunate oxen had already been
wantonly sacrificed to their malice; but at all events,
the day was too far spent to admit of our reaching
the scene of action before dark, and the night being
moonless, it was necessary that our attack should be
delayed until the following morning. The hateful
squaws had abandoned their kraal the preceding day,
and it was not unlikely that a party of the marauders
might be lurking in the hill, ready to fall upon the
waggons during our temporary absence. After much
consultation therefore, it was resolved to leave Claas
and Frederick, who confessed their inability to fight,
together with the two domestics, whose black beards
were calculated to instil terror into the stoutest
heart—starting ourselves with the other five Hottentots in the dead of night, in order if possible to
avoid creating suspicion of our departure. All the
preliminaries of a surprize thus skilfully arranged,
the best horses were selected and fastened to the
waggons, and one hundred rounds of ammunition
having been served out to each of the little band, we

retired to rest, leaving the watch in charge of
Cœur de Lion, with instructions to keep his eye steadily fixed upon the hands, and not fail to arouse us
when they pointed to the hour of twelve.

CHAPTER XXXIII.

NIGHT ATTACK ON THE MARAUDERS.

I was still broad awake, conjecturing the success of our projected Commando, when the watchful valet thrust his well furnished chin under the canvas curtains of the waggon, and in a tremulous voice proclaimed the midnight hour. A dram of spirits having been issued to each. Hottentot knight with the design of inspiring chivalrous sentiments, the skeleton steeds were silently saddled; and not a word having been spoken above a whisper, we commenced our march towards the enemy's position. The night was cold and clear, and withal gloriously starlight; and it was in truth a goodly sight to behold the motley band of gay cavaliers, girded about with their furniture of war, and carrying their heavy carbines on their shoulders, jauntily pricking over the plain. The distance of the Bushman castle not being less than eighteen miles, it was necessary, in order to arrive in proper time, that we should move as briskly as possible. Ever and anon, as we cantered blindly along, in momentary apprehension of losing each other, some one of the party was to be seen floun-

dering among the Meerkat burrows, with which the
soil was completely undermined. Herds of timid
Springbucks, upon whose repose we had unceremoniously obtruded, bounded panic stricken across our
path; and Gnoos, cantering inquisitively up at intervals, stood within pistol shot, whisking their streaming tails, and bellowing defiance. After three hours
journeying, we arrived on the bank of a narrow
stream, completely choaked with bulrushes and
tangled sedge; shortly after forcing our way through
which, with incredible difficulty and many casualties, we descried the Lilliputian fortress rising before
us in dim perspective. There being yet no glim-
mering of dawn, we halted for a few minutes
behind a group of rocks to reconnoitre; and a council of war being held, it was decided that we
should ascend the hill on the opposite side, and
having carried the enemy's position in reverse, by a
coup de main, should shoot all who made any show
of resistance. Dismounting therefore, and leading
our steeds, we noiselessly groped our way among
crags and brushwood to the summit of the hill,
which although rather abrupt in front, was spread
out into undulations behind. Here the horses having been fastened together by the bridles, were left in
charge of one of the Hottentots—the rest, with us,
creeping on all fours towards the table land occupied by the enemy, of whose increasing proximity,

our noses began now to apprize us. Cautiously
peeping with uncovered heads over a natural parapet
we could presently perceive their fires burning about
two hundred yards in advance; and thus securely
ambushed, scarcely daring even to breathe, we a-
waited the approach of dawn with a degree of nervous impatience which may be estimated by those
who recollect that upon its successful issue, the sal-
vation of our waggons and property almost entirely
depended.

While thus watching the cold darkness of night,
which seemed as though it would have lasted for-
ever, the bright morning star—that joyous herald
whose appearance I had never hailed with greater
delight, suddenly shot like a rocket above the horizon. A faint light immediately pervaded the Eastern
sky, before which as it gradually increased, the stars
appeared to fade away, while the earth still continued in night. Imperceptibly almost, this light had
presently given place to a ruddy tint, which speedily
extended itself over the whole vault of heaven; but
though the outline of objects in the extreme distance
could now be indistinctly traced, those immediately
about us were yet shrouded in darkness. Around,
all was silent as the grave, not a zephyr disturbing
the death-like stillness that was reigning. As objects became gradually plainer, the forms of several
conical huts could be distinguished, and lastly by a

still less dubious light, the prostrate carcases of many of our oxen became visible. Alas! it was then, as we had feared; but if indeed we were irretrievably ruined, our moment for taking vengeance had arrived. Stealing over the parapet, every rifle was noiselessly cocked, and a finger flew to every trigger, as with palpitating hearts and wary tread, we approached the wretched wigwams. Woe unto that luckless wight who had there been found sleeping—he would never have awoke again. But though smouldering fires were smoking in various directions, every cabin was deserted; and having visited each in succession, and diligently searched every nook and corner without being able to discover a solitary human being, we turned for a moment to contemplate the tragic scene before us. Nineteen of our gallant oxen swollen and disfigured with many a wanton wound, were stretched in the wild enclosure, from which arose the most sickening of savage odours. Lean dogs,

" Gorging and growling o'er carcase and limb"

held their carnival over the dead, but were too busy even to bark at our intrusion; while torpid vultures, distended to such a size, that they could with difficulty hop out of our way, were perched like harpies upon the surrounding rocks. It was by this time broad day light, and a few of our oxen being to our great delight perceived standing at the foot of the

hill, a party was immediately detached to take possession of them, while we glanced over the field of
slaughter, to ascertain the extent of our loss. Side
by side at our feet, and swollen almost to bursting,
from the effects of a subtile poison, were Holland
and Oliphant, the two sturdy wheelers of our choice
Naudè *span*,* which had never failed to extricate us
from every difficulty. Near them, and weltering in
a pool of blood, lay Lanceman and England, the
steadiest and staunchest of our leaders. Passing
onwards our attention was next attracted to a head-
less trunk, and at no great distance from it—the
white eyes glaring upon us as if still alive—was the
hornless cranium of *Mutlee*. Every eye turned
upon the caitiff Andries, and peals of ill-timed merriment burst from every Hottentot mouth. The arm
of retribution had for once descended on a right worthy victim. Maddened with rage at the heart-rend-
ing prospect before us, again and again did we
search every chink and cranny, and unweariedly did
we cast about for the trail of the marauders. "Grim
satyr-faced baboons" railed hoarsely at us from
their rocky clefts, and to whichever side we turned,
the slope of the hill was besprinkled with mouldering
human bones; but after the closest scrutiny, no object
could be discovered upon which to wreak our ven-

* Ten oxen usually compose a *span* or team.

geance. A Rheebuck, that our early approach had
disturbed, having bounded through the encampment,
and given the alarm, the "dwellers with owls and
bats," although doubtless spectators of all that we
were doing, had effectually concealed themselves
from observation, and after the strictest search, nine
tracks only could be discovered. Of these six were
females, and one was that of our bewitching acquaintance. Barely four inches in length, but yet fully
developed, there could be no mistaking *her* foot mark;
and it now became evident, that whilst she and her
elfin colleagues had been aiding and abetting to our
ruin from the very commencement, our luckless followers had fled—not from the overwhelming host
which their imaginations had conjured into existence
—but from the empty challenge of a woman given
from a position, to which either on horseback or on
foot, they could have ascended without the smallest
difficulty !

Completely frustrated in our endeavours to chas-
tise the authors of our heavy misfortunes, we at
length descended the hill in order to muster the remnant of our ill fated teams; and little less melancholy was the prospect that there awaited us. Ex-
clusive of the old cow, and the equally useless
black bull, neither of which were touched, seventeen
drooping wounded wretches, with glazed eyes, and
fallen crests, were huddled together—some shivering

in the last agonies of death—and many others barely able to rise. In addition to sundry wounds which had been inflicted by our merciless and malicious foes whilst urging them across the plain, the unfortunate animals had recently received many cold blooded gashes bestowed apparently with the design of rendering them unserviceable to us; and thus crippled it was not without infinite labour and difficulty that we eventually succeeded in driving them to the camp, which we reached long after dark. On our way thither, visiting the demon kraal, we found a filthy area, enclosed by masses of rock heaped together by the hand of nature, and overgrown with wild olives; but inhabited only by meagre curs, which had been left by the vindictive sprites, to guard during their absence, from the assaults of vultures, the garbage and putrid skins with which the trees were festooned.

Taking a review of the whole of this unfortunae affair, it was poor consolation to reflect that the catastrophe had been brought about by a tissue of the grossest neglect, pusillanimity, and mismanagement on the part of our followers. Next to the inexcusable want of vigilance, and subsequent credulity of Andries, in which the whole mischief had originated, came the needless and provoking loss of time on the morning of the 4th, followed by an extraordinary lack of energy and zeal, on the part of the Hottentots who were sent in quest of the truants. The retreat of the marauders, whose adroitness in driving off cattle has already been noticed, was doubtless greatly favored by the undulating character of the ground; but if instead of plodding on the trail, the mounted men had galloped in advance, and reconnoitred the country, there can be no doubt that the event would have been widely different. An examination of the footmarks showed that Piet, in the first instance, without any reason whatever, had turned back when actually within a quarter of a mile of the plunderers, whom he must have seen had he ridden to the brow of the next eminence. And even after the golden opportunity of retaking the greater portion of our oxen, had been thrown away through the cowardice of Andries and Cobus—still the day might have been retrieved, had those doughty characters been persuaded to accompany me to thehill, as I repeatedly urged them to do. In the end, it appeared that the former of these worthies, had some days before sold his ox to the latter for a stipulated sum which was to be paid on arrival at Graaff Reinet; and never was their apathy and indifference to the interest of their masters, more perfectly illustrated than on the present occasion—the irreparable loss which we, through their agency, had sustained, being totally merged in a dispute which had arisen between the two principal delinquents as to which was to be considered the owner and loser of the one eyed *Mutlee.*

It rained pitilessly during the night, and in the morning three of our oxen were stiff and cold, four others being quite unable to rise. The accursed women who had in a great measure been instrumental to this disastrous state of affairs, had nevertheless in some degree assisted us in finding the remedy —the pretty Bush girl having informed us that there was a Boor's habitation about two days' journey to the Westward of our camp. To that quarter every eye had been anxiously turned; and as another cheerless evening closed upon us, unusual columns of dust which arose in the distant horizon, appeared to be indicative of flocks returning from pasture. It was therefore resolved that I shouldset forth immediately in that direction in search of assistance, leaving Richardson to proceed to a point agreed upon, at whatever pace six suffering oxen could transport our heavy vans; and that failing to discover the Farmer's residence, of which even the existence was extremely uncertain, I should make the best of my way to the Colony, now probably less than one hundred miles distant, whence, having procured fresh teams, I could return to the relief of the wreck with all practicable expedition.

CHAPTER XXXIV.

EXCURSION ON HORSEBACK IN QUEST OF ASSIST-
ANCE, AND MEETING WITH THE EMIGRANT
FARMERS.

So dreadfully had our horses suffered during the
late campaign, that it was with considerable difficulty
I succeeded in selecting from the whole drove, three
that appeared fit for service. With these, and a
good supply of ammunition, I set out on the morning
of the 8th of January, attended by Andries, and
joyfully turned my back upon the disastrous hill, near
which we had been so long spell-bound. Proceeding
several miles to the Westward, we ascended a high
barren range, overlooking an extensive valley, and
soon discovered that the columns of dust which had
been greeted as the harbingers of relief from our
misfortunes, were occasioned by the mad careering
of troops of Gnoos. Thus disappointed, we swept
round to the Southward, and night closing in after
we had ridden about forty miles, we lay down to
sleep in an olive brake, on the bank of a small stream.
It rained very heavily for some hours, and the bushes
not keeping out the water, rather added to than diminished the discomfort, so that I had sufficient reason

to rejoice at the return of day light. Continuing our search in parallel lines along the heights, I
reconnoitred the whole country through a telescope,
and after having been twice deceived by herds of
Springbucks, at length discovered a *veritable* flock
of sheep, grazing in a distant valley. Overjoyed at
the discovery, I hastened towards the spot, and turning the flank of a detached range, a most cheering
prospect was suddenly opened to my view. Forty
Dutch Colonists with their kith and kin, were encamped on the banks of the Calf river, where it
wound between two ranges of hills; the assemblage
of snow white waggon tilts, around which herds of
oxen, and droves of horses were grazing, imparting
to the animating scene the appearance of a country
fair. Several women, attended by their husbands,
were washing linen in the river, but as both sexes
declined holding any communication with me, I rode
up to the nearest tent, and learnt from a slave boy
that it belonged to Christian Breck. Pipe in mouth,
the portly *Baas* or master presently sallied forth,
and after the customary salutation, I enquired how
many days' journey it was to the Great river. Instead of receiving any reply to this question however, I was elaborately catechized as to my age,
name, residence, calling, destination, and domestic
history. The mention of "Sillekat's land" while it
elicited an oath, and an exclamation of surprise,

procured me also an invitation to "saddle off;" and walking with mine host into the pall, I was minutely scrutinized through a pair of spectacles by the good vrouw, who was seated agreeably to Colonial custom, with her feet over a warming pan. Neither my ragged and weather beaten appearance, nor my patriarchal beard, were pleasing to the old lady on first acquaintance, but as I was now na accomplished Dutch scholar, we speedily became better friends; and after I had patiently satisfied *her* curiosity also, on all points connected with my private biography, a Hottentot girl was directed to set before me a plate full of mutton bones drowned in Chili vinegar; to which savory dish the mistress added an apology for the absence of bread. Over this frugal meal, I detailed my misfortunes, which provoked but little sympathy, although the offer of a bribe in tea and snuff readily induced Mynheer Breck to desire his son and nephew to accompany me with two *spans* of oxen, for the purpose of bringing up the waggons. Several other Boors joining the party whilst the preparations were being made, I fortunately succeeded in hiring a couple of horses from them, my own three being completely exhausted.

Escorted by my young Dutch friends, with two frisky teams, which had been selected from their numerous well conditioned herds, I again set forth at two o'clock, to rejoin my wrecked fellow traveller, who, advancing at a snail's pace, was not a little rejoiced at my speedy return. We encamped, from necessity, about eight miles South of the execrated hill, upon which the Hottentots, with a design of perpetuating their chivalrous exploits, had conferred the appellation of *Bushman's Kop.* It again brought us evil fortune. The timidity of our little flock of sheep had increased in the ratio of their reduction in numerical strength; and during this night, all efforts to keep them near the waggons proving abortive, they dashed for the last time into the wilderness, and we saw them no more. Leaving Frederick to hunt for his truant charge we pursued our journey at a merry pace in the morning, and after experiencing much difficulty in crossing the Calf river, the bottom of which is extremely muddy, we reached the *trek-boor's* encampment. Like most of the Cape Colonists, our juvenile allies held English men and English rifles in equal contempt; and until I had shot two Gnoos for their edification, at four hundred yards, were not to be persuaded that a barrel under four feet in length, or of smaller calibre than their own clumsy *roers*, could be of the slightest avail. The Gnoo and Spring-buck, although still abundant, had become now so exceedingly wild from constant persecution, that during the rest of our journey I found it requisite to display a red handkerchief on the muzzle of my rifle in order to inveigle the former within shot. This exhibition invariably produced the most violent excitement, and caused the herd to charge past in single file—following their leader—flinging out their heels, lashing their tails, and butting with their horns in so menacing a manner, that I was not unfrequently compelled to strike my colors.

Our object now being to recruit our teams and lighten the waggons of all redundant stores, we lost not a moment in opening a *winkel*, or shop—proposing to exchange for oxen, either tea, sugar, snuff, meal, lead, or gunpowder. But although these articles were all in especial demand, we found it impossible to negociate by barter—that being a mode of dealing which, strange to say, they appeared quite unable to comprehend. After repeatedly shaking the wheels of our admirable waggons, in order to ascertain whether they "ran lightly," we received many generous offers of shattered rickety vehicles, with a few indifferent oxen, in exchange for them; but ultimately we found ourselves obliged to refer to our treasury, which fortunately still containing two hundred and fifty rix dollars, we were enabled to purchase a few head of cattle to begin with—receiving back the cash in payment for our wares, and again disbursing it for more oxen—until, having realized the requisite number, we had still ten shillings left in our pockets to carry us to Graff Reinet.

In the course of conversation at a tea party given to the ladies and gossips of the Dutch camp, we learnt that they had left Colesberg three months before, and were on their way to join the Emigrants, who were assembled at the head of the Modder river, near the Rev. Mr. Archbell's Missionary station at Thaba Uncha, lying about two days journey Eastward of the scene of our catastrophe. The men spoke in the most contemptuous terms of Moselekatse, regarding whom, nevertheless, they were greatly inquisitive; informing us that they were awaiting the return of a Commando under *Gert Maritz,* our Graaff Reinet acquaintance, who had marched some time before to invade the Matabili territories and crush the despot. I must add also, that the circumstance of *our* having been well received by His Majesty, and suffered to escape with our lives—while it elicited every one's astonishment, appeared also to create a general feeling of jealousy and dissatisfaction.

Again there was a drenching rain all night, and two more of our finest oxen being completely powerless from their wounds, we presented them to young Breck, in part acknowledgment for his Father's assistance, and pursued our journey on the morning of the eleventh. Even to the Colonial boundary, we had still a weary distance before us, and grass was represented to be extremely scarce; but we now

travelled with fresh oxen along a beaten waggon
road, an accommodation to which we had been
strangers for several months. In the course of the
forenoon, we were met by a Farmer from Beaufort
on the Karroo, with a Hottentot *achter ryder*, or
footman, going to *kek* as he called it, or in other
words, to see how the Emigrants were likely to thrive,
before selling his own farm. On learning that we
were from Sillekat's land his first question was,
"How the Kafirs had happened to let us come out
in a sound skin?" And this in fact, wherever we
went, was the theme of wonder and astonishment—
few being able to understand the difference between
conciliating a savage with presents, and entering his
territories uninvited.

In the course of this day's journey, which occupied nine hours, we crossed the Riet river, and were
rejoined by Frederick, who reported that he had seen
the remnant of our flock safe in the hands of a party of Bushmen, whom, although mounted and armed himself, he durst not approach. It was waxing
late, when volumes of dust attracted our attention
to countless flocks of sheep that were being driven
from pasture; following which, and entering a gorge
in the hills, an astounding panorama burst upon the
sight. A lone green valley, which stretched between
two ranges of rocky hills, lay extended before us,
and, covered in every direction with white waggon

tilts, canvas palls, bell tents, oxen, horses, sheep, and human beings, literally presented the appearance of the encampment of a goodly army. Having obtained permission from a Dutchman named *Humans* to unyoke in an unoccupied spot, we again opened our *negotic winkel:* but coming from Moselekatse's country by the forbidden route, every one appeared suspicious of our object, and declined to barter their oxen. The next morning however, (the 12th) being on our journey some miles, we were overtaken by a youth with pack horses, who came from the Emigrant camp provided with monies for the purchase of leaden balls.

Advancing, we passed several filthy kraals of Griquas under *Dam Kok,* a hybrid Chieftain residing at Phillipolis; and halting for an hour at one of them, the fellows clamorously demanded to see the portrait of their arch enemy which they understood from the Hottentots I had brought. The Napoleon of Southern Africa having been accordingly exhibited at the end of the waggon, they spit at, and offered him every indignity—their Captain, a diabolical looking ruffian, whose head had been turned by "the school master" at his elbow, logically enquiring "whether he had not as good a right to put us to death for shooting ducks on his tank, without paying for the same, as Moselekatse to destroy the Griquas who hunted *Zeekoe's* in the Likwa ?" They at last became so exceedingly

insolent and overbearing, that we were fain to decamp; and Cobus and April, who had contrived to obtain some brandy from their country-women, attempting to desert at the same time, we narrowly escaped
adding the whole of our horses to the catalogue of our
losses.

Great had been the pointing of fingers, and long
and loud the discussions touching the Geographical
position of Phillipolis—one declaring his conviction
that it still bore to the South-east, and another to the
South-west.   About sunset however, having now
achieved upwards of three hundred and fifty miles, in
straight line from the Cashan mountains, a peak rose
to view, which being unanimously recognized, and
acknowledged to mark the position of the Missionary station, was hailed, as a beacon on the sea-shore
is hailed by mariners after a long and dangerous voyage.   Our followers were now as bold as lions; and
an unusually diminutive Bushman injudiciously presenting himself with the humble salutation of " Go-
en-dakha, tabakka," ("good morrow gentlemen,
some tobacco if you please,") was flogged with the
long waggon whip within an inch of his life.   Twenty-five miles the following day brought us to an extensive lodge of Griquas under Captain Abraham
Barend, where we passed the night, and in exchange
for tea and snuff, obtained from the civil old man the
luxuries of fowls and milk, to which we had so long
been entire strangers.

CHAPTER XXXV.

RETURN TO CIVILIZATION, AND ARRIVAL IN THE CAPE COLONY.

On the afternoon of the 14th, having advanced some sixteen miles through a dreadful storm of dust, which literally darkened the atmosphere, the rushing of mighty waters suddenly announced our approach to the Great river. Hastening to the bank, our mortification may be imagined at perceiving from the agitated and muddy tide, and the drift wood which was borne past by the impetuosity of the current, that it had only just then become swollen. A farmer had brought over his light horse waggon with some difficulty a quarter of an hour before, but to cross now was impossible. Two tedious days were passed in watching the willowed banks—the troubled waters now subsiding sufficiently to tantalize us with the prospect of being shortly able to pass over, and again receiving a fresh accession of the turbid element. Andries, who was in the bosom of his family, bore the calamity without a murmur, until certain misdeeds, committed when sent from Bok's fontein in pursuit of the truant horses, accidentally transpiring—even he was unable longer to bear the detention,

and he then obligingly informed us of the existence of
a raft, a few miles higher up the river, of which he had
hitherto carefully kept us in ignorance. Proceeding
thither we found the river straightened between rocky
sides, to one third of its usual breadth; and after we
had bribed a man to swim across in order to summon
the proprietor of the *float*, whose house was some
miles distant, our waggons were at length taken to
pieces, and transported wheel by wheel into the Colony.
This tedious operation occupied an entire day, and
so frightfully strong was the current, that in bringing
the oxen across, poor *Whitefoot*, the only survivor
of our *Naudé* team, that till now had escaped un-
scathed, and had never once failed us during our long
pilgrimage, was clumsily forced under the raft, and
drowned.   Some consolation, however, was to be derived from the information that our loss was comparatively trifling, a loaded waggon having a short
time before slipped off the raft, and gone bodily to
the bottom.

At length then, we were fairly standing upon the
civilized ground of the Hantam. Loud was the
shouting and huzzaing, and many were the discharges of musquetry, that proclaimed the fact, of which
however, the inhospitable conduct of an insolent boor,
named Pienaar, at whose farm we passed the night,
might almost have rendered us sceptical. Not a
blade of grass met the eye from this moment; and

as we were penniless, we could only obtain with
difficulty provisions in exchange for tea, sugar, and
tar; which last, being used in the composition for
greasing the wheels, (an operation which it was
found necessary to perform every other day) was
fortunately in great demand amongst the Boors.
Every Hottentot now tricked himself out in Ostrich
plumes, and dragged to light some hidden article of
finery which had been reserved against his return
amongst his clansmen, for whose especial edification
he had also prepared right wondrous tales of his
deeds in arms, and his perils by field and flood. The
town of Colesberg being known to possess a licensed retailer of ardent spirits, we preferred passing
the night of the 18th without water, to visiting it;
but after all, it was only by frequent pointed allu-
sions to field Cornets, and Clerks of the Peace, that
the impatient and thirsty souls were prevented from
absconding thither.

On the 21st we struck into the high road near
Dassies Fontein, where we had the happiness of
finding our ancient Kafir acquaintance inhaling his
Dacca with unabated industry. Our followers too
were unexpectedly met by a party of their cronies
with waggons from Graaff Reinet, who greeted them
as men risen from the dead, with the astounding intelligence that a report had gone forth in the Colony
of our whole party having been put to death by the

King. It was known that we were in the neighbourhood of the Emigrants at the time of their massacre,
and so long a time having elapsed without any tidings being received of our safety, the tongue of ru-
mour had not been idle, Our Colonial friends, who
had entertained so contemptuous an idea of our travelling capabilities, were by no means unprepared
for this dismal intelligence, which had spread far and
wide, and was even credited at the Cape.   Unimportant though it may appear, it had nevertheless
proved the death blow to the domestic happiness of
most of our followers—their faithless consorts having soon forgotten their plighted vows, and embraced the earliest opportunity of casting aside their
widow's weeds.   The report was subsequently traced to a Lothario from the frontier, who had actually
backed the offer of his hand and heart to Ethalduar's
relict, with the assurance that he had himself performed the last melancholy offices for her husband, to
whose corpse the infidels had offered indignities too
barbarous to be here recorded.

Sixty-nine casualties had already occurred amongst
our oxen; and on the 24th, another victim being
left in the Sneuwebergen, we had barely a sufficient number remaining to drag our waggons into
the village of Graaff Reinet. This dreadful mor-
tality, which, although partly attributable to the

rapidity of our march, was owing in a still greater
measure to the neglect and cowardice of the Hottentots, eventually swelled the expenses of the expedition to £800 sterling.   But it is proper to state for
the information of those of my Indian friends who
may resolve upon such a campaign, that by entertaining a sufficient number of Europeans to keep the Hottentots in awe; and, employing also a third waggon to
carry out grain for the best horses, as well as to bring
back ivory and rare quadrupeds to the Colony, the
expedition might be made to cover its own expenses.
In addition to the Sable Antelope, which had travelled
the whole way on my cot, and was, a source of constant anxiety, my collection consisted of two perfect
Crania of every species of game quadruped to be
found in Southern Africa, together with skins of the
Lion, Quagga, Zebra, Ostrich, &c., tails of the Cameleopard, and tusks of Elephants and Hippopotami, besides elaborate drawings of every animal
that interests the sportsman from the tall Giraffe to
the minutest Antelope.

The unlooked for return of the "two Indian Gentlemen" from the interior, together with the exhibition of these creditable trophies, most of which were
novelties to the oldest resident, created a considerable revolution of sentiment in our favor; hundreds
now declaring that had they only been aware of our
intention of visiting "the terror of the Interior,"

(whose portrait was not considered the least attractive of our curiosities,) nothing on earth should have deterred them from taking part in so interesting an adventure.   There is doubtless a wide difference betwixt setting out and returning, but I can assure these enterprising travellers, that unless the trackless desert hath charms for me, which it would not possess in the eyes of the less enthusiastic, they would have found no cause to repent of their rashness.   To all others I prefer a life of adventure—its very privations, when coupled with scenes such as I have attempted to describe, constituting an excitement peculiarly adapted to my humour.   The tracts through which we travelled extending into the temperate Zone, and being surrounded also on three sides by the ocean, while they possess the advantage of a moderate climate, are the nursery of the noblest quadrupeds.   There was something truly soul-stirring and romantic in wandering among these free born denizens of the desert—realizing as it were a new creation, in regions hitherto seldom, if ever, trodden by white man's foot.   During the whole period that we were absent from the Colony, I never once omitted to take the field at break of day, or as soon after as the weather would permit, frequently preparing my own breakfast, and never returning unladen with spoils.   Firmly determined to bring back correct delineations of the whole of the feræ naturæ inhabiting Africa, South of

the Tropic, I never moved without drawing materials
in my hunting cap, and found ample employment for
the pencil as well as for the rifle.

The Indian traveller who has been accustomed to
the accommodation afforded by tents and retinue, can
form little conception of the ten thousand difficulties,
distresses, and draw-backs, that beset the wanderer in
the African Desert. Nearly all my sketches were
made under a bush in the open air, and completed on
my knees in the waggon amid rain and wind—the
Zoological specimens, which I had in the first instance
realized and brought home myself, being subsequently prepared with my own hand. Nothing could exceed the annoyance given by the Hottentots, whose
indolence and indifference throughout the journey,
obliged us frequently to rise during the night—the
rain, which pursued us whithersoever we went,
heightening in no small degree the discomforts we
experienced. Nor shall I deny that we sometimes
sighed for the luxuries to which we had been accustomed; bread and meat, with simple tea or coffee,
forming for many months our monotonous diet. But
in spite of all these hardships and privations, toilsome and tedious as our journey frequently was,
across deserts of utterly hopeless sterility, we were
more than amply repaid by the unparalleled magnificence of the sport that we enjoyed; and I can safely
aver that some of the happiest days of my existence

have been passed in the wilds of Africa.   They form
a passage in my life which time can never efface from
the tablet of my recollection—a green spot in memory's waste, to which, in after years I shall revert with
intense and unabating pleasure.

CHAPTER XXXVI.

SKETCH OF THE EMIGRATION OF THE BORDER
COLONISTS.

THE abandonment of the Cape Colony by the old
Dutch inhabitants, to which I have so frequently had
occasion to allude, and which has in fact become completely interwoven with the thread of my narrative,
has no parallel in the history of British Colonial
possessions. Partial emigrations are by no means
uncommon, as the existence of the Colony itself
sufficiently proves, but here is an instance of a body
of between *five and six thousand* souls, who have
with one accord abandoned the land of their nativity,
and the homes of their forefathers—endeared to
them by every interesting association—and have
recklessly plunged into the pathless wilds of the interior; braving the perils and hardships of the wilderness, and, many of them already in the vale of
years—seeking out for themselves another dwelling
place in a strange and inhospitable soil.

The first question that presents itself must naturally be, what has led to so extraordinary an expatriation? The losses to which they have been

subjected by the emancipation of their slaves; the absence of laws for their protection from the evils of uncontrolled vagrancy, and from the depredations of the swarm of vagabonds by which the Colony is infested; but, above all, the insecure state of the Eastern frontier, and the inadequate protection afforded by the English Government against the aggressions of their wily and restless Kafir neighbours, by whose repeated predatory incursions the fairest spots have been laid desolate, and many hundreds of the border Colonists reduced to ruin, are the inciting causes assigned by the Emigrants, for the unprecedented and hazardous step they have taken.

If it be impossible to view the violent remedy sought by these oppressed but misguided men in other than a criminal light, yet no unprejudiced person who has visited the more remote districts of this unhappy Colony, will hesitate to acknowledge that the evils they complain of actually exist. Long subjected to the pilferings of a host of Hottentot vagrants, whose lives are passed in one perpetual round of idleness, delinquency, and brutish intoxication on the threshold of the gin-shop, the South African settler has lately, in too many instances, been reduced from comparative affluence to want, by being unseasonably, and without adequate compensation bereft of the services of his slaves : who, prone to villainy, and no longer compelled to labour,

44

have only served to swell the swarm of drones by
which it is his destiny to be persecuted. Far greater than these, however, are the evils that have arisen
out of the perverse misrepresentations of canting and
designing men, to whose mischievous and gratuitous
interference, veiled under the cloak of philanthropy,
is principally to be attributed the desolated condition
of the Eastern frontier; bounded as it is, by a dense
and almost impenetrable jungle, to defend which nine
times the military force now employed would barely
be adequate; and flanked by a population of eighty
thousand dire, irreclaimable savages, naturally inimi-
eal, warlike, and predatory, by whom the hearths of
the Cape Border Colonists have for years past been
deluged with the blood of their nearest and dearest
relatives. And whilst, during the unprovoked inroads of these ruthless barbarians, their wives and
helpless offspring have been mercilessly butchered
before their eyes; whilst their corn-fields have been
laid waste, their flocks swept off, and their houses
reduced to ruins, to add bitterness to gall, they have
been taunted as the authors of their own misfortunes,
by those, who strangely biassed by *ex-parte* state-
ments, have judged them unheard, at the distance
of several thousand miles, from the scene of pillage,
bloodshed, and devastation.

It does indeed furnish matter of amazement to
every thinking person, how such a state of things

should so long have been suffered to exist; how those who have legislated for the affairs of the Colony should not long ago, have seen the imperious necessity, dictated alike by reason, justice, and humanity, of exterminating from off the face of the earth, a race of monsters, who, being the unprovoked destroyers, and implacable foes of Her Majesty's Christian subjects, have forfeited every claim to mercy or consideration. Denied redress however, and deprived of the power of avenging themselves of the wrongs under which they have writhed, in utter hopelessness of recovering their property or even enjoying future tranquillity, the Border Colonists have at length thrown off the yoke of their allegiance; and whilst seeking out for themselves an asylum in other lands, are now retorting upon our allies, the injuries they have so long sustained at their hands.

My visit to Moselekatse, and subsequent return by the hitherto unexplored route of the Vaal river, afforded me opportunities of observing the proceedings beyond the boundary, of these voluntary exiles, and of making myself acquainted with their position in relation to the numerous native tribes, by which they are surrounded. Neither being correctly understood, I shall endeavour as briefly as possible to trace their steps from the commencement of the emigration.

Weary of the insecurity of their homes, several of the frontier Farmers, who had heard much of the soil and capabilities of Port Natal, resolved to decide for themselves on the accuracy of these reports, forming a large party, and with ten or twelve waggons, proceeded to explore the country. So well pleased were they with what they saw, that they formed a determination of locating themselves in that neighbourhood, and returned forthwith for their families, when the breaking out of the last Kafir war obliged them to postpone the execution of their design.

Shortly after the conclusion of hostilities, the first party of actual Emigrants, consisting of about thirty families, left the Colony under the guidance of an Albany Farmer, named Louis Triechard. Being desirous of eluding the Kafir tribes, they proceeded across the Great river in a North-easterly direction, skirting the mountain chain which divides Caffraria from Bechuana Land; with the intention, when they had cleared it, of turning to the East-ward, and gaining the neighbourhood of Port Natal. The features presented by this barrier are rugged and forbidding in the extreme; they have the appearance of innumerable pyramidical hills thrown together in the most grotesque and disorderly manner: one peak jutting beyond, or soaring above the other, as though precluding the possibility of any human foot, much less

any wheeled vehicle, from passing over; and, from
the imperfect knowledge possessed by the wanderers,
of that section of Southern Africa, the geography
of which is still veiled in considerable obscurity,
they were led by the course of the mountains far beyond the latitude of Port Natal and found themselves
about the end of May 1836, in a fertile but uninhabited waste, lying between the 26th and 27th parallels
of South latitude, on the Eastern banks of the large
and beautiful river, noticed in a former part of this
Narrative, which flows sluggishly through a level
tract in a North-easterly direction, and is said to
join the Oori or Limpopo, and discharge its waters
into the Bay of Delagoa.

From this point, in order to reach the unoccupied
country about Natal, it would have been necessary
to traverse the whole length of Dingaan's dominions,
a journey fraught with difficulties of the most formidable kind, and opposed by a climate of the most
destructive character.   And, as the newly discovered
country was abundantly watered, abounded in game,
and afforded all the materials requisite for building,
the further progress of the Emigrants was for the
present discontinued.

The example thus set by Louis Triechard was
speedily followed by many of his countrymen.   Numerous parties were formed on the frontier by the
Border Colonists, who, with their families and flocks,

crossed the Great river, and dived into the very
depths of the wilderness; with no very clear idea
perhaps of what their ultimate destination was to be,
but yet firmly determined to abandon their native
hearths for ever, and to fix their future residence in
some distant land. For the sake of obtaining pasturage for their numerous herds, and in opposition to
the advice of the Missionaries through whose stations
they passed, by whom they were warned of the imminent risk that they would incur from the native tribes,
they scattered themselves heedlessly along the luxuriant banks of the Likwa or Vaal river, with the design of remaining until the country in advance should
be explored, and their plans digested and arranged.

About the end of May, two parties headed by J.
S. Bronkhorst, and H. Potgeiter, left the Emigrant
camp for the purpose of exploring the country to
the North-eastward. They visited Louis Triechard
at the Zout-pans-berg, or salt pan hill, and penetrated sixteen days' journey beyond, through a lovely,
fertile, and unoccupied country, until they arrived
within six days' journey of Delagoa Bay, where
they met with two sons of the notorious Conrad
Buys, living amongst a friendly tribe of natives,
whom, from a peculiarity in the nasal prominence,
they nignified with the appellation of "knob-nosed
kafirs." Returning hence by a nearer route with

the account of their success, and of the discovery of
a land flowing with milk and honey, they found their
camp totally deserted, and the ground strewed with
the mutilated bodies of their friends and relations!
The migratory Farmers had been attacked three
days before, by Moselekatse, and twenty-eight of
their number had been butchered.

It will have been seen from the foregoing pages,
that the country over which this powerful and despotic Prince claims sovereignty, is of great extent,
and is bounded on the South by the Likwa, or Vaal
river, one of the two principal branches of the Gareep. From that direction he had been repeatedly
attacked by Jan Bloem, a notorious and often successful freebooter, and by other leaders of predatory
bands of Griquas, who had scoured his territories,
and swept away his cattle. In 1831, it has been
shown, he was last attacked by a strong Commando
of Barend Barend's Griquas, who succeeded in obtaining possession of the whole of the Matabili herds;
and, all the regular warriors of Moselekatse being
absent at the time on an expedition to the Northward, the ruin of the tribe had nearly been accomplished. Owing, however to a want of proper precaution on the part of the invaders, they were sig-
nally defeated by a mere handful of irregulars, who
attacked them during the night, and ere the day dawned, had slaughtered the greater part of them.

Since that occurrence, Moselekatse had publicly
and positively prohibited any trader or traveller
from visiting him, or entering his territories from
that quarter: whilst, to guard against the inroads of
his enemies, strong armed parties were frequently sent
to scour the country watered by the Likwa. But, on
the other hand, he declared his willingness to receive
as friends, those visiters who might find it convenient
to approach him by way of Kuruman or New Litakoo, having the most implicit confidence in Mr.
Moffat the enlightened Missionary at that Station,
through whose assistance only they could effect an
entrance.

Can it be wondered at, under these circumstances,
that Moselekatse should have viewed with a jealous
and suspicious eye, the sudden advance of so formidable a body of strangers from the forbidden quarter, to the very borders, if not actually within the
confines of his territories?   Without so fair a pretext as their open defiance of his commands afforded
him, would it have been surprising that the temptation afforded by the fat flocks and herds of his new,
opulent, and very unceremonious neighbours, should
have induced the despot to impart a lesson which
might inculcate the necessity of at least propitiating
him with presents, which are known to be the only
sure road to the friendship or good offices of a savage?   Towards the close of August, a Commando

consisting of about five hundred Matabili warriors, was despatched from Mosega *for this very purpose.* On their way to plunder the Emigrants, who were encamped in scattered detachments along the Vaal river, they accidentally fell in with Stephanus Erasmus, who had been on a hunting expedition still farther to the Northward, and was then on his return to the Colony by the forbidden route. Arriving at his waggons in the evening with one of his sons, and finding them surrounded by a host of armed savages, he precipitately fled to the nearest Emigrant camp, about five hours' ride on horseback from his own, where, having succeeded in persuading a party of eleven Farmers to accompany him, he returned towards the spot. On the way thither they were met by the barbarians, whose impetuous onsets obliged them to seek refuge within the encampment. A severe struggle ensued, but the enemy were finally repulsed with great slaughter, and the loss, on the part of the farmers, of only one man named Bronkhorst.

This was however but the prelude to a more bloody tragedy. A party of the Matabili soldiers had in the mean time detached itself from the main body, and fallen upon nine other waggons that were assembled at a distance from the principal camp. The waggons were saved, but the greater part of the flocks and herds were carried off, and twenty-four

45

persons massacred; viz. Barend Liebenberg, Sen,
Stephanus, Hendrick, and Barend Liebenberg, Jun.
Johannes de Toit, an English schoolmaster named
McDonald, Mrs. H. Liebenberg, Mrs. De Toit,
four children, and twelve black servants.

Six day's after this catastrophe, Erasmus's curiosity
prompted him to ascertain the fate of his family and
property. Proceeding to the spot he found the bodies of his five black slaves, and could distinguish
the wheel tracks of his five waggons going in a
northerly direction. Two of his sons, and a youth
named Carel Kruger, had been taken prisoners, and
it was afterwards ascertained that having attempted
to effect their escape, they were mercilessly put to
death on their way to the King.

CHAPTER XXXVII.

EMIGRATION OF THE BORDER COLONISTS,
CONCLUDED.

ALMOST immediately after this disastrous occurrence, being rejoined by the parties that had proceeded to explore the North-east country, the migratory Farmers fell back about four days' journey
from their first position to the South side of the Vaal
river; and encamped near the embouchure of the
Donkin—one of its principal tributaries, called by
the natives the Nama Hari. Here they remained in
blind and fancied security, without taking any steps
towards an amicable understanding with the King,
until the end of October. They had scarcely recovered from the confusion into which they had been
thrown by the first attack, when, to their great
consternation, they received intimation of the near
approach of another and far more formidable body
of Moselekatse's warriors. Retreat being impossible, they sedulously applied themselves to fortifying
their position. They drew up their fifty waggons
in a compact circle, closing the apertures between and beneath them with thorn bushes, which
they firmly lashed with leathern thongs to the

wheels and *dissel-booms;* * and constructing within
the enclosure so formed, a smaller one for the protection of the women and children. These arrangements
hastily completed, they rode forth to confront the
enemy, whom they presently met in number about
five thousand on their march towards the camp,
when some skirmishing took place in which several
of the Matabili were slain. It has already been
remarked that their principal weapon is a short spear,
or assegai termed *unkonto,* which is not thrown, as
with the Kafir tribes, but used for stabbing, for
which purpose they rush in at once upon their opponents. Terrible as is this mode of fighting to unwarlike nations, it is calculated to effect little against
muskets in the hands of cavalry. Their numbers
and impetuosity however rendering it impossible
to keep them from the waggons, the farmers retired
within the enclosure; where by the time their guns
were cleansed, they were furiously assailed by the
barbarian horde, who with savage yells and hideous
war cries, poured down like locusts upon the encampment. Closing around the circle, and charging the
abattis with determined resolution, again and again
did they endeavour to break through the line, or clam-
ber over the awnings of the waggons. Dealing
however with men whose lives were the stake, their

* Waggon poles.

attacks were as constantly repelled. Repeated vollies of slugs and buck-shot discharged at arm's length from the heavy bores of the besieged, ploughed through their crowded ranks;

> " Even as they fell, in files they lay,
>   Like the mower's grass at the close of day,
>   When his work is done on the levell'd plain;
>   Such was the fall of the foremost slain."

A desperate struggle of fifteen minutes terminated in their discomfiture. Hurling their javelins into the enclosure they retired in confusion over the heaps of slain, leaving upwards of one hundred and fifty of their number dead or disabled on the field.

In this affair, which took place on the 29th October, Nicholaas Potgeiter and Piet Botha were killed behind the stockade, and twelve other farmers were severely wounded. The assault was led in person by Kalipi, Moselekatse's principal Captain, and most confidential counsellor. Although shot through the knee, he contrived to make good his retreat, nor did he retire empty handed; the whole of the flocks and herds of the Emigrants amounting to six thousand head of cattle, and forty-one thousand sheep and goats, being swept away by the barbarians, and safely conducted to Kapain. Remounting their horses, the farmers took advantage of the retreat of their savage foes, to add a few more to the list of slain, until the sun dsscending below the horizon, let drop the curtain upon the scene of carnage.

This second gentle hint on the part of His Majesty had the desired effect. A portion of the farmers remained with the wreck of the late flourishing camp, whilst others, with all possible haste, conveyed the women and children to the Rev. Mr. Archbell's Missionary Station at Thaba Uncha; whence, having procured fresh oxen, the whole party fell back, and encamped near the sources of the Modder river. Here their numbers were shortly reinforced by a strong detachment of Emigrants under the guidance of Gert Maritz, a wealthy and ambitious burgher from Graaff Reinet, who soon contrived to cause himself to be elected Governor General. At this period the number of waggons assembled near the populous Barolong village of Thaba Uncha, amounted to about two hundred and fifty, and the number of souls may be estimated at above eighteen hundred.

Maritz's first step after assuming the reins of Government, was to assemble a force for the purpose of retaliating upon the Amazooloo Monarch, the injuries that the Emigrants had received at his hands: but for which in truth they had alone to thank their own obstinacy and imprudence. On the 3rd of January 1837, a Commando consisting of one hundred and seven Dutch farmers, forty of Peter

David's mounted Griquas, and sixty armed savages on foot, left Thaba Uncha on their march to invade Moselekatse's country, under the guidance of
a warrior, who, having been taken prisoner in the
affair of the 29th October, durst never again present
himself before his royal master. Keeping considerably to the Westward of North, they crossed the
head of the Hart river, and struck into the Kuruman
road—by this masterly manœvre approaching the
Matabili from the very quarter whence they were
least prepared to expect an attack. A lovely and
fertile valley, bounded on the North and Northeast
by the Kurrichane mountains, and in form resembling
a basin of ten or twelve miles in circumference, contained the military town of Mosega, and fifteen
other of Moselekatse's principal kraals, in which resided Kalipi, and a large portion of the fighting men·
To this spot were the steps of the Emigrant farmers directed. As the first streaks of light ushered
in the eventful morning of the 17th of January, Maritz's little band suddenly and silently emerged from
a pass in the hills behind the houses of the American Missionaries; and ere the sun had reached the
zenith, the bodies of four hundred chosen Matabili
warriors, the flower of barbarian chivalry, garnished
the blood-stained valley of Mosega. Not a creature
was aware of the approach of danger, and the entrance of a rifle ball by one of the bedroom

windows, was the first intimation received by the Missionaries of the impending onslaught. One of their
domestics, Baba, the converted Bechuana, who it
will be remembered, accompanied the author to the
King's residence in capacity of interpreter, being
mistaken for a Zooloo, was hotly pursued to the river, into which he plunged, hippopotamus-like, and narrowly escaped annihilation by counterfeiting death,
after three bullets had whistled past his protruded
head. So perfect were the military dispositions
which the information afforded by the captive had
suggested, that the valley was completely invested,
and no avenue of escape remained. The Matabili
flew to arms at the first alarm, and bravely defend-
ed themselves, but were shot like sparrows as fast
as they appeared outside of the enclosure, nor did
they succeed in perforating the leathern doublet of
a single Dutchman. But the star of Moselekatse
was still in the ascendant. At the time of this successful attack he was residing at Kapain, fifty miles
further to the Northward; and Kalipi, having singularly enough been summoned thither only the day
before, escaped the fate of a large proportion of his
brave but unfortunate followers.

Had Maritz followed up the advantage thus gained, and marched at once upon Kapain, Moselekatse could not possibly have effected his escape.
Inflated by the recent success of his arms, the

despot was basking in the sunshine of security little dreaming of so sudden an invasion. Struck at
that moment, another blow would have completed
the work of destruction, and left the Emigrants
to pursue their pilgrimage in safety. Blind, however, to the obvious course they should have pursued,
and content for the present with what they had
achieved, the Boors secured seven thousand head of
cattle and the waggons that had been taken from
Erasmus, with which they immediately set out on
their return, by forced marches; and, accompanied
by the American Missionaries, who whilst they rea-
sonably dreaded the summary vengeance of the exasperated savage, had now no further field for their
labours—arrived in a few days at Thaba Uncha,
without molestation or pursuit on the part of the
Matabili.

Magical indeed was the effect which the news of
this victory produced upon the Dutch Colonists. It
fanned the smouldering embers of the epidemic into
a flame, and caused the rage for emigration to burst
forth and spread like wild-fire. The promise of
land unlimited, and of relief from taxation, tempted
hundreds whose remoteness from the Border had
smothered the incentives which actuated the original
projectors of the scheme. Another class, who like
the bat in the fable, had been prudently watching the
turn that affairs would take, now openly avowed

their abhorrence of the English rule, and freed themselves from its trammels. Some having yielded to
the claims of relationship, went because their kins-
men had gone; others to gratify their ambition, their
love of adventure, or passion for a nomadic life; and
not a few from a natural desire to participate in the
loaves and fishes. For several weeks the whole of
the frontier line was in a state of ferment and commotion, and large caravans were daily to be seen
hurrying across the border and flocking to the standard of their expatriated countrymen. In the month
of April, Piet Retief, a gallant and distinguished
Field-cornet of the Winterberg, who with a very
large cavalcade was encamped at a distance from
Maritz, was induced after much entreaty and persua-
sion to accept the office of Governor and Commander in Chief—a post which he was eminently qualified to fill, and to which he was elected by the
unanimous voice of the United Emigrants. He appointed subordinate Officers, enacted wholesome laws,
and ratified treaties which had already been concluded with the neighbouring native Chiefs, the principal of whom are Sikonyela, king of the Manta-
tees ; Moshesh, Chief of the Basuto ; Moroko, Chief
of the Barolongs at Thaba Uncha ; Tauani, Chief
of the remnant of the Baharootzi; and Peter David,
Captain of the Lishuani Bastards. This last, it
will be remembered, is the father of Truëy theGri-

qua maid, and the successor of Barend Barends, whose exploits have already been sung. One and all are the deadly enemies of Moselekatse, ready to take up arms against him on the slightest reverse of his fortune.

These arrangements completed, the Emigrants once more advanced towards the scene of their former misfortunes, and in May last, (1837) upwards of one thousand waggons, and sixteen hundred efficient fighting men, with their wives, families, and followers, were assembled near the confluence of the branches of the Vet rivière. A Commando consisting of five hundred Farmers, was preparing to march on the 1st June, for the purpose either of arranging matters with the King, or completely subverting his power. This done, their march towards Louis Triechard's camp will be resumed—there the corner stone of their city is to be laid, and a NEW AMSTERDAM will rear its head in the very heart of the wilderness.

Such, in a few words, is the History of the Emigration of the Border Colonists—an event which, while it has materially weakened the North-eastern Frontier, has kindled a flame in the interior which can be only quenched with blood. The place vacated by every Dutch Farmer will doubtless be speedily filled by an industrious peasant; and when the Colony shall have recovered from the first shock,

it will probably be found not to have suffered
from the change. Yet, taking a political view
of this important feature in the Colonial History, it
cannot but appear extraordinary that so large a body
of disaffected subjects, from what cause soever their
discontent may have arisen, should have been permitted to detach themselves from their allegiance,
and cross the frontier in open defiance of existing
laws—taking with them their slaves, and forcibly
entering the territories of an ally, for the avowed
purpose of establishing themselves in a position,
where they might shortly become the most formidable of our enemies. Fortunately however, many and insuperable obstacles are arrayed against
the success of their scheme. The golden opportunity of crushing the formidable viper in their path
is gone; and Moselekatse having gained wisdom from
the past, is not likely to be assailed a second time
with success. No sooner had the tidings of his disastrous defeat at Mosega, reached the ears of his
hereditary foe Dingaan, than the Zooloo tyrant, despatched an army, with orders to complete what the
Emigrant Farmers had, in his eyes, so laudably be-
gun. Already harassed by a long march, in the
course of which they had suffered the severest privations, the invaders were promptly met by the
Matabili, and routed with terrible slaughter. Taking advantage of the confusion, a band of vagabond

Griquas and Korannas, slunk jackal-like into the
Amazooloo territories from the Westward, and
were actually in full retreat with a considerable booty
in cattle, when they too were overtaken by a party
of the Matabili warriors, and utterly destroyed.
Thus badgered and worried on all sides, the Lion of
the North will not again be found sleeping; and
granting that the superior strength of the Emigrants
enables them eventually to despise his opposition,
their situation will still be far from enviable. Shut
out from Natal, as a sea-port, by their remote loca-
tion from the coast; and excluded from the advantages of Delagoa Bay by the jealousy of the Portu-
guese, their supplies, more especially of ammunition, must necessarily be extremely limited. By an
old Colonial law, the transit of gunpowder across
the border is contraband, and by a late act of Par-
liament, offences committed within the 25th parallel
of South Latitude have been rendered capitally cog-
nizable. Their horses must speedily perish by the
epidemic already described, and thus precluded from
hunting they will become solely dependent for support upon domestic resources. Admitting that intestine dissensions have not already caused a division, the necessity of obtaining pasturage for their
numerous herds will shortly compel them to break
up into small parties; and want of water, the curse
of unhappy Africa, will couple a similar contin-

gency with any attempt at cultivation. Thus situated, the isolated, ammunitionless Emigrant will fall an easy prey to the lurking and predatory savage—repenting when it is too late, of the folly that induced him to resign himself to the hazards of so wild an adventure.

Much then, as these deluded exiles have already suffered, and deluged as their path has already been with blood, even they can form at present but a very inadequate conception of the dangers and difficulties with which their undertaking is fraught. Hemmed in on one side by Moselekatse, who will never lose sight of the past, but tiger-like, will watch his opportunity of revenge, with unceasing and savage vigilance; and on the other hand by Dingaan, who cannot fail to regard their obtrusion with an eye of jealousy and suspicion; surrounded too, by a whole host of marauders, who, whatever they may pretend to the contrary, are ever on the alert to enrich themselves at the expense of their more opulent neighbours, the position of the migratory Farmers can hardly be said to be improved by the step they have taken. They have cast off the yoke of a Government which they felt burthensome, and whilst they flourish, are the judges and the avengers of their own cause. But to an unprejudiced observer, their path would seem strewed with difficulties, and beset

with perils. Thus far their course has been marked
with blood, and with blood must it be traced to its
termination, either in their own destruction, or in
that of thousands of the native population of Southern Africa.

APPENDIX.

DESCRIPTION

OF

THE FERÆ NATURÆ

THAT INHABIT
SOUTHERN AFRICA.*

Order. FERÆ.

Genus. FELIS.

1. *Felis Leo.* The Lion. Leuew *of the Cape Colonists.* Tao *of the Matabili, and Bechuana.*

Adult male about three feet eight inches high at the shoulder, and less at the rump. Extreme length usually about ten feet six inches. Tail three feet long, tufted with black hair at the extremity. Ears round and black. Five toes on the fore feet, four on the hind. Claws retractile, each concealed by a tuft of blackish hair. Hair on the body and extremities short, of a tawny yellow color, darker on the back, and lighter on the belly. The upper parts of the head, the chin, neck, shoulders, and belly, covered with long shaggy hairs forming a copious mane. The color varying between tawny, brown, and black, according to the age of the animal. A black spot at each corner of the mouth. Whiskers strong and white. Eyes yellow. Lioness smaller, and without any appearance of a mane.

---

* With few deviations, I have followed the classification adopted by Dr. Smith, in his copious "*African Zoology.*" The descriptions have all been drawn up from numerous specimens killed by myself.

Inhabits variously; usually found amongst reeds in open plains. Gregarious, and very common.

2. *Felis Leopardus.* The Leopard. Tiger *of the Cape Colonists.*

Adult male about two feet seven inches high at the shoulder, and seven feet six inches in extreme length. Claws retractile. Chin, neck, breast, belly, and insides of extremities, white. The rest varying in different specimens between tawny, fulvous, and reddish brown, irregularly marked with spots of black, which vary greatly in number, size, and appearance, at different ages or seasons. Tail about three feet eight inches long, ringed with black. Whiskers strong and white. Eyes yellow.

Female similar, but smaller.

Inhabits thick coverts. Monogamous, or solitary.

3. *Felis Jubata.* The Hunting Leopard. Luipaard *of the Cape Colonists.* 'Nquāne *of the Bechuana.*

Size of both sexes about that of a greyhound. Body slender; legs very long; claws semi-retractile. Belly and insides of extremities white; the rest pale yellow, studded with small round black spots, larger on the back and outside of thighs. Hair of the upper part of the neck and withers, rather long, forming a small mane. A black stripe on the ears, and another from the corners of the eyes to the angle of the mouth. Tail annulated with black and white bars, and tipped with white.

Inhabits open places. Not common.

Genus. Hyæna.

4. *Hyæna Crocuta.* The Spotted Hyæna. Wolf *of the Cape Colonists.* Impeese *of the Matabili.*

Height at the shoulder of both sexes, about two feet six or eight inches; much less at the rumps. Extreme length about five feet ten inches. Feet with four toes;

nails not retractile. Head short, and very broad ; muzzle and nose black. Lower part of the head, throat, belly, and inner surfaces of the extremities, dingy white. General color of the other parts fulvous brown, irregularly blotched with circular black spots. Tail sixteen inches ; the lower two thirds of its length furnished with long black hairs forming a tassel. Hair on the back of the neck and withers, long, forming a reversed mane. Both sexes furnished with a glandular pouch below the tail.

Very common every where.

5. *Hyæna Fusca.* The Fuscous Hyæna. Strand Wolf *of the Cape Colonists.*

Usual height at the shoulder, about two feet four inches ; much lower behind. Extreme length about four feet ten inches. Hair very long and shaggy on the upper parts of the neck, back, and tail. General color reddish grey, brindled with brown and black stripes and spots. Extremities yellowish, with deep black, transverse bands. Tail twelve inches ; black, with red hairs towards the tip.

Female similar.

Less abundant than the preceding, but common.

6. *Hyæna Venatica.* The Wild Dog. Wilde Hond *of the Cape Colonists.*

Height at the shoulder under two feet; rather lower behind. Length about four feet three inches. Form slight; muzzle pointed. Ground color of the hair sandy bay, or ochraceous yellow, irregularly blotched and brindled with black and variegated spots of exceedingly irregular shape. Face, nose, and muzzle, black. Tail bushy like that of a fox, divided about the middle by a black ring, above which the color is sandy, and below, white.

Hunts in large organised packs.

Order. PACHYDERMATA.

Genus. ELEPHAS.

7. *Elephas Africanus.* The African Elephant. Oliphant *of the Dutch Colonists.* Maclou *of the Matabili.*

Male attains the height of twelve feet at the shoulder; droops behind. Extreme length between eighteen and nineteen feet. Skin, black, rough, and nearly destitute of hair. Tail short, tufted at the end. Head rounder, forehead more convex, and ears much larger than in the Asiatic Elephant. The latter extremely flat, reaching to the legs, and overlapping each other on the top of the neck. Five toes on all the feet. Tusks arched; between eight and nine feet in length, and weighing one hundred pounds. Female upwards of eight feet; usually provided with tusks about four feet in length. Mammæ two, placed between the fore legs.

Solitary or gregarious in large troops. Common in the extensive plains and forests of the interior.

Genus. HIPPOPOTAMUS.

8. *Hippopotamus Amphibius.* The Hippopotamus. Sea Cow or Zeekoe *of the Cape Colonists.* Imfooboo *of the Matabili and Kafirs.*

Between four and five feet high at the shoulder, and from ten to eleven feet long. Body ponderous and shapeless; legs very short, terminating with four toes. Head thick and square, muzzle broad; eye very small, placed in a prominence; ears small, round, and approximated. The upper incisors and canine teeth greatly developed; the latter forming tusks. Skin rough, hard, and very thick: entirely destitute of hairs, a few scattered bristles on the lips, ears, and tail, excepted. General color pinkish brown, with freckles on the flanks and belly. Tail twelve inches.

Female smaller. Mammæ two.

Amphibious. Inhabits the rivers and lakes of the interior.

Genus. SUS.

9. *Sus Larvatus.* The Wild Hog. Bosch Vark *of the Cape Colonists.*

Height at the shoulder about two feet four or five inches. Extreme length between five and six feet. Four toes on all the feet, the two middle ones only touching the ground. Nose elongated, and cartilaginous. Canine teeth very strong; those of the upper jaw projecting norizontally, those of the lower, upwards. A tuberculous excrescene covered with coarse hair, upon the chaffron. Color dirty brown. Bristles very long, especially on the neck and back. Tail slightly tufted, and upwards of a foot in length. Mammæ twelve.

Gregarious. Inhabits the plains and forests.

Genus. PHASCOCHÆRUS.

10. *Phascochœrus Africanus.* The African Boar. Vlacke Vark *of the Cape Colonists.* Ingooloob *of the Matabili.*

Height at the shoulder about two feet six inches. Extreme length, six feet two inches. Color reddish brown, The top of the head, upper part of the neck, shoulders, and back, covered with long rigid bristles ; those on the top of the head diverging like the radii of a circle. Canine teeth very large and long, and directed upwards. Head extremely large, and muzzle very broad. A large fleshy wen behind each eye, and a prominent warty excrescence on each side of the muzzle, between the eye and tusks. Eyes small and sinister. Tail tufted with bristles; twenty inches in length, straight and thin.

Gregarious. Inhabits the plains and forests.

Genus. RHINOCEROS.

11. *Rhinoceros Africanus.* The African Rhinoceros. Rhinaster *of the Cape Colonists.* Chukuroo *of the Matabili.*

Upwards of six feet high at the shoulder, and above thirteen feet in extreme length. Body very robust and clumsy. Legs short and small, each with three toes. Head long and large. Eyes small and lateral. Snout hooked, and resembling that of a tortoise: armed with two horns * on the muzzle, placed one behind the other; the anterior usually from one to two feet long; the posterior generally small, but capricious—in some specimens attaining the same, or nearly the same length. Ears pointed and approximated, placed on the neck. Skin naked; very thick, rugous, and knotty, 'but without plaits or folds. Colour brownish black. Tail about two feet long, laterally compressed at the end, and furnished with a few bristles.

Female similar but smaller. Mammæ two. Very common in the interior.

12. *Rhinoceros Sinusus.* The White Rhinoceros Witte Rhinaster *of the Cape Colonists.* Chicore *of the Matabili and Bechuana.*

Six feet six or eight inches high at the shoulder, and above fourteen in extreme length. Head, four feet long. Muzzle truncated, upwards of eighteen inches in breadth; furnished with two horns placed one behind the other as in the last species; the anterior robust at the base, tapering, and about three feet in length; the posterior a mere excrescence, five or six inches long. Ears pointed and approximated, placed on the neck. A square hump immediately behind them. Eyes very diminutive and late

---

* The horns of no two specimens of this animal that came under my observation, were exactly the same. Disease or accident not unfrequently renders the anterior horn the shorter of the two.

ral. Legs short and straight, terminating in three toes. Tail about two feet long, compressed and bristled at the extremity. Hide very rough and knotty, extremely thick, with folds and plaits about the neck. Color varying; usually dirty brownish white.

Female similar but smaller. Mammæ two. Very common in the interior after passing Kurrichane.

Genus. EQUUS.

13. *Equus Zebra.* The Zebra. Wilde Paard *of the Cape Colonists.*

About four feet high at the shoulder, and eight feet two inches in extreme length. Shape light and symmetrical. Legs very slender. Feet small, terminating in a solid hoof. Head light and bony. Ears and tail asinine; the latter blackish, about sixteen inches long, and tufted at the extremity. Ground color of the hair white. The whole of the body, neck, head, and legs, covered with narrow black bands, placed wider or closer together; the upper ones connected with the dorsal line, but not extending over the belly, or inside of thighs. Mane erect and bushy, alternately banded white and black. Two transverse black bands on the ears. Brown stripes on the face terminating in a bay nose. A bare spot a little above the knee on all four of the legs.

Female with two inguinal mammæ.

Gregarious. Found within the Cape Colony. Inhabits mountainous regions only.

14. *Equus Burchellii.* Burchell's Zebra. Bonti Quagga *of the Cape Colonists.* Peechey *of the Bechuana and Matabili.*

Four feet six inches high at the shoulder, and eight feet six inches in extreme length. Body round. Legs robust. Crest arched and surmounted by a standing mane, five inches high, banded, black and white. Ears

48

and tail equine; the latter thirty five inches long flowing
and white. Muzzle black. General ground color of the
head, neck, and body, sienna, capriciously banded with
black and deep brown transverse stripes forming various
figures, and unconnected with the dorsal line, which
widens towards the croup. Belly and legs pure white.
Bare spots above the knees on the inside.

Female an udder with four mammæ.

Inhabits the plains of the interior beyond the Gareep
in immense herds.

15. *Equus Quagga.* The Quagga. Quagga *of the
Cape Colonists.*

About the height of Burchell's Zebra, but of a more
robust form. Ears and tail equine as in the preceding;
the former marked with two irregular black bands. Crest
very high, surmounted by a standing mane banded alternately brown and white. Color of the head, neck, and
upper parts of the body, reddish brown, irregularly banded and marked with dark brown stripes, stronger on the
head and neck, and gradually becoming fainter until lost
behind the shoulder. Dorsal line broad, belly, legs, and
tail, white.

Still found within the Cape Colony. Inhabits the open
plains South of the Vaal river in immense herds.

Order. RUMINANTIA.

Genus. CAMELOPARDALIS.

16. *Camelopardalis Giraffa.* The Giraffe. Kameel
of the Cape Colonists. Intootla *of the Matabili.*

In stature the tallest of mammiferous animals. Adult
male, twelve feet high at the shoulder and eighteen at
the crown of the head. Legs slender, seven feet in
length. Feet terminating in a divided hoof. No succentorial hoofs. Body short. Withers elevated, a scanty

upright, rufous mane extending along the whole neck. Back oblique. Tail thirty-four inches long, terminating in a tuft of bristly black hair about the same length, which reaches to the hocks. Head light and tapering, thirty-four inches long; provided with osseous penduncles, (common to both sexes) covered with a hairy skin and terminating in in a tuft of black hair. A tuberculum on the chaffron. No muzzle. Upper lip entire. Eyes large and melting. No lachrymary sinus. Ears pure white, and ample. Callosity on the breast. Tongue very long, pointed, and flexible. General color, deep sienna, with large angular ferruginous spots, variously disposed over the whole; each spot darker in the centre. Belly and cheeks white, with dark blotches.

Female sixteen or seventeen feet in height at the crown, of a dirty white color with pale ferruginous spots as in the male. Mammæ four.

Gregarious in small troops. Inhabits the great plains of the interior.

Genus. Bos.

17. *Bubulus Caffer.* The Cape Buffalo. Buffel *of the Cape Colonists.* 'Neaat *of the Matabili,* Bokolokolo *of the Bechuana.*

Adult male about five feet six inches high at the shoulder, and upwards of twelve in extreme length. Structure very powerful. Body ponderous. Neck short. Breast and shoulder deep, and slightly dewlaped. Back straight and hunchless. Limbs short and solid, terminating in a divided hoof, which is nearly circular. Succentorial hoofs very long. Tail three feet long, terminating in a tuft of coarse black hair, which reaches below the hocks. Head short, and small in proportion to the animal's bulk. Eyes small and sinister, overshadowed by rough and ponderous dark colored horns, nearly in contact at

the base, spreading horizontally, and turned upwards
and inwards at the tips, which measure about four feet
between. Hide bluish black, and naked with exception of
a few distichous bristles. No lachrymary sinus. Muzzle bovine, square, and naked.

Female similar but smaller, with smaller and more
vertically disposed horns. An udder with four mammæ.

Still found within the Colony. Inhabits the plains
and forests of the interior in large herds.

Genus. CATOBLEPAS.

18. *Catoblepas Gnoo.* The Gnoo. Wilde Beest *of
the Cape Colonists.* Gnoo *of the Hottentots.* Impa-
toomo *of the Matabili.*

Adult male upwards of four feet high at the shoulder,
nine feet in extreme length. General contour very muscular, and exhibiting great energy. Head large and
square. Muzzle large, spread out, and flattened, with
narrow linear nostrils. Above the muzzle is situated a
conspicuous tuft of black bristling hairs, radiating laterally, and resembling a blacking brush. A tuft of similar hair beneath each eye, concealing a gland which dis-
tils a viscous humour. Eye wild and fiery. Ears short
and pointed. White bristles surrounding the eye, like
the radii of a circle. Numerous white bristles on the upper lip. Horns broad, and approximated at the base; fur-
rowed upon the summit of the head ; scarcely advancing
from the skull, they taper out sideways over the eyes,
and uncinate up into a pointed hook, sweeping with a regular curve, and producing a sinister and suspicious aspect. Shoulder deep. Neck thick, and much arched.
Body round. A pillow of fat on either haunch. Legs slender and long. A full vertical mane on the neck, composed of wiry white hairs. A bushy black beard on the

under jaw and throat; and a bush of full black hair
between the fore legs, extending some distance along the
belly. Tail equine, white, and reaching to the ground.
General color of the hair, deep brown. Hoofs pointed,
blueblack.

Female similar, but slighter. Base of horns less approximated. An udder with four mammæ,

Very gregarious. Abundant on the plains South of
the Vaal river.

19. *Catoblepas Gorgon.* The Brindled Gnoo. Blauw
Wilde Beest *of the Cape Colonists.* Kokoon *of the Bechuana and Matabili.*

Adult male about four feet six inches high at the shoulder, and nine feet eight inches in extreme length. Withers very elevated. Neck not arched. Nose aquiline,
and covered with coarse black hair. Muzzle broad and
square: bare, with large hanging nostrils. Horns black,
placed horizontally on the head; the points turned upwards, and then acutely inwards; a few rugosities at the
base. A long flowing mane on the neck, extending
beyond the withers. Chin covered with a copious bristly
black beard, descending down the dewlap to the breast.
Tail black, flowing, and reaching to the heels. Ears small
and pointed. Eyes very high in the head. A large glan-
dulous naked spot, of an oblong form below each eye,
distilling a viscous humour. Legs slender. General
color dirty dun, or sepia grey, variegated with obscure
streaks or brindles. Four or five cross streaks on each
arm.

Female precisely similar, but on a smaller scale.

Gregarious. Inhabits the plains beyond the Orange
river in vast herds.

Genus. DAMALIS.

20. *Boselaphus Oreas.** The Impoofo. Eland *of the Cape Colonists.* Impoofo, or Pooffo *of the Bechuana and Matabili.*

Adult male six feet six inches high at the shoulder, and about twelve in extreme length. Facial line straight. Muzzle broad. Forehead square, covered with a cluster of strong wiry brown hair, margined on either side by a yellow streak, commencing above the eyes, and nearly meeting half way down the face. Horns placed on the summits of the frontals; about two feet long, massy, and nearly straight, with a ponderous ridge ascending in a spiral direction nearly to the tips. Proportions of the body like those of a bull. Neck very thick. Shoulders very deep. Larynx very prominent. A broad deep dewlap, fringed with long wiry brown hair, descending to the knees. A crest of bristles from the forehead, passing upwards and recurrent along the edge of the neck. Legs short. Hind quarters very large. Tail two feet three or four inches long, with a large tuft of coarse brown hair. Hide black. Hair very short. General color rufous dun, or ashy grey tinged with ochre. A muzzle. No suborbital sinus.

Female smaller and slighter, with longer and more slender horns. No dewlap, but a tuft of hair on the larynx. Color redder. An udder with four Mammæ.

Gregarious. Inhabits the open plains of the interior in vast herds.

---

* The *Bastard Eland* of the Cape Colonists, (*Boselaphus Canna*) is doubtless identical with B. *Oreas,* and cannot be considered a distinct species.

21. *Strepsiceros Koodoo.* The Koodoo. Eechlongole *of the Matabili.*

Adult male upwards of five feet high at the shoulder; above nine feet in extreme length. Horns bulky and compressed, having an anterior ridge which forms with them, two complete spiral circles : the tips turned outwards and forwards; length about three feet; color brown; the tips black with a white point. Chaffron straight. Muzzle very broad. Ears oblique, very broad, and pointed at the tips, of a light brown color. Neck thick. Withers elevated. Dewlap anteriorly square. Forehead black. A white line passing over the orbits unites on the chaffron. Three white spots on either cheek, below the eye. Chin white bearded. A long fringe of variegated black and white hair on the dewlap, and a standing mane on the neck and withers. General color of the hair, a buff grey, or sky blue, marked with a white line along the spine, and intersected by five or six transverse lines running downwards to the belly, and four more over the croup. Buttocks white. Legs rufous below the knees. Tail two feet long, rufous, edged with white, tapering to a point, and black at the tip. No suborbital sinus. An entire moist muzzle.

Female slighter, hornless, and with fewer and fainter white markings. Has an udder with four mammæ.

Gregarious. Still found within the Colony. Inhabits thickets and wooded hills.

22. *Acronotus Caama.* The Caama. Hartebeest *of the Cape Colonist*—Intoosel *of the Matabili.* Caama *of the Bechuana.*

Adult male about five feet high at the withers, and nine in extreme length. Shoulders very elevated, and head very large and long. The whole animal made up of triangles. Horns placed upon a high ridge above the frontals; very close at the base; robust, divergent, and again approximating so as to form a lozenge, with double flexures strongly pronounced, turned forwards, and the points backwards, with several prominent knots on the anterior surface. A black spot at their base, above the forehead, continued behind, and terminating in front of the ears. A black streak down the nose, commencing below the eyes, and terminating at the nostrils. Chin black. A narrow black stripe down the back of the neck. A black streak on the fore leg commencing about mid shoulder; another down the hind leg commencing about the middle of the buttock. A triangular spot of white immediately above on each buttock, and a white spot above each eye. Tail reaching to the hocks, covered with posteriorly directed black hair. General color, bright sienna, with a deep red cast. A half muzzle. No suborbital sinus, but a mucous discharge. Eyes fiery red.

Female similar, but smaller, with more slender horns. Mammæ two.

Inhabits the plains of the interior beyond the Orange river, in immense herds.

23. *Acronotus Lunata.* The Sassayby. Bastard Hartebeest *of the Cape Colonists.* Sassabe *of the Matabili and Bechuana.*

Adult male four feet six inches high at the shoulder, four feet at the croup. Eight feet two inches in extreme length. Horns robust, about twelve inches long, placed on the summit of the frontals, turning outwards, and forming two crescents with the points inwards; marked with from twelve to fifteen incomplete annuli. Neck short. Body rather bulky. Legs slender. Withers very elevated. Head long, narrow and shapeless. Facial line strait. A dark streak from between the horns to the nose. Ears fawn color, nine inches long. General color deep blackish purple brown above, fulvous beneath. A dab of slate color extends from the middle of the shoulder to the knee; and another from the middle of the flank to the hock, outside. A band of the same color passes across the inside of both fore and hind legs, upon a fulvous ground. Lower part of the legs, deep fulvous. Tail twenty two inches long, rufous, and covered with posteriorly directed black hair. Rump fawn color. Eyes fiery red. A half muzzle, and very indistinct lachrymary perforation.

Female precisely similar, but smaller, with more slender horns. Mammæ two.

Gregarious. Inhabits the country of the Bechuana, in considerable herds.

Genus. ANTILOPE.

24. *Aigocerus Harrisï.* The sable Antelope. *Undescribed by Naturalists. Unknown to the Matabili.*

Adult male four feet six inches high at the shoulder; nearly nine feet in extreme length. Horns thirty seven inches over the curve; placed immediately above the eyes; flat, slender, sub-erect, and then strongly bent back scimitarwise; at first gradually diverging, and then running parallel to each other; three fourths annulated with about thirty strongly pronounced incomplete rings, more rigid on the edges, but chiefly lost on the outside of the horn; the remaining one fourth smooth, round, slender, and pointed. Head somewhat attenuated towards the muzzle, and compressed laterally. Carcase robust. Withers elevated. Neck broad and flat. Hoofs black, obtuse, and rather short. Hair close and smooth. General color of the coat, intense glossy black, with an occasional cast of deep chesnut. A white streak commencing above each eye continued by a pencil of long hairs covering the place of the suborbital pouch, (of which cavity no trace is to be found,) and then running

49

down the side of the nose to the muzzle, which is entirely
white; the same color pervading the throat and one half
of the cheek. Ears ten inches long; narrow, tapering,
and pointed; white within, lively chesnut without, with
black pencilled tips. A broad half crescent of deeper
chesnut at the base of each ear, behind. A small entire
sharp black muzzle. A copious standing black mane,
somewhat inclined forwards, five and a half inches high,
extending from between the ears to the middle of the
back. Hair of the throat and neck longer than that of
the body. Belly, buttocks, and inside of thighs, pure
white. A longitudinal dusky white stripe behind each
arm. Fore legs jet black inside and out, with a tinge of
chesnut on and below the knees. Hind legs black, with
a lively chesnut patch at and below the hock. Tail
black; long hair skirting the posterior edge, terminating in a tuft which extends below the hocks.

Female smaller than the male, with smaller but similarly shaped horns. Color deep chesnut brown verging
upon black,

Very rare. Gregarious in small families. Inhabits
the great mountain range which threads the Eastern portion of the Matibili country.

25. *Aigocerus Equina* *—The Roan Antelope. Bastard Gemsbok *of the Cape Colonists.* Etak *of the Matabili.*

Adult male about five feet high at the shoulder, and
nine is extreme length. Horns very robust, above two
feet in length, strongly bent back scimitarwise, and
nearly parallel; with from twenty-five to thirty prominent rings, more remote from the orbits, and extending
to within about four inches of the points. Face and head

---

* If the *Blue Antelope,* (*Aigocerus Leucophœa*) ever did exist, it
is now extinct. I am disposed to regard it as a variety of the Roan
Antelope, and Daniel's *Takhaitze,* (*A. Barbata,*) is probably so too

hoary black, with a large white streak before and behind each eye, formed of a pencil of long hairs. A white spot between the horns, and a white muzzle. Ears of asinine dimensions, fourteen inches long, pointed, and the tips bent back very eccentrically. Tail descending to the hocks, slender black, and tufted. Hair coarse, loose, and undulating; mixed red and white, forming a roan. Beneath the throat longer and whiter. Neck furnished with a stiff upright mane, terminating at the withers. A half muzzle. No suborbital sinus.

Female similar, but hornless. Mammæ two. Gregarious in small families or herds, but rare. Inhabits the elevated ridges near the source of the Vaal river.

26. *Aigocerus Ellipsiprymnus.* The Water Buck. Phitomok *of the Matabili.*

Adult male four feet six inches high; nearly nine feet in extreme length. Horns upwards of thirty inches; upright, curved forwards and sometimes inwards, but always diverging; of a whitish green color; the first third slightly compressed; the other two thirds nearly cylindrical; very strongly annulated along the front and outside to within six inches of the points. Face deep brown. Forehead, base of horns, and behind the eyes, rufous. A white patch on the throat. Under lip and muzzle white. A white streak before each eye, and a white elliptical band encircling the tail. Ears round and large; white inside; brown without. General color of the hair greyish brown; in texture coarse, and resembling split whale bone; shorter on the body, but on the neck long and reversed, having the semblance of a mane. Hide black. Legs dark brown. Tail brown and tufted, not quite reaching to the hocks. A muzzle. No suborbital indent.

Female precisely similar, but hornless. Mammæ two.

Gregarious. Found only on the banks of rivers near the Tropic, the Limpopo and Mariqua, especially.

27. *Oryx Capensis* The South African Oryx. Gemsbok *of the Cape Colonists.* Kookaam *cf the Matabili
and Bechuana.*

Adult male three feet ten inches high at the shoulder;
ten feet in extreme length. Horns upwards of three feet
long; straight, or very slightly bent; horizontal, divergent, and tapering to the points; the lower part annulated with from twenty five to thirty rings. Eyes high in
the head. Black space between the base of the horns
descending in a streak down the forehead; another passing through the eyes to the corner of the mouth, connected by a third which runs round the head over the
nose; a fourth passes from the base of the ears under the
throat completing the appearance of a head-stall: the
rest of the head white. Ears round; white with black
edging. General color of the coat vinous buff. The
breast, belly and extremities white. A tuft of bristly black hair on the larynx, and the latter edged
with black. A mane reversed; and a black list stripe
from the nape of the neck along the back, widening an-
gularly over the croup, and terminating in a bushy black
tail, three feet long which sweeps the ground. A broad
black bar across the elbow, passing along the flank, and
ending in a wide angular space on the thigh above the
hocks; and a black spot upon each leg between the
knee and fetlock. Nose ovine. No suborbital sinus.

Female similar, with longer horns. An udder with two
mammæ.

Gregarious. Principally found in the Karroo, or in
the open plains of Namaqua land.

28. *Gazella Euchore.* The Spring Buck. Spring-bok
of the Cape Colonists. Tsepe *of the Matabili and Bechuana.*

Adult male about two feet eight inches high at the
shoulder, and two feet ten at the croup. Extreme length

about four feet ten inches. Head and face white, resem·
bling a lamb's. Horns black, lyrate, robust, with about
twenty complete rings; the tips turned inwards, and ⁻
generally either forward or backwards. General color
of the hair, yellow dun, with a white croup consisting of
long hairs which can be erected or depressed at pleasure.
Belly, throat, and inside of limbs, white, separated from
the dun by a broad rich chesnut band along the flanks;
another along the edges of the folds of the croup; and a
streak from the back of the horns through the eyes to
the nose. A truly ovine nose. Small indistinct lachrymary sinus. Ears long, attenuated, and dirty white.
Eyes very large, dark, and expressive. Tail eight
inches long; white, with a tuft of posteriorly directed
black hairs.

Female similar, but smaller, with very slender horns,
and few indistinct annuli. Mammæ two.

Scattered over the plains in countless herds.

29. Gazella Albifrons. The White Faced Antelope.
Bles-bok *of the Cape Colonists.* Nunni *of the Bechuana.*

Adult male three feet eight inches high at the shoulder, and six feet three inches in extreme length. Head
long and narrow. Muzzle broad. Horns from twelve to
fifteen inches in length, white, very robust at the base;
divergent, with ten or twelve semi-annuli on the anterior
side. A patch of chocolate colored hair at the base of the
horns, divided by a narrow white streak, which suddenly
widens between the eyes to the whole breadth of the face,
down which it passes to the nose. Ears rather long and
white. Sides of the head and neck deep purple chocolate.
The back and shoulders hoary bluish white as if glazed.
Flanks and loins brown. Belly white. Legs brown outside, white within. Croup and chest rufous. Tail reaching to the hocks; seventeen inches long, with much posteriorly directed brown and white hair. Linear nostrils.

Very indistinct muzzle. Small circular lachrymary perforation.

Female precisely similar, but slighter, less vividly colored, and with more slender horns. Mammœ two.

Very gregarious. Inhabits the plains South of the Vaal river in immense herds.

30. *Gazella Pygarga.* The Pied Antelope. Bontebok *of the Cape Colonists.*

Rather larger than the preceding. Head long, narrow, and shapeless, with a very broad muzzle. Horns fifteen inches long; black, divergent, erect, very robust at base, with ten or twelve incomplete annuli, broken in the middle and striated between. Forehead and face white, as in the Bles-bok. Ears long and reddish. Sides of the head, neck, and flanks, deep purple brown. Back bluish lilac, as if glazed. Legs perfectly white from the knees and hocks downwards. Belly and inside of thighs white, and a large white patch on the croup. Tail reaching to the hocks; white above, with a tuft of posteriorly directed black hairs. Small detached lachrymary perforation. Linear nostrils. Very indistinct muzzle.

Female precisely similar, but on a slighter scale, with more slender horns. Mammæ two.

Gregarious. Still found in Zoetendal's V'ley near Cape L'Agulhas. Common in the interior.

31. *Antilope Melampus.* The Pallah. Rooye-bok *of the Cape Colonists.* Pallah *of the Matabili and Bechuana.*

Adult male about three feet three or four inches high at the shoulder, and six in extreme length. Very high on the legs. Horns about twenty inches in length, ascending obliquely upwards, outwards, and backwards; and midway at an obtuse angle, obliquely inwards and forwards; black, coarsely annulated and striated between

for about two thirds of their length; the tips smooth.
Ears round, seven inches long, tipped with black. Tail
thirteen inches long; pointed, white, with a dark brown
streak down the middle. Color of the head, neck, and
upper part of the body, deep fulvous. Sides and hinder
parts yellow dun. Belly white. A dark brown streak
down each buttock. A dark spot in place of spurious
hoofs, which do not occur in this species. A large cush-
ion of brown hair between the hock and fetlock. A
white spot before each eye. A dark spot between the
horns. No trace of a suborbital sinus. Small bare space
for a muzzle.

Female similar, but hornless. Eye very large, soft
and full. Mammæ two.

Gregarious in small families or herds. Inhabits the
banks of rivers chiefly in the Bechuana country.

32. *Tragelaphus Sylvatica.* The Bush Buck. Bosch-
bok *of the Cape Colonists.*

Adult male about two feet eight inches high and five
feet two inches long. Form elegant; somewhat receding from the typical structure of true Antelopes, and assuming that of the goat. Horns about twelve inches
long; erect, spiral, and sublyrate; marked with an obsolete ridge in front, and one in rear; black, and closely
wrinkled at the base; points a little bent forward. General color brilliant chesnut black above, marked with a
narrow white streak along the spine; two white spots on
each cheek; several on the flanks, and two on each fetlock. Inside of thighs, and chin white. Forehead deep
sienna. A broad naked black band encircling the neck
as if worn off by a collar. Tail nine inches long; brown
above, white beneath. Ears large and round. Moist
naked muzzle. No lachrymary opening.

Female similar, but without horns. Mammæ four.

Monogamous or solitary. Inhabits the forests on the
sea coast.

33. *Redunca Eleotragus.* The Reit Buck. Reit bok *of the Cape Colonists.* Inghalla *of the Matabili.*

Adult male about two feet ten inches high at the shoulder, and four feet ten inches long. Horns ten or twelve inches long; advanced beyond the plane of the face; divergent, and regularly curved with the points forward; wrinked at the base, and annulated with obsolete rings in the middle. Ears six inches. Tail ten inches long. General color of the coat ashy grey tinged with ochre beneath white; hair of the throat white and flowing. A small muzzle, and imperfect suborbital opening.

Female similar but smaller and hornless. Mammæ four.

Gregarious in small families, or solitary. Resides variously, principally among reeds.

34. *Redunca Lalandii.* The Nagor. Rooye Rhee bok *of the Cape Colonists.*

Adult male two feet eight inches high at the shoulder, and five feet in length. Horns about six inches long, approximating at base, sub erect, nearly parallel and hooked forward at the point, with five or six semi-annuli striated between. Legs, head, and neck, tawny. Chin and lower parts white. Body fulvous brown with a cast of purple. The hair long, loose and whirling in various directions. Tail ten inches; grey with long white hair along the edges. Muzzle small. Suborbital opening barely perceptible.

Female similar, but hornless. Mammæ four. Found amongst rocks in small troops.

35. *Redunca Capreolus.* The Rhee Buck. Rheebok *of the Cape Colonists.* Peeli *of the Bechuana and Matabili.*

Adult male two feet five inches at the shoulder, and

about five feet in length. Body very slender. Neck long. Head small, and ears pointed. Horns about nine inches in length; straight, slender, vertical, and pointed, with from ten to fifteen rings at the base. Hair very soft and villous, resembling wool. General color whitish grey, with a cast of buff; beneath, white. Tail about five inches; grey, tipped with white. Muzzle naked and moist. Suborbital perforation low down, but distinct.

Female similar, but smaller, without horns. Mammæ four.

Found within the Colony, in small troops amongst hills and rocks.

36. *Redunca Scoparia.* The Ourebi. Ditto *of the Cape Colonists.* Subokoo *of the Matabili.*

Less than two feet high at the shoulder, and about four in extreme length. Very slight. Horns four or five inches long; black, round, and nearly vertical : wrinkled at the base, with four or five annuli in the middle. A white arch above the eyes. Tail short and black. General color, pale tawny; beneath white; long white hair under the throat; fulvous tufts below the knees. A small muzzle. Lachrymal opening well developed.

Female similar, but smaller, and hornless. Mammæ four.

Found in grassy plains, usually in pairs.

37. *Oreotragus Saltatrix.* The Klipspringer. Ditto *of the Cape Colonists.*

Adult male about twenty-two inches high at the shoulder, and thirty-six in extreme length. Tail three inches long. Form square and robust. Head short and broad. Horns about four inches long; round, distant, vertical, but slightly inclined forwards; obscurely wrinkled at the base, and annulated in the middle. Legs robust.

Pasterns very rigid. Each hoof subdivided into two segments, and jagged at the edges, so as to give it the power of adhering to the steep sides of smooth rocks. Fur very thick and long; hard, brittle and spirally twisted; ashy at base, brown in the middle, yellow at the tips, forming an agreeable olive. Suborbital sinus conspicuous. Muzzle pointed and small.

Female hornless, in other respects resembling the male. Mammæ two.

Common in the Colony. Inhabits rocks and precipices, in pairs.

38. *Tragulus Rupestris.** The Steenbuck. Steenbok *of the Cape Colonists.* Eoolah *of the Matabili.*

About twenty inches high at the shoulder, twenty-two at the croup and thirty-five in length. Head short and oval. Snout pointed. Muzzle black, ending in a point upon the ridge of the nose. Horns vertical, parallel, and nearly strait; four inches in length, slender, round, and pointed, with one or two rudiments of wrinkles at the base. Ears large, round, and open. Tail barely an inch long, having the appearance of a stump, beyond which the hair does not protrude. General color rufous, with occasionally a cast of brown or crimson. Belly white. Groin naked and black. No accessory hoofs. Pasterns very rigid. A detached suborbital sinus.

Female similar, but without horns. Mammæ four.

Monogamous or solitary. Inhabits the bushes of high ground. Common in the Colony.

39. *Tragulus Melanotis.* The Grysbok. Ditto *of the Cape Colonists.*

Adult male from twenty to twenty-two inches high at

* The *Vlackte Steenbok*, (Tragulus Rufescens,) and the *Bleekbok* (T. Pediotragus) appear to be merely varieties of this Antelope, and not distinct species.

the shoulder, and about thirty-six in length. Head very broad and short. Snout obtusely pointed. Horns about three and a half inches long; smooth, round, slender, and vertical, or slightly inclining forwards. Ears round, open, and broad. Color deep chocolate red, intermixed with numerous single white hairs; beneath rufous. A black horse shoe on the forehead. Detached suborbital sinus, and small muzzle.

Female similar, but hornless. Mammæ two.

Monogamous or solitary. Common in the Colony, among the wooded tracts along the sea coast.

40. *Cephalopus Mergens.** The Duïker. Duikerbok *of the Cape Colonists.* Impoon *of the Matabili.*

Adult male about two feet high at the shoulder, and three feet eight inches in extreme length. Horns four inches long, approximated, somewhat reclining, bending outwards, with a longitudinal ridge on the front travers- ing four or five annuli on the middle, but not traversing the wrinkles of the base. Forehead covered with a patch of long bright fulvous hair. A dark streak on the chaf- fron. Three dark striæ on each ear inside. A dark streak down the front of the legs, terminating in a black fetlock, as if booted. Color various; usually cinereous olive above, and white beneath. Tail eight inches long; black, tipped with white. Spurious hoofs scarcely devel- oped. A long suborbital slit down the side of the face, and a small naked muzzle.

Female similar, with very small horns, completely con- cealed by long rufous hair. Mammæ four.

Solitary or Monogamous. Common in the Colony, es- pecially along the coast, among bushes.

---

* *Cephalopus Burchellii* would appear to be a variety only of this species, of which no two specimens are exactly alike.

41. *Cephalopus Cærula.* The slate-colored Antelope. Blauwbok and Kleenebok *of the Cape Colonists.*

Adult male about fifteen inches high, and twenty-eight inches long. Head very long and pointed, with a spacious muzzle, resembling a rats both in shape and expression. A bare spot round the eyes. Ears short and round, like a rats. Horns black, conical, reclined, slightly turned inwards and forwards, two inches in length, closely and strongly annulated. General color, dull brownish buff, or mouse color, above; beneath whitish. Legs and rump rufous. Tail two inches long, dark above, white beneath. No suborbital sinus, but a suborbital sack lower down, marked by a lengthened streak upon the cheek.

Female similar but hornless, and more diminutive.

Solitary. Inhabits the forests along the sea coast.

FINIS.

PROSPECTUS

OF

CAPTAIN HARRIS'S AFRICAN VIEWS.

––––––

THE author of this Narrative proposes to publish by subscription, TWENTY-EIGHT ORIGINAL PAINTINGS, executed during his Expedition into the Interior of Africa.

It has been his object to combine in them, as far as possible, information which might be useful to the Naturalist, the Sportsman, and the lover of Wild Scenery. They comprise accurate delineations of the whole of the South African Game Quadrupeds, from the Elephant and Giraffe to the smallest Antelope, drawn from repeated measurements upon a uniform scale of one and a half inches to a foot. One or more of each species is depicted in the fore ground of an appropriate Landscape twelve by seventeen inches, with groups in the distance or middle ground.

This arrangement has enabled him to convey an accurate idea of the nature of the country inhabited by each species; also their manner of living, in numerous herds, in small families, or singly. Another advantage gained, also, is that the kinds of trees aad plants, most common in the districts the different animals inhabit, are distinctly shown.

As the expense of publishing has been estimated at about £ 5,000, it will be necessary, when 500 Subscribers shall have been obtained, to call upon each to pay the sum of Rupees 50, or £ 5, in advance; the remainder, which will not exceed, but may fall short of 50 Rupees or £ 5, to be paid in shares on the delivery of each number.

More than two hundred and fifty names have already been obtained in India. Gentlemen desirous of becoming Subscribers, are solicited to signify their wishes, if by letter, Post paid, to either of the following Agents.

Calcutta. Messrs. R. & T. P. Morrell. No. 10. Chowringhee.

Madras. Messrs. Arbuthnot & Co.

Bombay. Mr. J. Malvery. Circulating Library.

London. Messrs. Lucas & Parkinson, 9. Argyll St. Regent Street.

LIST OF SUBSCRIBERS

TO CAPTAIN HARRIS'S

NARRATIVE OF AN EXPEDITION INTO SOUTHERN AFRICA.

The Right Hon. Lord AUCKLAND, G. C. B.,
Governor General of India

The Right Hon. Lord ELPHINSTONE, G. C. H.,
Governor of Madras

The Hon'ble JAMES FARISH, Esquire,
Governor of Bombay.

H. E. Lt. Genl. Sir JOHN KEANE, K. C. B., G. C. H.
Commander-in-Chief, Bombay

Aga Mahomed Jaffer Esq.
Ahmednuggur Station Library
Aked, Ensign J. S. 4th N. I.
Ardaseer, Cursetjee Esq.
Aston, Lieutenant, H.
Augusto, A. C. Mr.
Awdry,The Hon. Sir John
Ayrton, Lieutenant, F. Artillery
Arriens, Col. H. N. M. S.
Arbuthnot, J. A. Esq. Madras
Anderson, W. B. Esq. do.

Baber, T. II. Esquire, C. S.
Bagnold, Mrs. Colonel,
Barnes, Captain, W. M. B.; Q. T.
Bate, Lieut. J. C. 11th N. I.
Baxter, William Esq.

Beckwith, J. Esq. Calcutta
Bell, The Hon. Col. C. B. Cape
Town
Bell, D. C. Esq. Surgeon, 15th
N. I.
Bell, W. W. Esq. C. S.
Bellasis, Capt. 9th N. I.
Bettington, A. Esq. C. S.
Billamore, Major, 1st Gr. N. I.
Bird, J. Esq. Surgeon,
Birdwood, William, Esq. C. S.
Bishop, Major General, Madras
Blair, Brigadier, Nizam's Cavalry,
Blake, Ensign, 7th N. I.
Blane, G. J. Esq. C. S.
Bombay Branch Royal Asiatic So-
ciety, two copies

Bombay, Right Rev. Thomas, Lord Bishop of
Bonamy, Captain, H. M. 6th
Book Society, 3d N. I.
Book Society, 5th N. I.
Boswell, Mr. A. B.
Bourchier, F. Esq. C. S
Bowstead, J. Esq. Assist. Surg.
Boyd, Capt. G. 2d. Gren. N. I.
Boyd, W. S. Esq. C. S. five copies
Boyé, Lieut. 22d N. I.
Brett, Lieut. H. Artillery
Briggs, E. H. Esq. C. S.
Brodie, Captain John
Brough, Major, Queen's Royals
Brown, Rob. Esq. M. D.
Brown, Capt. 7th N. I.
Bruce, T. Esq.
Bruce, W. C. Esquire, C. S.
Burnes, Captain, A. Cabool
Burnes, Lieut. 17th N. I.
Burnes, Jas., LL.D.; K.G.H.
Burnes, Mrs. James
Burnes, Adam Esq. Montrose
Burnes, David Esq. M. D. London
Burt, Capt. Bengal Engineers
Book Club, 40 Regt. B. N. I.
Barnard, Captain, W. 54 do.
Bird, G. Esq. Madras
Bower, The Revd. M. do.
Barrow, J. Esq. do.
Balfour, Lieut. D. W. Artillery do.

Campbell, G. A. Esq. C. S.
Campbell, Major, N. Actg. Qr. Mr. General
Carruthers, Major, H. M. Q R.

Cavaye, Major W. 21st Regt.
Chambers, Lieut. 13th N. I.
Chambers, R. C. Esq. C. S.
Clibborn, Capt. C. 1st Gren. Regt.
Cloete, Hon'ble H. Esq. Cape of Good Hope
Cocke, Major, Jas. Artillery
Cockburn, M. D. Esq. C. S. Madras
Collett, & Co. Booksellers, Two copies
Collins, H. Esq.
Corsellis, Captain 18th N. I.
Cracklow, Major, 22d N. I.
Crawford, Lieut. Engineers
Crawford, R. W. Esq.
Crawley, Major 4th N. I.
Cruickshanks, Lieut. Engineers
Cursetjee Jamsetjee, Esq.
Clerk, R. Esq. Madras
Cherry, A. J., Esq C. S. do.
Choix, J. B. Esq. do.
Cullen, Col. W. do.
Cotterill, Rev. H. do.

Dallas, E. H. Esq. C. S.
Dallas, E. W. Esq. C. S.
Davidson, Captain, Depy. Commissary General
Davidson, Lieut. 18th N. I.
Davies, J. M. Esq. C. S. Two copies
Davis, G. H. Esq. Surg. Artillery
Davies, Rev. M. Chaplain
Deacon, W. Esq. Assist. Surgeon
Dutton, Major H. M. S.
Dickinson, Lieut. Col. Engineers
Dickinson, Ensign H. M. Q. R.

Davidson, D. Esq. C. S.
Dickson, Capt. 13th N. I.
Delamotte, Lieut. C. D. 1st Gr. Regt.
Doig, John Esq. Assist. Surgeon
Donnelly, Captain, T. 1st N. I.
Downey, C. Esq. Garrison Surgeon
Duncan, Lieut. Assist. A. G. Hussingabad
Dunlop, J. A. Esq. C. S.
Durack, Captain, Actg. Assist. Q. Mr. Genl.
D'Urban, Lt. Genl. Sir B., K. C. B.; G. C. H.
Dacca, Library,
Dent, J. Esq. Madras
Dhackjee Dadajee, Esq.
Dadabhoy Pestonjee, Esq.

Earle,. Captain E. M 24th N. I.
Eastwick, Ensign 6th N. I.
Eastwick, Lieutenant, 12th N. I.
Edmond W. Esq.,
Elliott, E. E. Esq. C. S.
Elliott, H. R. Esq. Assist. Surgeon
Elliott, G. L. Esq. C. S.
Elliott, Walter, Esq. C. S. Madras
Elphinstone, A. Esq. C. S.
Elphinstone, Mr.
Ennis, Captain, E. M. 21st N. I.
Erskine, J. Esq. C. S.
Evans, Lieut. W. E., B. E. R.
Ewart, Peter, Esq.
Eyre, Lieut. 3rd L. C.
Ewer, W. Esq. Landour

Farquharson, Captain, Artillery

Fawcett, H. Esq.
Fletcher, Rev. W. K. Chaplain,
Fogerty, W. Keys Esq.
Foulerton, Capt. 1st Gr. Regt.
Foquett, Captain 20th N. I.
Forbes, Major D. 2d Gr. Regt.
Forjett, Mr. C. Judl. Commissioner
Fraser, Captain, T; G. B. E. R.
French, Captain, 23rd N. I.
Frith, & Co., Messrs., Bombay
Fulljames, Lieut. G. 25th N. I.
Faber, Captain, E. Madras
Framjee Cowasjee, Esq. two copies
Fanning, Ensign 1st Gr. Regt.

Geographical Society, Bombay, two copies
Gibson, Major, Artillery
Glass, H. H. Esq. C. S.
Glen, J. Esq. Surgeon
Good, P. L. Esq. Bengal C. S.
Godfrey, Lieut. 17th N. I.
Golding, B. Esq. C. S.
Gordon, Colonel W.
Gordon, H. G. Esq.
Gordon, Lieut 19th N. I.
Graham, Lieut. W. Engineers.
Graham, Lieut. D. 19th N. I.
Graham, J. Esq. Deputy Post Mr. General
Grant, Ensign, 3d N. I.
Grant, Dr. J. Calcutta
Grant, Lady
Grant, Lewis, Esq.
Green, Lieut. E. 21st N. I.
Greenhill, D. Esq. C. S.

Greenway, G. Esq. Madras C. S.
Gresley, Captain Nizam's Service.
Garrow, G. Esq. Madras
Guichard, C. Esq. Madras C. S.
Grant, A. Esq. do.
Gordon, Rev. J. W. do.
Grant, Ensign J. P.

Hadow, A. Esq.
Haines, Lieut. G. 18th M. N. I.
Hale, Captain 22nd N. I.
Hamerton, Captain, 15th N. I.
Hamilton, Capt. 1st L. C.
Harrison, F. Esq. Assistant, Surgeon
Harrison, W. H. Esq. C. S.
Hart, Captain, 22nd N. I.
Hart, Lieutenant, 2nd Gr. N. I.
Hartley, Lieut. 2d Gr. N. I.
Hay, Captain, Agra
Hebbert, Lieut. Engineers
Henderson, J. W. Esq.
Henderson, Major, B. E. R.
Hendley, Lieut. 21st N. I.
Hennell, Captain, 12th N. I.
Hicks, Lieut. Artillery
Heighington, Capt. 1st Gr. Regt.
Hobson, Captain, 20th N. I.
Hockin, Parr, Esq. Assist Surgeon,
Holland, Captain, Jas. Depy. Qr. Mr. Genl.
Holmes, Lieut. John 12th N. I.
Honner, Lieut. C. F. 2d L. Cavalry
Honner, Capt. R. W. 4th N. I.
Horne, Lieut. 8th Regt. N. I.
Horton, The Right Hon'ble Sir R. W., G. C. H. Bart

Howard, W. Esq.
Hutchinson, Mr. F.
Harris & Co. Messrs. London,
Hart, W. B. Esq. Madras
Hubert, Lieut. Col. do.

Inverarity, J. D. Esq. C. S.
Jackson, Lieut. 2d L. C.
Jackson, Lieut. B. E. R.
Jacob, Lieut. Engineers
James, Colonel, Jaulna
Jameson, Captain, 1st Assist. Mil. Audr. Genl.
Jaulna, Book Society
Jemsetjee Cursetjee, Esq.
Jervis, Major, Engineers,
Johnston, H. Esq. Surgeon
Jopp, Major, Engineers
Jugunauth Sunkersett, Esq.
Jemsetjee Jejeebhoy, Sons & Co. Two copies

Kane, C. Esq. Surgeon
Keane, Lieutenant, A. D. C.
Keith, Major, Depy. Adjt. General
Kennedy, R. H. Esq. M. D.
Kennett, Capt. 13th N. I.
King, Colonel, Bengal Cavalry
Kirkland, N. Esq. C. S.
King, T. Col. Madras
Key, T. B. Esq. Madras

Lavie, Lieut. 13th N. I.
Law, J. S. Esq. C. S.
Law, W. C. Esq. Madras Army
Leckie, R. Esq.
Leggett, Mr. F.
LeGeyt, P. W. Esq. C. S.

LeMessurier, A. L. Esq. Advocate Genl.

Lewis, Colonel, Royal Engineers Cape Town

Lewis, Lieut. R. 22d N. I.

Library, H. M. 40th Regt.

Library, 25th Regt. N. I.

Liddell, Capt. 23rd N. I.

Liddell, Capt. J. 1st L. C

Liddell, H. Esq. C. S.

Little, J. Esq.

Lloyd, Lieut. G. B. 7th N. I.

Lockley, Ensign E. 2d Gr. N. I.

Lumley, J. R. Esq. Sholapoor

Langstaff, Dr. Bengal Med. Board

Lash, Lieutenant, J. J. Madras

Line, John Esq. do.

Logan, Lieut. Colonel H. M. 63rd Regt. Madras

Luard, J. K. Major, Madras

Macdonald, Major Ranald, K. H.

Mackenzie, Lieut. H. M. 41st Regt.

Mackie, William Esq.

McGrigor, Ensign J. 21st Regt.

Mainwaring, Rev. E. Chaplain,

Malcolm, Rear Admiral Sir Charles,

Malcolm, G. Esq. C. S.

Malet, A. Esq. C. S.

Malet, H. P. Esq. C. S.

Malvery, Mr. J. J. Circulating Library

Mant, Capt. Depy. Judge Adv. Genl.

Manson, Lieut. Col. C. B. Art.

Marriott, H. E. Esq.

Marriott, Cornet, 2d L. C.

Martin, Captain, Artillery

Martinant, Mr. F.

Mathews, Lieut. A. 15th N. I.

McLeod, Crawford, Esq.

Mess, H. M. 6th Regt.

Mill, John, Esq. Bengal Artillery

Mills, Capt. 19th N. I.

Moore, Major, Depy. Mily. Audt. Genl.

Morris, Lieut. Bheel Corps Candiesh

Morse, Brigadier James

Morse, Lieut. B. E. R.

Munbee, Lieut. Engineers

Madras Literary Society

Montgomerie, H. Esq. C. S.

Manackjee Cursetjee, Esq.

Mess, 1st Gr. Regt.

Mess 2d Gr. Regt.

Mess, 19th Regt. N. I.

Mess, 22d Regt. N. I.

Nicholson, Lieut. P. Bengal Army

Nicolson, Captain, A. D. C. to Gov. Genl.

Noton, B. Esq.

Ogilvy, T. Esq. C. S.

Oliphant, A. Esq. Cape Town

Orlebar, Professor A. B.

Orton, Jas. Esq. Med. Board

Ottley, Lieut. 2d B. L. C.

Outram, Captain, Jas. Two copies

Owen, Lieut. 1st B. L. C.

Oglander, Major, Genl. Cawnpore

Ouchterlony, J. Esq. Madras

Opling, T. Esq.

Parr, Lieut. 23d. N. I.

Pears, Lieutenant, Madras Engineers

Peacocke, Ensign 1st Gr. Regt.

Pelly, J. H. Esq. C. S.

Phillips, J. L. Esq.

Pope, Capt. 17th N. I.

Powell, Lieut. Col. Adjt. Genl.

Prendergast, C. J. Esq. C. S.

Prother, Lieut. 4th N. I.

Public Library, Calcutta; Three copies

Pickwick Club., Calcutta

Quin, Capt. H. M. Ship. Raleigh,

Rolland, Ensign H. 19th. N. I.

Ramsay, Lieut G. 25th. B. N. I.

Ravenscroft, A. W. Esq. C. S.

Reid, L. R. Esq. C. S.

Remington, Lieut. 15th. N. I.

Reynolds, Ensign 14th. N. I.

Richardson, A. Esq. C. S.

Richardson, W Esq. C. S. five copies

Rigby, Ensign. 5th. N. I.

Roberts, Major H. G. 13th N. I.

Robinson, J. C. Esq. Bengal

Robinson, Major, Indore

Ross, J. Esq.

Salmon, Lieut. 2d L. C.

Salter, Brig, General

Salter, Mrs. General

Saunders, Major. J. 15th N. I.

Saunderson Capt. P. 15th N. I.

Schuler, Lieut. Col. Artillery

Scobie, Captain 14th Regt. N. I·

Seton, Captain B. Town Major

Shaw, A. N. Esq. C. S.

Shortt, Captain J. M. 13th N. I.

Shortrede, Capt. R. 14th N. I.

Sims, Charles Esq. C. S.

Simson, J. B Esq. C. S.

Sinclair, Captain, Artillery

Sinclair, Jeffrey Amherst Esq. Surgeon

Skinner, C. B. Esq.

Skinner, John, Esq.

Sleigh, Major General, C. B.

Smee, Captain 5th N. 1.

Smith, D. B. Esq.

Smith, R. Esq.

Smyttan, G. Esq. M. D. Med. Board

Sonnenkalb, T. H. Esq

Spens, A. Esq. C. S.

Spiers, Col. Pol. Agent Bengal

Spiers, W. Esq. Calcutta

Spiller, Captain, Royal Artillery

Spooner, R. Esq. C. S.

Stalker, Major, 19th N. I.

Stanton, Captain, Artillery

Stewart, G. A. Esq. Sup. Surgeon.

Stewart, Lieut. Col. Madras

Stokes, H. Esq. C. S. Madras

Strong, Captain, B. E. R.

Supple, Lieut. J. C. 13th N. I.

Sutherland, Lieut. Col. Resident Gwalior

Shortt, Lieut. H. M. 4th Foot Madras

Sewell, R. B. Esq. Madras

Shaw, J. A. Esq. C. S.

Tanner, Mr. Indian Navy
Tawse, Alexander Esq. Surgeon
Taylor, Capt. Nizam's Service
Thomas, Lieut. 8th N. I.
Todd, G. Esq. Bengal C. S.
Tomkyms, Major, Nizam's Service
Turner, Capt. W. 2d L. C.
Tytler, G. E. F. Esq. C. S.
Templar, J. W. Esq. C. S. Patna
Taylor, Captain, C. Madras
Thompson, J. Esq. do.
Trewman, Lieut. Col. do.

Unwin, Lieut. Artillery
Underwood, W. E. Esq. Madras

Valiant, Col. K. H.; H. M. 40th Regt.
Vaughan, J. Esq. Madras C. S.
Verreaux, Mons. Cape Town
Vardon, Lieut. Engineers, Madras

Waddington, Capt. Engineers
Walker, Jas. O. Esq. M. D.
Walker, Lieut. R. Bengal Artillery
Wallace, Lieut. 18th N. I.
Warburton, Lieut. Marine Battalion

Ward, Captain W. 15th N. I.
Ward, Rev. Randall
Wathen, W. H. Esq. C. S. five copies
Watson, L. T. Esq. Bengal Med. Staff
Weekes, T. P. Esq. Medical Board
Welland, Lieut. Artillery
Wemyss, Lieut. Engineers
Wenn, Captain, 13th N. I.
Wheatley, Lieut. 4th Regt. N. I.
Williams, Lieut. I. N.
Willis, Brigr. General R. A.
Willoughby, J. P. Esq. C. S.
Wilson, Captain 14th N. I.
Wilson, Rev. John, D. D.
Wilson, Lieut. Col. 2d L. C.
Wingate, Lieut. H. M. Q. R.
Wingate, Lieut. Engineers
Wood, Lieut. Engineers
Woodhouse, Captain, 6th N. I.
Wright, James Esq.
Wyllie, Captain, 21st N. I.
Watson, Major C. W. Madras
Wells, Capt. C. H. 26th N. I.
Welsh, Major Genl. Jas. Madras

Young, D. S. Esq. Surgeon Nizam's Army

ADDITIONAL LIST.

Bagshaw, Capt. F. 5th N. I.   Brown, H. Esq. C. S.
Book Society, 3rd N. I.   Crawford, J. H. Esq. C. S

Several of the Bengal and Madras lists have not been received.

The agent for the sale of Capt. Harris's Narrative in London, is Mr. J. M. Richardson, Bookseller, 23 Cornhill, and orders will be received in Edinburgh for the work, as well as for the African Views, at the Office of W. A. Lawrie, Esq. W. S., Her Majesty's. Gazette Printer for Scotland.